MAP 1 - GREATER EDINBURGH

PLACES TO STAY
1 Edinburgh Caravan Club Site
3 Queen Margaret College
7 Mortonhall Caravan Park

OTHER
2 Lauriston Castle
4 Edinburgh Zoo
5 Murrayfield Rugby Stadium
6 Heriot-Watt University
8 Craigmillar Castle

KT-513-633

FIRTH OF FORTH

See Leith Map

LEITH
DOCKS

NORTH
LEITH

SOUTH
LEITH

WHAVEN

RONNINGTON

NONMILLS

BROUGHTON

B900

PILRIG

A900

Lindsay Rd

Commercial St

Pitt St

Leith Walk

Salamander St

RESTALRIG

MEADOWBANK

A199

Seafield

Seafield Rd East

PORTOBELLO

Portobello Rd

See Map 5

GREENSIDE

CALTON

ABBEYHILL

A1

CANONGATE

See Edinburgh Walking Tour
& The Royal Mile Map

HOLYROOD
PARK

NEWINGTON

See Map 7

See Holyrood Park Map

Portobello Rd

A1140

WILLOWBRAE

A1

DUDDINGSTON

Duddingston Loch

Duddingston
Golf Course

A6106

A199

A1

BINGHAM

BRUNSTANE

A199

A1

NEWCRAIGHALL

A6095

To Musselburgh,
Prestonpans,
& North Berwick

A700

Prestongfield Golf Course

A7

PRESTONFIELD

A6106

A6095

NIDDRIE

Musselburgh

A1

MAYFIELD

GRANGE

Mayfield Road

A701

Dalkeith Road

CRAIGMILLAR

Old Dalkeith Rd

8

Craigmillar
Castle
Road

A6106

B6415

Blackford
Hill

BLACKFORD

Craigmillar Park
Golf Course

Liberton Road

Kingston Road

A772

DANDERHALL

Old Dalkeith Road

See Map 3

A701

MORTONHALL

LIBERTON

7

MOREDUN

GRACEMOUNT

B701

Gilmerton Road

GILMERTON

MIDLOTHIAN

A6106

id Hills Public
Golf Course

B701

The City of Edinburgh By-Pass

A720

To Penicuik, Peebles

A772

A68

To Dalkeith,
Lauder & Melrose

River North Esk

A768

Edinburgh
1st edition – March 1999

Published by
Lonely Planet Publications Pty Ltd A.C.N. 005 607 983
192 Burwood Rd, Hawthorn, Victoria 3122, Australia

Lonely Planet Offices
Australia PO Box 617, Hawthorn, Victoria 3122
USA 150 Linden St, Oakland, CA 94607
UK 10a Spring Place, London NW5 3BH
France 1 rue du Dahomey, 75011 Paris

Photographs
Many of the images in this guide are available for licensing from
Lonely Planet Images.
email: lpi@lonelyplanet.com.au

Front cover photograph
Reflections of pedestrians in Leith (Paul Harris, AllStock/PNI)

ISBN 0 86442 580 5

text & maps © Lonely Planet 1999
photos © photographers as indicated 1999

Printed by Colorcraft Ltd, Hong Kong

All rights reserved. No part of this publication may be reproduced,
stored in a retrieval system or transmitted in any form by any means,
electronic, mechanical, photocopying, recording or otherwise, except
brief extracts for the purpose of review, without the written permission
of the publisher and copyright owner.

Although the authors
and Lonely Planet try
to make the informa-
tion as accurate as
possible, we accept
no responsibility for
any loss, injury or
inconvenience sus-
tained by anyone
using this book.

Contents – Text

PLACES TO STAY 85

PLACES TO EAT 91

ENTERTAINMENT 101

SHOPPING 106

EXCURSIONS 110

GLOSSARY 135

INDEX 137

MAP LEGEND back page

METRIC CONVERSION inside back cover

Contents – Maps

The Author

Tom Smallman

Tom lives in Melbourne, Australia, and had a number of jobs before joining Lonely Planet as an editor. He now works full time as an author and has worked on Lonely Planet guides to Canada, Ireland, Dublin, Australia, New South Wales, Sydney, Britain, Scotland, Western Europe and Pennsylvania.

THANKS

My gratitude goes to the following: Sue Graefe for her patience and support; Lindy Mark for her invaluable information, Lyn, Flora and Alex Sharpe and Sue, Jeff and Holly Ross for their hospitality; Jeff Ross for adding a Scottish perspective; Marie, Joe and Narelle for their insider tips on Edinburgh; Graeme Cornwallis for his contributions above and beyond the call of duty; and to all those people who patiently answered my questions.

This Book

From the Publisher

This book was edited in Melbourne, Australia by Chris Wyness with help from Arabella Bamber, Ada Cheung, Liz Filleul and Craig MacKenzie. Ann Jeffree did the design, maps and layout with help from Rachel Black and Anthony Phelan. Simon Bracken designed the cover.

Foreword

ABOUT LONELY PLANET GUIDEBOOKS

The story begins with a classic travel adventure: Tony and Maureen Wheeler's 1972 journey across Europe and Asia to Australia. Useful information about the overland trail did not exist at that time, so Tony and Maureen published the first Lonely Planet guidebook to meet a growing need.

From a kitchen table, then from a tiny office in Melbourne (Australia), Lonely Planet has become the largest independent travel publisher in the world, an international company with offices in Melbourne, Oakland (USA), London (UK) and Paris (France).

Today Lonely Planet guidebooks cover the globe. There is an ever-growing list of books and there's information in a variety of forms and media. Some things haven't changed. The main aim is still to help make it possible for adventurous travellers to get out there – to explore and better understand the world.

At Lonely Planet we believe travellers can make a positive contribution to the countries they visit – if they respect their host communities and spend their money wisely. Since 1986 a percentage of the income from each book has been donated to aid projects and human rights campaigns.

Updates Lonely Planet thoroughly updates each guidebook as often as possible. This usually means there are around two years between editions, although for more unusual or more stable destinations the gap can be longer. Check the imprint page (following the colour map at the beginning of the book) for publication dates.

Between editions up-to-date information is available in two free newsletters – the paper *Planet Talk* and email *Comet* (to subscribe, contact any Lonely Planet office) – and on our Web site at www.lonelyplanet.com. The *Upgrades* section of the Web site covers a number of important and volatile destinations and is regularly updated by Lonely Planet authors. *Scoop* covers news and current affairs relevant to travellers. And, lastly, the *Thorn Tree* bulletin board and *Postcards* section of the site carry unverified, but fascinating, reports from travellers.

Correspondence The process of creating new editions begins with the letters, postcards and emails received from travellers. This correspondence often includes suggestions, criticisms and comments about the current editions. Interesting excerpts are immediately passed on via newsletters and the Web site, and everything goes to our authors to be verified when they're researching on the road. We're keen to get more feedback from organisations or individuals who represent communities visited by travellers.

Lonely Planet gathers information for everyone who's curious about the planet – and especially for those who explore it first-hand. Through guidebooks, phrasebooks, activity guides, maps, literature, newsletters, image library, TV series and Web site we act as an information exchange for a worldwide community of travellers.

Research Authors aim to gather sufficient practical information to enable travellers to make informed choices and to make the mechanics of a journey run smoothly. They also research historical and cultural background to help enrich the travel experience and allow travellers to understand and respond appropriately to cultural and environmental issues.

Authors don't stay in every hotel because that would mean spending a couple of months in each medium-sized city and, no, they don't eat at every restaurant because that would mean stretching belts beyond capacity. They do visit hotels and restaurants to check standards and prices, but feedback based on readers' direct experiences can be very helpful.

Many of our authors work undercover, others aren't so secretive. None of them accept freebies in exchange for positive write-ups. And none of our guidebooks contain any advertising.

Production Authors submit their raw manuscripts and maps to offices in Australia, USA, UK or France. Editors and cartographers – all experienced travellers themselves – then begin the process of assembling the pieces. When the book finally hits the shops, some things are already out of date, we start getting feedback from readers and the process begins again …

WARNING & REQUEST

Things change – prices go up, schedules change, good places go bad and bad places go bankrupt – nothing stays the same. So, if you find things better or worse, recently opened or long since closed, please tell us and help make the next edition even more accurate and useful. We genuinely value all the feedback we receive. Julie Young coordinates a well travelled team that reads and acknowledges every letter, postcard and email and ensures that every morsel of information finds its way to the appropriate authors, editors and cartographers for verification.

Everyone who writes to us will find their name in the next edition of the appropriate guidebook. They will also receive the latest issue of *Planet Talk*, our quarterly printed newsletter, or *Comet*, our monthly email newsletter. Subscriptions to both newsletters are free. The very best contributions will be rewarded with a free guidebook.

Excerpts from your correspondence may appear in new editions of Lonely Planet guidebooks, the Lonely Planet Web site, *Planet Talk* or *Comet*, so please let us know if you *don't* want your letter published or your name acknowledged.

Send all correspondence to the Lonely Planet office closest to you:

Australia: PO Box 617, Hawthorn, Victoria 3122
USA: 150 Linden St, Oakland, CA 94607
UK: 10A Spring Place, London NW5 3BH
France: 1 rue du Dahomey, 75011 Paris

Or email us at: talk2us@lonelyplanet.com.au

For news, views and updates see our Web site: www.lonelyplanet.com

HOW TO USE A LONELY PLANET GUIDEBOOK

The best way to use a Lonely Planet guidebook is any way you choose. At Lonely Planet we believe the most memorable travel experiences are often those that are unexpected, and the finest discoveries are those you make yourself. Guidebooks are not intended to be used as if they provide a detailed set of infallible instructions!

Contents All Lonely Planet guidebooks follow the same format. The Facts about the Country chapters or sections give background information ranging from history to weather. Facts for the Visitor gives practical information on issues like visas and health. Getting There & Away gives a brief starting point for researching travel to and from the destination. Getting Around gives an overview of the transport options when you arrive.

The peculiar demands of each destination determine how subsequent chapters are broken up, but some things remain constant. We always start with background, then proceed to sights, places to stay, places to eat, entertainment, getting there and away, and getting around information – in that order.

Heading Hierarchy Lonely Planet headings are used in a strict hierarchical structure that can be visualised as a set of Russian dolls. Each heading (and its following text) is encompassed by any preceding heading that is higher on the hierarchical ladder.

Entry Points We do not assume guidebooks will be read from beginning to end, but that people will dip into them. The traditional entry points are the list of contents and the index. In addition, however, there is a complete list of maps and an index map illustrating map coverage.

There's also a colour map that shows highlights. These highlights are dealt with in greater detail in the Facts for the Visitor chapter, along with planning questions and suggested itineraries. Each chapter covering a geographical region begins with a locator map and another list of highlights. Once you find something of interest in a list of highlights, turn to the index.

Maps Maps play a crucial role in Lonely Planet guidebooks and include a huge amount of information. A legend is printed on the back page. We seek to have complete consistency between maps and text, and to have every important place in the text captured on a map. Map key numbers usually start in the top left corner.

Although inclusion in a guidebook usually implies a recommendation we cannot list every good place. Exclusion does not necessarily imply criticism. In fact there are a number of reasons why we might exclude a place – sometimes it is simply inappropriate to encourage an influx of travellers.

Introduction

Studded with volcanic hills, Edinburgh has an incomparable location on the southern edge of the enormous Firth of Forth. The city's superb architecture ranges from the Greek-style monuments on Calton Hill (for which it was called the 'Athens of the North'), to extraordinary 16th century tenements to monumental Georgian and Victorian masterpieces. All are dominated by the castle on a precipitous crag in the city's heart. Sixteen thousand buildings are listed as architecturally or historically important, in a city which is a World Heritage Site.

The geology and architecture combine to create an extraordinary symphony in stone. The Old Town, with its crowded tenements and bloody past, stands in contrast to the orderly grid of the New Town with its disciplined Georgian buildings. Most of the city's sights are contained within these two districts. The largely medieval Royal Mile, running down from Edinburgh Castle to the Palace of Holyroodhouse, is the Old Town's

spine. In the New Town, Princes St, though less architecturally inspiring, is Edinburgh's chief thoroughfare.

There are vistas from every street – sudden views of the Firth of Forth, the castle, the Pentland Hills, Calton Hill with its memorials, and rugged Arthur's Seat. Huge Holyrood Park, dominated by Arthur's Seat and a series of other hills, is the Scottish countryside come to the city.

Beyond the centre, once outlying villages are now part of Edinburgh's municipality. To the north, Leith, Edinburgh's main port, has survived a period of decline to become a fashionable area of pubs and restaurants. Portobello to the east is where Edinburgh's citizens spend time on the beach when the weather is warm enough. To the west, medieval South Queensferry sits in the shadow of the two large bridges that span the Firth of Forth. To the south, near Holyrood Park, is picturesque Duddingston.

Since it became a royal capital in the 11th century, all the great dramas of Scottish

Across Edinburgh, from the National Gallery past the Balmoral Hotel to the National Monument

9

history played at least one act in Edinburgh. Following the union of 1707 with England it remained the centre for government administration (now the Scottish Office), the separate Scottish legal system and the Presbyterian Church of Scotland.

When the Stone of Destiny was returned to Scotland in 1996 after centuries in England, Edinburgh became its new home. And, at the beginning of the new millennium, a Scottish Parliament will once again sit here, after nearly three centuries.

In some ways, however, it's the least Scottish of Scotland's cities due to the impact of tourism, its closeness to England, and because of its multicultural, sophisticated population.

Edinburgh has a reputation for being formal and reserved, especially in comparison with intense and gregarious Glasgow.

However, the universities and colleges create a large and lively student population for much of the year and there's a small but thriving gay and lesbian community which, next to Amsterdam's, is one of the largest of any city in Europe.

There's also a vibrant pub and late night club scene, lots of good restaurants and enough theatres and music venues to satisfy most tastes.

Special events occur throughout the year, but every August the city's dynamism unleashes a series of international festivals that includes the world's greatest arts and fringe festivals.

The flipside to all this, however, is the grim reality of life in the bleak council housing estates surrounding the city, the serious drugs scene and the distressing AIDS problem.

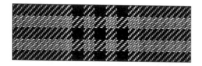

Facts about Edinburgh

HISTORY
First Immigrants

Scotland's earliest inhabitants were hunter-gatherers who began arriving about 6000 years ago from England, Ireland and northern Europe. Over the next few thousand years these colonisers came in waves to different parts of the country. There are indications of Baltic cultures in east Scotland and Irish cultures on the islands of the west. Mesolithic flints from northern France have been found at many sites.

The Neolithic era, beginning in the 4th millennium BC, brought a new way of life, with agriculture, stock breeding and trading. Unprecedentedly large populations were the result and more complex patterns of social organisation evolved to control them. With organised groups of workers, more ambitious construction projects were now possible.

Between the late Neolithic and the early Bronze Age the Beaker People reached the British Isles from mainland Europe. They were so named because they burned pottery with their dead but they also introduced bronze for knives, daggers, arrowheads and articles of gold and copper. Some sources claim that they were the original Celts.

Edinburgh's Castle Rock, a volcanic crag with three vertical sides, dominates the city centre. This natural defensive position was probably what first attracted settlers, and on Arthur's Seat, Blackford Hill and Craiglockhart Hill the earliest signs of habitation date back to around 850 BC.

The Iron Age reached Scotland around 500 BC, with the arrival of Celtic settlers from Europe.

Roman Attempts at Colonisation

The Romans didn't have much success in the north of Britain. In 80 AD, the Roman governor Agricola (whose son-in-law, Tacitus, named this region Caledonia) marched north and spent four years trying to subdue the wild tribes the Romans called the Picts (from the Latin pictus, meaning painted). The Picts were the most numerous of many Celtic peoples occupying this area at the time.

By the 2nd century, Emperor Hadrian decided that this inhospitable land of mists, bogs, midges and warring tribes had little to offer the Roman Empire and built the wall (122-28 AD) that took his name. Two decades later Hadrian's successor, Antoninus Pius, invaded Scotland again and built the turf rampart, the Antonine Wall, between the Firth of Forth and the River Clyde. Roman legions were stationed there and at hill forts at Inveresk in Musselburgh, Cramond and Dalkeith for about 40 years, before they again withdrew.

Celts & Northumbrians

When the Romans finally left Britain in the 4th century, there were two indigenous Celtic peoples in northern Britain, then known as Alba: the Picts and, in the Lothian region, the Britons. The chief tribe in Lothian was the Votadini, who had settlements on Castle Rock, Arthur's Seat and Blackford Hill. Following Roman withdrawal they made Castle Rock their capital. Under their descendants, the Gododdin, it became known as Din Eidyn (also spelled Duneideann) meaning Fort of Eidyn.

The historian, Bede, attributes Christianity's arrival in Scotland to St Ninian who established a centre in Whithorn (in Dumfries & Galloway) in 397. It's likely, however, that some of the Romanised Britons in southern Scotland adopted Christianity after the religion was given state recognition in 313.

In the 6th century a third Celtic tribe, the Scotti (the name given to them by the Romans), reached Scotland from northern Ireland (Scotia) and established a kingdom in Argyll called Dalriada. These Irish Celts spoke Q-Celtic or Gaelic which they introduced into Scotland.

In the 7th century, Northumbrian Angles from north-east England colonised south-east Scotland. They built their own fortress on Castle Rock which they called Edwinesburh.

Despite their differences, all these tribes had converted to Christianity by the late 8th century at which time a new invader appeared.

In the 790s, raiding Norsemen in longboats sacked the religious settlement at Iona off Mull that had been founded by St Columba in 563. The monks fled with St Columba's bones to found a cathedral in the Pictish Kingdom at Dunkeld. The Norsemen continued to control the entire western seaboard until Alexander III broke their power at the Battle of Largs in 1263.

Kenneth MacAlpin & the Makings of a Kingdom

In the meantime, the Picts and Scotti were drawn closer together by the threat from the Norsemen and by their common Christianity. In 843 Kenneth MacAlpin, king of the Scotti of Dalriada and son of a Pictish princess, took advantage of the Pictish custom of matrilineal succession to make himself king of Alba. Scotland north of the Firth of Forth was thus united into one kingdom. He made Scone his capital to which he also took the sacred Stone of Destiny used at the coronation of Scottish kings. Thereafter the Scotti gained cultural and political ascendancy, the Pictish culture disappeared and Alba eventually became known as Scotia.

Nearly 200 years later, MacAlpin's descendant, Malcolm II (954-1018) defeated the Northumbrian Angles led by King Canute at Carham near Roxburgh on the River Tweed. This victory brought Edinburgh and Lothian under Scottish control and extended the border to the Tweed.

Canmore Dynasty

Shakespeare's Malcolm was Malcolm III, a Canmore, who killed Macbeth at Lumphanan in 1057. With his English queen, Margaret, he founded a solid dynasty of able Scottish rulers. They introduced new Anglo-Norman systems of government and religious foundations.

Tanistry: Finding a King

Unlike the matrilineal Picts, the Scots preferred tanistry – the selection of a suitable male heir from anyone in the family who could claim a king as great grandfather. The chosen successor was known as the tanist. This had dire consequences for Scottish history, with many successions decided by the murder of one's predecessor. Shakespeare demonstrated this to great effect in *Macbeth*, but seen in a historical context Macbeth was no more a villain than anyone else. While the play isn't historically or geographically accurate, it certainly manages to evoke the dark deeds, bloodshed and warring factions of the period.

Edinburgh really began to grow in the 11th century when markets developed at the foot of the fortress, and from 1124 when their son, David I, held court at the castle and founded the abbey at Holyrood. Queen Margaret had been a deeply religious woman and either David I or his brother, Alexander I, built a church in her honour on Castle Rock. Today this is known as St Margaret's Chapel, and is the city's oldest building. David I increased his influence by adopting the Norman feudal system, granting land to great Norman families in return for their acting as what amounted to a government police force.

David I made Edinburgh a royal burgh (a self-governing town with commercial privileges) along with several other centres including Canongate, Berwick, Roxburgh, Stirling and Forfar. These traded wool from the monasteries of the Borders for Flemish cloth or wine from Burgundy. Most of the population, however, eked out a subsistence from the land. Malcolm IV, David I's successor, made the castle in Edinburgh his chief residence.

Inaccessible in their glens, the Highland clans remained a law unto themselves. A cultural and linguistic divide grew up between Gaelic-speaking Highlanders, and the Lowland Scots who spoke Lallans, a language made up of English, Norse and Gaelic constituents.

Wars of Independence

Two centuries of the Canmore dynasty effectively ended in 1286 when Alexander III fell to his death into the Firth of Forth at Kinghorn, Fife, and was succeeded by his four-year-old granddaughter, Margaret (the Maid of Norway). She was engaged to the son of England's Edward I, but died in 1290.

There followed a dispute over the succession to the throne for which there were no less than 13 'tanists' or contestants, but in the end it came down to two: Robert Bruce of Annandale and John Balliol. Edward I, as the greatest feudal lord in Britain, was asked to arbitrate and chose Balliol. However, instead of withdrawing, Edward I sought to formalise his feudal overlordship and travelled the country forcing clan leaders to sign a declaration of allegiance to him. Balliol allied himself with the French in 1295, thus beginning the enduring Auld Alliance with France.

In a final blow to Scottish pride Edward I removed the Stone of Destiny, the coronation stone on which the kings of Scotland had been invested for centuries, and sent it from Scone to London. Resistance broke out throughout the country, some of it serious, and Edward's response earned him the title Hammer of the Scots. In 1296 he laid siege to and captured Berwick, Edinburgh, Roxburgh and Stirling.

In 1297, William Wallace's forces defeated the English at the Battle of Stirling Bridge. After further skirmishes Wallace was betrayed, captured and executed – hanged, drawn, emasculated, burnt and quartered – at Smithfield in London in 1305. He's still remembered as the epitome of patriotism and a great hero of the resistance movement.

Robert the Bruce (grandson of Robert Bruce of Annandale) emerged as contender. He murdered his rival, John Comyn (also called Red Comyn), in February 1306 and

William Wallace, a great Scottish patriot, was executed by the English in 1305

had himself crowned king of Scotland in March. However, he was defeated in battle first at Methven (19 June) by the English under the Earl of Pembroke, then at Dalry (11 August) by John MacDougall of Lorne, a kinsman of John Comyn.

According to myth, while Bruce was on the run he was inspired by a spider's persistence in spinning its web to renew his own efforts. He went on to defeat the English at the Battle of Bannockburn in 1314, a turning point in Scotland's fight for independence from England.

After his death, the country was ravaged by endless civil disputes and plague epidemics. The Wars of Independence helped strengthen links with France and Europe; the Auld Alliance with France was constantly renewed up to 1492.

The Stewarts & the Barons

Bruce's son became David II of Scotland, but was soon caught up in battles with Scots disaffected by his father and aided by England's Edward III. Edinburgh was occupied several times by English armies during this troubled period. David II suffered exile and imprisonment, but was released after agreeing to pay a huge ransom and made Edinburgh Castle his main residence. He appointed Edward's son as his heir, but when David II died in 1371 the Scots quickly crowned Robert Stewart (Robert the Bruce's grandson), the first of the Stewart dynasty.

The early Stewart kings were ruthless in their attempts to break the power of the magnates. These were not peaceful years. Time and again the king met with an untimely death and clans like the Douglases and the Donalds (Lords of the Isles after the Norsemen were driven from the Hebrides in 1266) grew to wield almost regal power.

By the mid-15th century Edinburgh was the de facto royal capital of Scotland. The coronation of James II (1430-60) was held in the abbey at Holyrood and the Scottish parliament met in the Tolbooth on High St or in the castle. The city's first effective town wall was constructed at about this time and circled today's Old Town and the area around Grassmarket. This restricted, defensible zone became a medieval Manhattan, forcing its densely packed inhabitants to build tenements that soared to 12 storeys.

James IV & the Renaissance

James IV married the daughter of Henry VII of England, the first of the Tudor monarchs, thereby linking the two families. This didn't, however, prevent the French from persuading James to go to war with his in-laws. He was killed at the battle of Flodden Hill in 1513, along with 10,000 of his subjects. To protect Edinburgh from a possible English invasion its citizens built the Flodden Wall around the city.

James IV's death ended a golden era that had seen the foundation of the Royal College of Surgeons, the establishment of a supreme law court and the introduction of printing in Edinburgh. Much graceful Scottish architecture dates from this time, and examples of the Renaissance style can be seen in alterations made to the palaces at Holyrood, Stirling, Linlithgow and Falkland. The building of collegiate churches and universities brought opportunities for education at home, along French lines. St Andrews University was founded in 1410, Glasgow in 1451 and Aberdeen in 1495.

Renaissance ideas flourished in Scotland during James' reign. Scottish poetry thrived. The intellectual climate was fertile ground for the ideas of the Reformation, a critique of the medieval Catholic church, and the rise of Protestantism.

Mary Queen of Scots & the Reformation

In 1542, James V died – broken-hearted, it is said, after his defeat by the English at Solway Moss. His baby daughter, Mary, became Queen of Scots.

At first the country was ruled by regents, who rejected Henry VIII's plan that Mary should marry his son, and sent her to France. Henry was furious, and his armies ravaged the Borders and sacked Edinburgh in a failed attempt to force agreement – the Rough Wooing, as it was called. Mary eventually married the dauphin and became queen of France as well as Scotland.

While Mary, a devout Catholic, was in France, the Reformation of the Scottish church was under way. The wealthy Catholic church was riddled with corruption and the preachings of John Knox, pupil of the Swiss reformer, Calvin, found sympathetic ears. In 1560 the Scottish Parliament created a Protestant church that was independent of Rome and the monarchy. The Latin mass was abolished and the pope's authority denied.

Following her husband's death, Mary returned to Scotland. Still only 18 and a stunning beauty, she was a headstrong Catholic and her conduct did nothing to endear her to the Protestants. She married Henry Darnley in Holyrood and later gave birth to a son in Edinburgh Castle. However, domestic bliss was short-lived and, in a scarcely believable train of events, Darnley was involved in the murder of Mary's Italian secretary Rizzio (rumoured to be her lover). Then Darnley himself was murdered, presumably by Mary and her lover and future husband, the Earl of Bothwell.

Forced to abdicate in favour of her son, James VI, Mary was imprisoned in the castle in the middle of Loch Leven, but escaped to England and her cousin, the

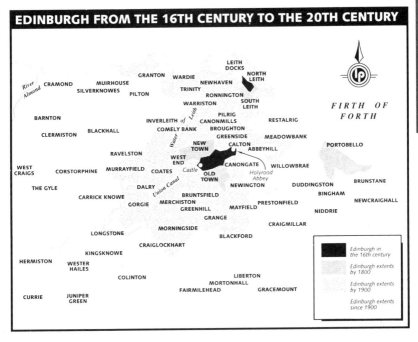

EDINBURGH FROM THE 16TH CENTURY TO THE 20TH CENTURY

Protestant Elizabeth I. Since Mary had claims to the English throne, and Elizabeth had no heir, she was seen as a security risk and Elizabeth kept her locked in the Tower of London. It took her 19 years to agree to sign the warrant for Mary's execution. When Elizabeth died in 1603, James VI of Scotland united the crowns by also becoming James I of England.

He moved the court to London and, for the most part, the Stewarts ignored Edinburgh. James VII's reign, however, did see the foundation of the Town College in 1582 which later became the University of Edinburgh.

Religious Wars of the 17th Century

Religious differences led to civil war in Scotland and England. The fortunes of the Stuarts (spelt the French way following Mary's Gallic association) were thereafter bound up with the church's struggle to establish independence from Rome. To complicate matters, religious reform in Scotland was divided between Presbyterians, who shunned all ritual and hierarchy, and less-extreme Protestants who were more like the Anglicans south of the border. The question of episcopacy (rule of the bishops) was particularly divisive.

Earning himself the nickname of the Wisest Fool in Christendom, James VII pursued a moderate policy despite the reformers' fervour. But he also insisted that his authority came directly from God (the Divine Right of Kings) and was therefore incontestable, and encouraged the paranoia which led to witch hunts, with many innocent people, set up as scapegoats, suffering appalling deaths by torture and burning.

In 1625 James was succeeded by his son, Charles I, a devout Anglican who attempted to impose a High Anglican form of worship on the church in Scotland.

In 1637 the Dean of St Giles' Cathedral in Edinburgh was reading the English prayer book (a symbol of episcopacy) when he was floored by a stool thrown by Jennie Geddes, an Edinburgh greengrocer. The common people wanted a common religion and riots ensued which ended with the creation of a document known as the National Covenant. The Covenanters sought freedom from Rome and from royal interference in church government, the abolition of bishops and a simpler ritual.

The dispute developed into civil war between moderate royalists and radical Covenanters. The Marquis of Montrose is still remembered as a dashing hero who, though originally a Covenanter, eventually held out for the king. He was betrayed to the English Republicans while hiding at Ardvreck Castle in Loch Assynt and executed as a traitor.

The Flodden Wall

In 1513 the English defeated the Scots at the Battle of Flodden – King James IV and 10,000 of his followers were killed. The citizens of Edinburgh were thrown into such despair by this episode that in order to protect the city they reluctantly decided to separate it from the outside world altogether. To that end they built the Flodden Wall (1513-60), which was over 1¼ miles long, 25 feet high and 5 feet thick.

As a result, rather than growing outwards, the city (today's Old Town) grew upwards. The wall enclosed West Port, Grassmarket, Greyfriars, St Mary's St (where it crossed the Royal Mile at Netherbow Port on High St) and the area south of Cowgate. Parts of it can still be seen at the western end of Greyfriars Kirkyard, in the vennel off West Port and in the basement of the World's End pub on the corner of High and St Mary's Sts.

In the meantime, civil war raged in England. Charles I was defeated by Oliver Cromwell and beheaded in 1649. His exiled son, Charles, was offered the crown in Scotland as long as he signed the Covenant. He was crowned in 1650 but was soon forced into exile by Cromwell, who invaded Scotland and captured Edinburgh.

After Charles II's restoration in 1660, episcopacy was reinstated. Many clergymen rejected the bishops' authority and started holding outdoor services, or Conventicles. His successor, James II, a Catholic, appeared to set out determinedly to lose his kingdom. Among other poor decisions, he made worshipping as a Covenanter a capital offence.

The prospect of another Catholic king was too much for the English Protestants, so they invited William of Orange, a Dutchman who was James' nephew and married to his eldest Protestant daughter, to take power. In 1689 he landed with a small army; James broke down and fled to France. In the same year, episcopacy was abolished.

Union with England in 1707

The wars had left the country and economy ruined. During the 1690s, famine killed up to a third of the population in some areas.

Anti-English feeling ran high. Graham of Claverhouse (Bonnie Dundee) raised a band of Highlanders and routed the English troops at Killiecrankie (1689), near Pitlochry. The situation was exacerbated by the failure of an investment venture in Panama set up by the Bank of England to boost the economy, which resulted in widespread bankruptcy in Scotland.

In 1692, people were horrified by the treacherous massacre, on English government orders, of MacDonalds by Campbells in Glencoe, for failing to swear allegiance to William. The massacre became Jacobite (Stuart) propaganda that still resonates today.

In this atmosphere, the lure of trade concessions to boost the economy and the preservation of the Scottish church and the legal and education systems (along with financial inducements to ensure the

St Giles' Cathedral, Old Town

A piper plays a Scottish lament

The winter sun sets on Edinburgh Castle

NEIL WILSON

Edinburgh's Historical Timelin

850 BC
Early settlement at Holyrood Park; Earliest habitation of Castle Rock.

1800s BC
Arrival of Beaker People; Construction of stone circles.

TOM SMALLMAN

1313
Holyrood Abbey demolished by Robert the Bruc
Photo: Palace of Holyroodhouse with ruined Abbey to the le

1437
James II crowned in Holyrood Abbey; First town wall constructed.

Photo: Heraldic plaque of James V, originally from Holyrood Abbey

BETHUNE CARMICHAEL

1128
David I founds Holyrood Abbey (St Margaret's Chapel); Edinburgh made a royal burgh.

1440s
Craigmillar Castle constructed.

600
Fortress constructed on Castle Rock (Edwinesburh), later to become Edinburgh Castle.

Photo: Stained glass window, Edinburgh Castle

BETHUNE CARMICHAEL

BETHUNE CARMICHAEL

1477
Grassmarket market established.

Photo: Wall plaque, Grassmarket

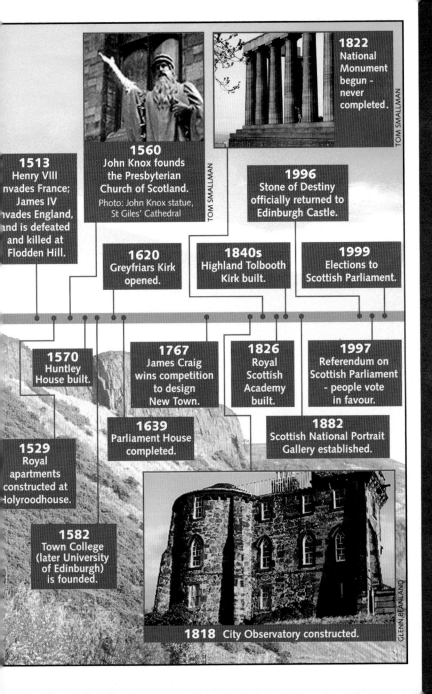

1513
Henry VIII invades France; James IV invades England, and is defeated and killed at Flodden Hill.

1560
John Knox founds the Presbyterian Church of Scotland.
Photo: John Knox statue, St Giles' Cathedral

TOM SMALLMAN

1822
National Monument begun - never completed.

TOM SMALLMAN

1996
Stone of Destiny officially returned to Edinburgh Castle.

1620
Greyfriars Kirk opened.

1840s
Highland Tolbooth Kirk built.

1999
Elections to Scottish Parliament.

1570
Huntley House built.

1767
James Craig wins competition to design New Town.

1826
Royal Scottish Academy built.

1997
Referendum on Scottish Parliament - people vote in favour.

1639
Parliament House completed.

1882
Scottish National Portrait Gallery established.

1529
Royal apartments constructed at Holyroodhouse.

1582
Town College (later University of Edinburgh) is founded.

1818 City Observatory constructed.

GLENN BEANLAND

Royal Mile, Old Town

A balloon headdress, Waverley Shopping Centre

St Cuthbert's Church and West Princes Street Gardens

compliance of the nobility) persuaded the Scottish Parliament to agree to the Act of Union of 1707. This act united the two countries under a single parliament and further reduced Edinburgh's importance, but the union was unpopular with most ordinary Scots.

The Jacobites (1715-45)

The Jacobite rebellions, most notably of 1715 and 1745, were attempts to replace the Hanoverian monarchy (chosen by Parliament to succeed the house of Orange) with Catholic Stuarts. Despite Scottish disenchantment with the Act of Union, however, there was never really much support for the Jacobite cause outside the Highlands, owing to the fear of inviting Catholicism back into Scotland.

James Edward Stuart, known as the Old Pretender, was the son of the exiled James VII. With support from the Highland clans he made several attempts to regain the throne but fled to France after the unsuccessful 1715 rebellion.

In 1745, James's son, Charles Edward Stuart (Bonnie Prince Charlie) landed in Scotland to claim the crown for his father. He was at first successful, getting as far south into England as Derby, but back in Scotland after retreating north the Young Pretender and his Highland supporters suffered catastrophic defeat at Culloden in 1746. Dressed as a woman, the prince escaped via the Western Isles assisted by Flora MacDonald.

After 'the '45' (as it became known), the government banned private armies, wearing the kilt and playing the pipes. Many Jacobites were transported or executed, or died in prison; others forfeited their lands.

Scottish Enlightenment

Edinburgh may have declined in political importance but its cultural and intellectual life flourished. In the Scottish Enlightenment of the 18th century, the philosophers David Hume and Adam Smith emerged as influential thinkers nourished on generations of theological debate.

After the bloodshed and fervent religious debate of the Reformation, people applied themselves with the same energy and piety to the making of money and the enjoyment of leisure. There was a revival of interest in vernacular literature, reflected in Robert Fergusson's satires and Alexander Mac-Donald's Gaelic poetry. The poetry of Robert Burns, a man of the people, achieved lasting popularity. Sir Walter Scott, the prolific poet and novelist, was an ardent patriot and responsible for the Scottish crown jewels being put on public display in Edinburgh Castle.

There was also an architectural renaissance in Edinburgh led by James Craig and Robert Adam. To relieve the city's overcrowding, non-existent sanitation and pollution from thousands of domestic fires (which gave it its nickname, Auld Reekie), in the second half of the 18th century the council sponsored a competition to design a new part of the city. Craig's design of the New Town, which was to be across the ravine to the north, won; Adam designed many of its buildings. The wealthy fled here from Auld Reekie.

The 19th Century

The Industrial Revolution of the 19th century caused Edinburgh's population to increase rapidly, quadrupling in size to 400,000, not much less than it is today. The old city's tenements were taken over by refugees from the Irish famines and there was severe overcrowding, malnutrition and disease. A new ring of crescents and circuses was built south of the New Town, and grey Victorian terraces sprung up. Urbanisation spread further after the arrival of the railways, with outlying villages like Portobello absorbed into the conurbation. Towards the end of the century, however, the academic Patrick Geddes (who also discovered chlorophyll) was able to help revive the Old Town.

The city's industries included baking, brewing, distilling, book printing and the manufacture of machinery.

Edinburgh's growth was considerable, but Glasgow's was massive and it became Scotland's largest city during this time. Thus began a tale of rivalry between the two cities which continues to this day.

The 20th Century

In the 1920s the city's borders were extended again to swallow Leith in the north, Cramond in the west and the Pentland Hills in the south. Following the reorganisation of Scottish local government in 1975, the city expanded westward to absorb South Queensferry, Ratho and Kirkliston. Inner-city slum dwellers were moved into new housing estates ringing the city, which now foster massive social problems.

In the 1920s and 30s Edinburgh was the focus of a Scottish political and literary revival led by the nationalist poet Hugh MacDiarmid, co-founder of the Scottish Nationalist Party (SNP).

Following WWII, the city's cultural life blossomed, initiated by the Edinburgh International Festival and its fellow traveller the Edinburgh Fringe Festival, both now recognised as world class arts festivals. The University of Edinburgh established itself as an international force in higher learning, with important research in areas such as medicine and electronics. In the 1960s and 70s some of Edinburgh's unique architectural heritage was destroyed by city planners. However, a strong conservation movement emerged to preserve and restore its old buildings and to control the impact of any new developments on the city's character.

Scottish Self-Rule

From 1979 to 1997, the Scots were ruled by a Conservative government for which the majority of Scots hadn't voted. Nationalist feelings, always present, grew stronger. In 1967 the SNP won its first seat, and support for it grew in this period.

Both the Labour and Conservative parties had toyed with offering Scotland devolution, or a degree of self-government. In 1979 Scots voted in a referendum on whether to set up a directly elected Scottish Assembly, but the majority of Scots voted against it.

Following the landslide victory of the British Labour Party in May 1997, another referendum was held over the creation of a Scottish Parliament. This time voters chose overwhelmingly in favour. The new parliament will be in Edinburgh and, following elections in 1999, will convene in the year 2000. Its temporary home will be the Assembly Rooms of the Church of Scotland near the castle. In the meantime, a new building that will be its permanent home is under construction near the Palace of Holyroodhouse.

GEOGRAPHY & GEOLOGY

Edinburgh's latitude is 55° 57' north, its longitude 3° 13' west. The city occupies about 5 miles of sloping land between the Pentland Hills in the south and the broad Firth of Forth estuary to the north. Within the city's boundaries are five extinct volcanoes. The solidified lava flows of Arthur's Seat, Calton Hill and Castle Rock form part of one. Glacial ice once flowed around Castle Rock, depositing to its east the debris of a lateral moraine upon which the Old Town was built. The surrounding valleys were cut by glacial action during the Pleistocene era.

In the centre of Edinburgh, Holyrood Park is a real wilderness with a varied landscape of hills, lochs, fields and moorland.

Edinburgh's only river, the Water of Leith, runs from the Pentlands north to the Firth of Forth and broadly marks the north-western border of the New Town.

CLIMATE

Scotland has a cool temperate climate. Considering just how far north the city lies (Edinburgh is on a similar latitude to Moscow), you might expect the climate to be colder than it is, but the winds from the Atlantic are warmed by the Gulf Stream. The east coast tends to be cool and dry. August is the warmest month when temperatures average a high of 18°C; winter temperatures rarely drop below 0°C, although winds off the North Sea can rattle your teeth. The average annual rainfall is around 650mm.

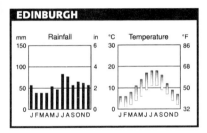

The weather changes quickly – a rainy day can often be followed by a sunny one. March and April are generally the driest, sunniest months, and July the wettest, but you can expect rain at any time. Storms are rare from April to August.

ECOLOGY & ENVIRONMENT

Edinburgh first earned its sobriquet of Auld Reekie (Old Smokey) from the huge number of domestic fires in the city. With the coming of the Industrial Revolution, pollution from factories added to the grime which darkened its buildings. Beginning in the 1950s a series of smokeless zones were set up which now encompass the whole city. This has encouraged the cleaning of the exterior of many of its buildings, which has restored them to their original colour.

To reduce traffic congestion and vehicle pollution, a scheme encouraging greater bus use has been set up (see the Greenways boxed text in the Getting Around chapter).

Edinburgh is the first city in the UK to try out a 'car free' housing development, 2 miles from the city centre. Space usually allocated to car parking will be given to children's playgrounds, sports facilities and cycle paths. With the aim of increasing cycle use in Edinburgh, a network of city centre cycling routes has been identified with about 16 miles constructed.

Organisations

A number of organisations concerned with the environment have their headquarters in Edinburgh including:

John Muir Trust
(☎ 0131-554 0114), 12 Wellington Place, Leith, Edinburgh EH6 7EQ; cares for some of the wilder areas of Scotland accessible to the public.

National Trust for Scotland (NTS)
(☎ 0131-226 5922), 5 Charlotte Square, Edinburgh EH2 4DU; a voluntary conservation body which cares for around 185,000 acres of countryside (as well as owning historic buildings); reciprocal membership agreements with the National Trust (for England, Wales and Northern Ireland).

Royal Society for the Protection of Birds (RSPB; ☎ 0131-557 6275), 12 Regent Terrace, Edinburgh EH7 5BN; has reserves around Scotland which are open to the public.

Scottish Natural Heritage
(☎ 0131-447 4784), 12 Hope Terrace, Edinburgh EH9 2AS; a government agency responsible for the conservation of Scotland's wildlife, habitats and landscapes; designates and manages National Nature Reserves (NNRs) and Sites of Special Scientific Interest (SSSIs).

Scottish Wildlife Trust
(☎ 0131-312 7765), 16 Cramond Glebe Rd, Edinburgh EH4 6NS; a voluntary agency that owns and runs 116 nature reserves.

GOVERNMENT & POLITICS

When the new Scottish parliament convenes in 2000 it will have 129 members, will sit for four-year terms and be responsible for education, health, levying income taxes, and other domestic affairs. Westminster will still control areas such as defence, foreign affairs and social security.

In the meantime the Secretary of State for Scotland, a member of the British Cabinet, will continue to be responsible for Scotland's administration in the form of five departments: education and health; development; planning; agriculture and fisheries; and the judicial system. The secretary operates from the Scottish Office in Edinburgh.

There are 72 Scottish members in the House of Commons and all Scottish peers have a seat in the House of Lords.

The main political parties are the same as for the rest of Britain – Labour, Liberal Democrat, Conservative – with the addition of the Scottish Nationalist Party. As a result of the 1997 British general election there were no remaining Conservative MPs in Scotland.

The Conservative Party was largely opposed to devolution (the transfer of government powers from Westminster to Scotland), but the long-term goal of the Scottish Nationalists is complete independence.

There are 32 administrative regions in Scotland, roughly corresponding to the old counties (eg Argyll, Perthshire etc) which existed prior to the 1975 reforms.

Responsibility for Edinburgh's local government is divided between two councils. The Lothian Regional Council is in charge of education, environment, transport, social services, and police and fire services in Edinburgh and the Lothians. The City of Edinburgh District Council is responsible for housing, libraries, museums and recreational facilities in the city itself. Both councils are popularly elected and serve four-year terms.

ECONOMY

Edinburgh has one of the richest urban economies in the UK. Of Edinburgh's traditional industries, only brewing continues on a major scale, but closures, takeovers and 'rationalisations' have reduced the size of the workforce. Publishing and printing also continue but on a smaller scale. Electronics and engineering are now the main industrial employers.

Edinburgh's economy is largely based on services (accounting for 85% of employment) most notably in finance and tourism; in both sectors Edinburgh is second only to London. Other important service industries include education, law, local government and medicine. The city's growth areas are in research, information technology, computer software and biotechnology.

The Royal Bank of Scotland, the Bank of Scotland and other financial bodies have their headquarters in the city.

Edinburgh has two ports, Leith and Granton, both on the Firth of Forth just north of the centre, which handle most imports and exports. Granton is also an important fishing centre.

On the down side, unemployment is higher than the UK average and is chronic in the outlying housing estates, especially among young people. Lothian & Edinburgh Enterprise Limited (LEEL), part of the Scottish Enterprise Network, is a quasi-government body that promotes businesses and jobs at a local level.

POPULATION & PEOPLE

Edinburgh's population of 409,000, is made up of white-collar and blue-collar workers in roughly equal proportions. In fact, with so many people employed in education, finance, government, law and medicine it has Scotland's largest middle class population. Immigration has added to the city's ethnic mix, but on a smaller scale than other European capitals. Following the 19th century famines in Ireland, many Irish settled here, as have a considerable proportion of English. There are also many smaller ethnic communities including Italians, Poles, Indians and Chinese. For much of the year the large student population adds to the city's cosmopolitanism.

ARTS

Edinburgh (together with Glasgow) dominates the arts in Scotland. It has an energetic cultural scene, partly reflected by its world-class festivals, which showcase an extraordinary range of performers and artists. Historically, however, although the Scots have had a disproportionate impact on science, technology, medicine and philosophy, they are, except for literature, underrepresented in the worlds of art and music.

The arts never seem to have caught the Scottish popular imagination – or at least not in a form recognised by modern culture vultures. It has been suggested that perhaps the need for creative expression took different, less elitist paths – in the *ceilidh* (see Society & Conduct), in folk music and dance, oral poetry and folk stories.

Literature

Scotland has a rich literary heritage and there are many works that have been inspired by or set in Edinburgh.

Most books are published in different editions by different publishers in different countries. As a result, a book might be a hardcover rarity in one country while it's readily available in paperback in another. Fortunately, bookshops and libraries search by title or author, so your local bookshop or library is best placed to advise you on the availability of the following.

Sir Walter Scott's prodigious output did much to romanticise Scotland and its historical figures. In the *Heart of Midlothian* he used an existing house in St Leonard's as the home of the fictional character Jennie Deans.

Several Robert Louis Stevenson novels have Scottish settings; *Kidnapped*, set on the island of Mull, Edinburgh and Rannoch Moor, captures the country most vividly. Although *Dr Jekyll and Mr Hyde* is set in London, Stevenson drew inspiration from the streets of Edinburgh.

Arthur Conan Doyle, creator of Sherlock Holmes, was inspired by his daily walk to the University of Edinburgh as a student past Salisbury Craigs for the setting of his novel *The Lost World*.

Sir Arthur Conan Doyle used his experiences as a student in Edinburgh for *The Lost World*

Robert Louis Stevenson drew inspiration from Edinburgh for the settings of several novels

Many of John Buchan's adventure stories are set at least partly in Scotland. In *The Thirty Nine Steps* the heroes take the train from London to Edinburgh and beyond in pursuit of the villain.

Muriel Spark's shrewd portrait of 1930s Edinburgh, *The Prime of Miss Jean Brodie*, was made into an excellent film. In sharp contrast, Irvine Welsh's novels, like *Trainspotting* which was also made into a successful film, take the reader on a guided tour of the modern city's underworld of drugs, drink, despair and violence. His latest novel is called *Ecstasy*. Ian Rankin's detective stories, which include *Hide and Seek*, also depict the seedy side of Edinburgh life.

St Leonard's Hall, just outside Holyrood Park, was occupied for a time by a girl's school called St Trinnean's. It was reputedly the inspiration for the St Trinian stories of Robert Earle whose daughter was a pupil there.

Collections of ballads and poems by the popular national bard Robert Burns, who spent some time in Edinburgh, are widely

Robert Burns

Best remembered for penning the words of *Auld Lang Syne*, Robert Burns is Scotland's most famous poet, and a popular hero whose birthday (25 January) is celebrated as Burns Night by Scots around the world.

He was born in 1759 in Alloway. Although his mother was illiterate and his parents poor farmers, they sent him to the local school where he soon showed an aptitude for literature and a fondness for the folk song. He began to write his own songs and satires, some of which he distributed privately. When the problems of his arduous farming life were compounded by the threat of prosecution from the father of Jean Armour, with whom he'd had an affair, he decided to emigrate to Jamaica. He gave up his share of the family farm and published his poems to raise money for the journey.

The poems were so well reviewed in Edinburgh that Burns decided to remain in Scotland and devote himself to writing. He went to Edinburgh in 1787 to publish a second edition, but the financial rewards were not enough to live on and he had to take a job as a customs officer in Dumfriesshire. He contributed many songs to collections published by Johnson and Thomson in Edinburgh, and a third edition of his poems was published in 1793. Burns died in Dumfries in 1796, aged 37, after a heart attack.

While some dispute Burns' claim to true literary genius, he was certainly an accomplished poet and songwriter, and has been compared to Chaucer for his verse tale *Tam o'Shanter*. Burns wrote in Lallans, the Scottish Lowland language derived from Anglo-Saxon that isn't very accessible to the foreigner; perhaps this is part of his appeal. He was also very much a man of the people, satirising the upper classes and the church for their hypocrisy.

available. Scotland's finest modern poet was Hugh MacDiarmid, who trained as a teacher in Edinburgh and later co-founded the SNP. Perhaps the city's worst poet was Edinburgh-born William MacGonagall, celebrated for the sheer awfulness of his rhymes. His *Poetic Gems* offers a taster.

Architecture

Scottish architecture can be divided into six periods: Celtic (up to the 11th century), Anglo-Norman (up to the 16th century), post-Reformation or Renaissance (up to the 17th century), Georgian (18th century), Victorian Baronial (19th century) and 20th century (which so far evades simple characterisation).

Interesting buildings can be seen throughout Scotland, but Edinburgh and the country around it have a particularly remarkable heritage of superb architecture from the 12th century to the present day.

Anglo-Norman The Normans were great builders, and their Romanesque style – with its characteristic round arches – can still be seen in David I's church at Dunfermline across the Firth of Forth. The oldest building in Edinburgh is the simple, stone St Margaret's Chapel in Edinburgh Castle built by David I (or his brother Alexander I) around 1130.

Military architecture was also influenced by the Normans in castles like Caerlaverock (1290) and, later, at Stirling (1496). Most feudal lords, however, built more modest tower, or peel, houses, like Smailholm (14th century) near Kelso. These had a single small entrance, massively thick stone walls and a single room at each of about five levels.

As the Gothic style developed in England and Europe, it was brought to Scotland and adapted by the religious orders. The characteristic pointed arches and stone vaulting can be seen in the ruins of great Border abbeys like Jedburgh (12th century).

Post-Reformation After the Reformation most churches were modified to suit the new religion, which frowned on ceremony and ornament. In some areas, tower houses and castles became less relevant because of the increasing effectiveness of artillery. The gentry therefore had the luxury of expanding their houses and at the same time making them more decorative. Features like turrets, conical roofs, garrets and gables became popular in buildings such as Thirlestane Castle in Lauder.

Georgian Edinburgh has a rich legacy of Georgian architecture. The greatest exponents of the austere, symmetrical Georgian style in Scotland were the Adam family, in particular Robert Adam. Among many of the buildings he designed in the mid-18th century are the Old College of the University of Edinburgh, Register House on Princes St, Charlotte Square (possibly the finest examples of Georgian architecture anywhere) and Hopetoun House near South Queensferry.

Baronial Victorian As the Scottish identity was reaffirmed by writers like Burns and Scott, architects turned to the towers and turrets of the past for inspiration. Fanciful buildings such as Scott's home, Abbotsford near Melrose, were created, and the fashion was also exhibited in many of the civic buildings.

Victorian architects also looked to Europe for inspiration, but whereas the Georgians looked to Greece, the Victorians tended to look to Italy. The Royal Scotland Museum in Chambers St has a Venetian Renaissance façade, for example, while the Scottish National Portrait Gallery is modelled on the Doge's Palace in Venice.

20th Century In general, the quality of modern building hasn't been high. Scotland's most famous 20th century architect and designer was Charles Rennie Mackin-

tosh, one of the most influential exponents of Art Nouveau, though he never designed anything in Edinburgh. The few good examples of modern Scottish architecture tend to be outside Edinburgh. The one exception is the Edinburgh International Conference Centre, on Morrison St, with its huge circular auditorium.

Edinburgh, like other larger towns and cities, suffered badly under the onslaught of the motor car, shoddy council housing and bad planning. Many citizens still haven't forgiven the university for pulling down much of George Square, to build featureless office blocks. Much of Princes St's north side has given way to bland shopfronts, and St James Shopping Centre round the corner on Leith St is just plain ugly. Waverley Market shopping centre, between the Balmoral Hotel and Princes Gardens, however, is unobtrusively tucked into the hillside. A few fine 19th century buildings have survived on Princes St including Jenners, the world's oldest department store.

Painting

There are few internationally known figures in the visual arts, although the National Gallery in Edinburgh has important Scottish collections.

Scottish painting only really emerged in the mid-17th century with portraits by George Jameson and John Wright. Scottish portraiture reached its peak during the Scottish Enlightenment in the second half of the 18th century in the figures of Alan Ramsay and Henry Raeburn. At the same time, Alexander Nasmyth emerged as an important landscape painter whose work had immense influence on the 19th century. One of the greatest artists of the 19th century was David Wilkie whose paintings depicted simple, rural Scottish life.

The Trustees' Academy in Edinburgh, particularly under the direction of William Scott Lauder, was very influential and taught many of the great painters of the 19th century, most notably William McTaggart. Exhibitions at the Royal Scottish Academy in Edinburgh also helped to promote Scottish painters.

Since the end of the 19th century, Glasgow has dominated the Scottish scene, partly thanks to the Glasgow School of Art, which has produced several outstanding artists. These included Charles Rennie Mackintosh, whose Art Nouveau style upset more traditionalist painters, and Mary Armour who was a student there in the 1920s.

In the 1890s, the Glasgow Boys, which included James Guthrie and EA Walton in their ranks, were stylistically influenced by the French impressionists. They were succeeded by the Scottish Colourists whose striking paintings drew upon French postimpressionism and Fauvism. In the same period the Glasgow Girls, exponents of decorative arts and design, drew upon Art Nouveau and Celtic influences. Among their members were Jessie Newbery, Anne Macbeth and the MacDonald sisters, Margaret and Frances.

The Edinburgh School of the 1930s were modernist painters who depicted the Scottish landscape. Chief among them were William Gillies, William MacTaggart (not to be confused with his earlier namesake) and Ann Redpath. Following WWII, artists such as Alan Davie and Eduardo Paolozzi gained international reputations in abstract expressionism and pop art, but their work isn't particularly 'Scottish'. Today's new wave of painters includes the New Glasgow Boys whose work is characterised by a concern for social issues.

Music

The Scottish Opera was founded in the 1960s and is based in Glasgow, but performs two to three times a year in Edinburgh in places such as the Edinburgh Festival Theatre and Usher Hall.

In the 1950s and 1960s many people's idea of Scottish music was represented by the likes of Kenneth McKellar and Andy Stewart, who sang mostly sentimental ballads accompanied by the accordion and

occasionally the bagpipes. They often wore the kilt when they performed. In the 1970s the most recognised Scottish pop band was the Bay City Rollers (the Spice Girls of their day) from Edinburgh. They sang simple ditties and wore outrageously baggy tartan trousers and can still be seen performing in small venues around the country.

Scotland has always had a strong folk tradition and in the 60s and 70s Robin Hall and Jimmy MacGregor, the Corries and the hugely talented Ewan McColl worked in the pubs and clubs up and down the country. During this time the Incredible String Band and the Boys of the Lough successfully combined folk and rock and have been followed by the Battlefield Band, Runrig (who write songs in Gaelic), Alba, Capercaillie and others. Rock musicians like Simple Minds and the Pogues borrowed from Scottish themes.

Some other Scottish artists who have been very successful in rock music include Edinburgh-born Iain Anderson, front man for Jethro Tull, and Mike Scott of the Waterboys. Barbara Dickson, Nazareth and Vipond all hail from Dunfermline across the Forth. Sheena Easton came from Bellshill and now lives in Beverley Hills and Aberdeen's greatest musical export is Annie Lennox. The Jesus & Mary Chain came from East Kilbride, while Glasgow has produced the BMX Bandits, Aztec Camera, Hue & Cry, Tears for Fears, Deacon Blue, Wet Wet Wet, Texas – and Lulu. Stuart Sutcliffe, one of the original members of the Beatles, was born in Edinburgh.

Cinema

Scotland has been the setting for many films, but Edinburgh itself surprisingly few. In such films as *Chariots of Fire* (1981), *Mary Reilly* (1995) and *Jude* (1996) parts of the city were used to depict locations elsewhere.

The two film versions of John Buchan's *The Thirty Nine Steps*, the first starring Robert Donat, the second Kenneth More, are partly set in the city. The story of

Actor Sean Connery was born and brought up in Fountainbridge, and as a boy earned a living delivering milk from a horse-drawn cart

Greyfriars Bobby, the Skye terrier who maintained a vigil on his master's grave, also made it into the movies twice – first as *Challenge to Lassie* in 1949, then as *Greyfriars Bobby* in 1960.

The comedy *Battle of the Sexes* (1959) with Peter Sellers was set in an Edinburgh textile factory.

Maggie Smith starred in the adaptation of Muriel Spark's novel, *The Prime of Miss Jean Brodie* (1969), about a 1930s Edinburgh schoolteacher, for which she received an Oscar.

Restless Natives (1985) is about two young men from a council housing estate who become famous after robbing tourists.

Trainspotting (1996), starring Ewan MacGregor and Robert Carlyle, was the grim film rendition of Irvine Welsh's bleak novel. Ewan MacGregor had also starred in the earlier *Shallow Grave* (1994) about three people whose new flatmate dies of a heroin overdose; they decide to bury him and keep his money. Though set in Edinburgh, it was mostly shot in Glasgow.

SCIENCES

It's not overstating it to say that the intellectual output of Scottish scientists has transformed modern civilisation. John Napier invented logarithms and Lord Kelvin revealed the second law of thermodynamics. James Clerk Maxwell, who described the laws of electromagnetism, and James Hutton, the founder of modern geology, were both born in Edinburgh and studied at the university.

The technologists include James Watt, who revolutionised steam power and John Dunlop, who invented the pneumatic wheel. John McAdam, invented the road surface that bears his name (but spelt differently) and Charles Mackintosh invented a waterproof material to use in the raincoat that is named after him. Alexander Graham Bell, inventor of the telephone, was another who studied in Edinburgh. John Logie Baird invented TV and Sir Robert Watson Watt, radar.

In medicine, John and William Hunter pioneered anatomy while Sir Joseph Lister pioneered the use of antiseptics. Alexander Fleming co-discovered penicillin. In 1996, a team of Scottish embryologists working at

James Watt, the Scottish engineer and inventor who revolutionised steampower in the 1700s

the Roslin Institute near Edinburgh scored a first when they successfully cloned a sheep, Dolly, from the breast cell of an adult sheep. They added to this success when Dolly was mated naturally with a Welsh ram; in April 1998 she gave birth to a healthy lamb, Bonnie.

The philosophers and thinkers include David Hume, author of *A Treatise on Human Nature* and Adam Smith who wrote *The Wealth of Nations.*

Many reasons have been given for this extraordinary roll-call, but one of the most obvious is the long tradition of high-quality education that can be traced back as far as the earliest monastic institutions.

SOCIETY & CONDUCT

Outside Scotland, Scots are often stereotyped as being a tight-fisted bunch, but nothing could be further from the truth – most are in fact extremely generous. Scots may appear reserved, but they are passionate in their beliefs whether they're about politics, religion or football. They generally treat visitors courteously, and the class distinctions that so bedevil England are less prevalent. The influence of religion is declining. Scotland is mainly an urban society with most people living in the south from the Firth of Clyde to the Firth of Forth.

Edinburgh is Scotland's most middle-class city, and those with the financial wherewithal enjoy the highest quality of urban life in the UK. The city's social problems have largely been pushed out to the big public housing estates where unemployment, drug abuse and AIDS are endemic.

Traditional Culture

Bagpipes One of the oldest musical instruments still used today is the bagpipe. Although no piece of film footage on Scotland is complete without the drone of the pipes, their origin probably lies outside the country. The Romans used bagpipes in their armies, and modern versions can be heard

as far away from the Highland glens as India and Russia.

The Highland bagpipe is the type most commonly played in Scotland. It comprises a leather bag inflated by the blowpipe and held under the arm; the piper controls the flow of air through the pipes by squeezing the bag. Three of the pipes, appropriately known as the drones, play all the time without being touched by the piper. The fourth pipe, the chanter, is the one on which tunes can be played.

Queen Victoria did much to repopularise the bagpipe, with her patronage of all things Scottish. When staying at Balmoral she liked to be wakened by a piper playing outside her window.

Ceilidh The Gaelic word ceilidh (pronounced 'kaylee') means 'visit' since a ceilidh was originally a social gathering in the house after the day's work was over. A local bard (poet) presided over the telling of folk stories and legends, and there was also music and song. These days, a ceilidh means an evening of entertainment including music, song and dance.

Clans A clan is a group of people who claim descent from a common ancestor. In the Highlands and Islands, where the Scottish clan system evolved between the 11th and 16th centuries, many unrelated families joined clans to be under the clan chief's protection. So, although they may share the same name, not all clan members are related by blood.

Clan members united in raiding parties into the more prosperous Lowlands or into neighbouring glens to steal other clans' cattle. After the 18th century Jacobite rebellions the suppression of Highland culture brought the forced breakdown of the clan system, but the spirit of clan loyalty still remains strong, especially among the 25 million Scots living abroad. Each clan still has its own chief, like the Queen merely a figurehead, and its own tartan (see Tartans later).

Highland Games Highland Games occur throughout the summer, and not just in the Highlands. The Edinburgh International Highland Games take place in late July and early August. Assorted sporting events with piping and dancing competitions attract locals and tourists alike.

The original games were organised by clan chiefs and kings who recruited the strongest competitors for their armies and as bodyguards. Even now the Queen never fails to attend the Braemar Gathering, the best known, and most crowded, of all Highland Games in September.

Some events are peculiarly Scottish, particularly those that involve the Heavies in bouts of strength testing. The apparatus used can be pretty primitive – tossing the caber involves heaving a tree trunk into the air. Other popular events in which the Heavies take part are throwing the hammer and putting the stone.

Tartans The oldest surviving piece of tartan, a patterned woollen material now made into everything from kilts to key-fobs, dates back to the Roman period. Today, tartan is popular the world over, and beyond – astronaut Al Bean took his MacBean tartan to the moon and back.

The *plaid* is the traditional Scottish dress, with a long length of tartan wrapped around the body and over the shoulder. Particular *setts* (patterns) didn't come to be associated with certain clans until the 17th century, although today every clan, indeed every football team, has a distinctive tartan.

The wearing of Highland dress was banned after the Jacobite rebellions but revived under royal patronage in the following century. For their visit in 1822, George IV and his English courtiers donned kilts. Sir Walter Scott, novelist, poet and dedicated patriot, did much to rekindle interest in Scottish ways. By then, however, many of the old setts had been forgotten – some tartans are actually Victorian creations. The modern kilt only appeared in the 18th century and was reputedly invented by Thomas Rawlinson, an Englishman!

More about Tartans

There's some contention over the origin of the word 'tartan', but according to the Scottish Tartans Society, the word originally described the way a woollen thread was woven to make the fabric: a single thread passed over two threads then under two etc. The tartan textile that it created, however, was too light to keep the wearer warm.

Today, tartan is the name given to the colourful pattern of cloth that derives from Highland dress. A tartan pattern is created from a list of coloured threads called a thread count. Broad strips of colour called the 'under check' are often decorated with narrower lines of colour called the 'over check'. Reading a tartan involves locating two unique points within the pattern called 'pivots'. Over 2500 tartan patterns have been recorded in the Register of All Publicly Known Tartans. Two of the largest groups of tartans are the Black Watch (named after the Highland regiment) and Royal Stewart.

If you'd like to learn more about tartans and/or whether your family has one, contact the Scottish Tartans Society (☎ 044-01796 474079, fax 01796 474090, www.tartans.electric scotland.com), Port-na-Craig Rd, Pitlochry PH16 5ND. New tartans can't be declared genuine without its approval. It's a charity which offers both academic and individual research on tartans and is keeper of the Register of All Publicly Known Tartans. It also runs the Scottish Tartans Museum (map 4, ☎ 0131-556 1252), 3rd Floor, The Scotch House, 39-41 Princes St, which displays some rare tartans.

Dos & Don'ts

Though using the term British is fine, the Scots understandably don't like being called English. The Scots' passion for football (soccer) creates intense rivalry between Heart of Midlothian and Hibernian. In the past this rivalry was exacerbated by religious divisions (Hearts was the Protestant team, Hibs the Catholic) but this has diminished. All the same, if you find yourself in the company of football fans it may be wise to express your neutrality in some way. Whenever subjects like religion or Scottish nationalism come up, as a visitor it's probably a good time for you to practise your listening skills, at least until you're sure of the situation.

Treatment of Animals

If you find any injured birds or animals contact the Scottish Society for the Prevention of Cruelty to Animals (☎ 339 0222), Braehead Mains, 603 Queensferry Rd, Edinburgh EH4.

RELIGION

It's probably true that religion has played a more influential part in Scotland's history than in other parts of Britain. This remains true today: while barely 2% of people in England and Wales regularly attend church services, the figure for Scotland is 10%.

Christianity reached Scotland in the 4th century although in some places vestiges of older worship survived. As recently as the 18th century, Hebridean fishing communities conducted superstitious rites to ensure a good catch. With the Reformation the Scottish Church rejected the pope's authority. Later a schism developed amongst Scottish Protestants, the Presbyterians favouring a simplified church hierarchy without bishops, unlike the Episcopalians.

Two-thirds of Scots belong to the Presbyterian Church (or Kirk) of Scotland, which is also the largest religious denomination in Edinburgh. There are two Presbyterian minorities: the Free Church of Scotland (known as the Wee Frees) and the United Free Presbyterians, found mainly in the Highlands and Islands. In Edinburgh, other denominations include Episcopalians, Methodists, Baptists and Roman Catholics. There are also small communities of Jews, Moslems and Hindus.

LANGUAGE

The ancient Picts spoke a language that may have been of non Indo-European origin; Pictish is described as P-Celtic (the same family as Welsh, Cornish and Breton). It survives mainly in place names beginning with 'Pit' (eg Pitlochry).

With the coming of Gaelic-speaking Celts (Gaels or Scotti, later called Scots) from northern Ireland from the 4th to 6th centuries, Gaelic (pronounced gallic in Scotland) became the language spoken in almost all Scotland. This predominance lasted until the 9th or 11th centuries when Anglo-Saxon arrived in the Lowlands. Gaelic then went into a long period of decline, and it was only in the 1970s that it began to make a comeback. The language is now encouraged with financial help from government agencies and the EU.

Lallans or Lowland Scots evolved from Anglo-Saxon and has Dutch, French, Gaelic, German and Scandinavian influences. It's the language of Robert Burns and Sir Walter Scott and it too is undergoing a revival.

And then there's English, whose influence grew following union in 1707. Aye, but the Scottish accent can make English almost impenetrable to the *Sassenach* (an English person or a Lowland Scot) and other foreigners, and there are numerous Gaelic and Lallan words that linger in everyday English speech. Ye ken?

See the Glossary for some common words you may come across.

Facts for the Visitor

WHEN TO GO

In terms of weather the best time to visit Edinburgh is May to September, but whenever you go, you're likely to see both sun and rain. April and October are also acceptable weather risks. In summer, daylight hours are long and Edinburgh evenings are seemingly endless. In winter the weather's cold and daylight hours are short, but with so much going on, Edinburgh is still worth visiting.

The city becomes impossibly crowded during the main festival period – August to early September – so book well ahead if you plan to visit then.

See also Climate in the Facts about Edinburgh chapter.

ORIENTATION

The most important landmark is Arthur's Seat, the 251m (823 feet) extinct rocky peak south-west of the city centre. The Old and New Towns are separated by Princes St Gardens, with the castle dominating both of them.

The main shopping street, Princes St, runs along the north side of the gardens. Buildings are restricted to its north side, which has the usual High St shops. At the east end, Calton Hill is crowned by several monuments. The Royal Mile (Lawnmarket, High St and Canongate) is the parallel equivalent in the Old Town.

The TIC is between Waverley train station and Princes St, above the Waverley Market shopping centre. The bus station in the New Town is trickier to find; it's off the north-east corner of St Andrew Square, north of Princes St.

Bear in mind that the same street may be subdivided into different names. For example Leith Walk is variously called Union Place and Antigua St on one side, Elm Row and Greenside Place on the other.

MAPS

The foldout maps produced by the Scottish Tourist Board, A-Z, Bartholomew (a local cartographic company) and Collins are good for most purposes. For more detail A-Z, Bartholomew and Collins also produce handy street atlases; there's also the *Super Red Book of Edinburgh* which is two colour and easy to read.

However, if you really want to explore the wynds, loans and closes of the city the Ordinance Survey *Edinburgh Street Atlas*, produced in large and pocket-size formats, is the most comprehensive. The print in the pocket-size version, though, may be too small for some users. It's testimony to the intricacies of the Old Town that not even the OS includes some of its tiniest nooks and crannies.

TOURIST OFFICES
Local Tourist Offices

The Scottish Tourist Board (STB, ☎ 0131-332 2433, fax 0131-315 4545, www .holiday.scotland.net) has its headquarters at 23 Ravelston Terrace (PO Box 705), Edinburgh EH4 3EU. In London, contact the STB (☎ 0171-930 8661, or, from 22 April 2000, ☎ 020-7930 8661), 19 Cockspur St, London SW1 5BL, off Trafalgar Square.

The busy main TIC (Map 5, ☎ 0131-557 1700), Waverley Market, 3 Princes St, opens November to March, Monday to Saturday from 9 am to 6 pm, plus Sunday from 1 to 6 pm in April and October. In May, June and September it opens Monday to Saturday from 9 am to 7 pm, Sunday from 11 am to 7 pm; July and August, Monday to Saturday from 9 am to 8 pm, Sunday from 11 am to 8 pm. There's also a branch at Edinburgh airport (☎ 333 2167). They sell an *Essential Guide to Edinburgh* (50p) and have information about all of Scotland.

At the Backpackers Centre (Map 7, ☎ 0131-557 9393), 6 Blackfriars St beside Haggis Backpackers, you can get valuable information about hostels and tours, and book tickets for National Express, Stena Line, P&O and many other services.

Tourist Offices Abroad

Overseas, the British Tourist Authority (BTA; www.bta.org.uk) represents the STB and stocks masses of information, much of it free. Contact the BTA before leaving home because some discounts are available only to people who have booked before arriving in Britain. Travellers with special needs (disability, diet etc) should also contact the nearest BTA office.

Some overseas offices include:

Australia
(☎ 02-9377 4400, fax 02-9377 4499)
Level 16, The Gateway, 1 Macquarie Place, Circular Quay, Sydney, NSW 2000
Canada
(☎905-405 1840, fax 905-405 1835)
Suite 120, 5915 Airport Road, Mississauga, Ontario L4V 1T1
France
(☎ 01 44 51 56 20)
Tourisme de la Grand-Bretagne, Maison de la Grande-Bretagne, 19 Rue des Mathurins, 75009 Paris (entrance in Rues Tronchet and Auber)
Germany
(☎ 069-97 1123)
Westendstrasse 16-22, 60325 Frankfurt
Ireland
(☎ 01-670 8000)
18-19 College Green, Dublin 2
Netherlands
(☎ 020-685 50 51)
Stadhouderskade 2 (5e), 1054 ES Amsterdam
New Zealand
(☎ 09-303 1446, fax 09-776 965)
3rd Floor, Dilworth Building, corner Queen & Customs Sts, Auckland 1
USA
(☎ 1 800 GO 2 BRITAIN)
625 N Michigan Ave, Suite 1510, Chicago IL 60611 (personal callers only)
551 Fifth Ave, Suite 701, New York, NY 10176-0799

DOCUMENTS
Visas

A visa is a stamp in your passport permitting you to enter a country for a specified period of time. Depending on your nationality, the procedure may be a mere formality. Sometimes you can get a visa at borders or airports, but not always – check first with the embassies or consulates of the countries you plan to visit.

There's a variety of visa types, including tourist, transit, business and work visas. Transit visas are usually cheaper than tourist or business visas, but they only allow a very short stay and can be difficult to extend.

Visa requirements can change, and you should always check with embassies or a reputable travel agent before travelling. If you're travelling widely, carry plenty of spare passport photos (you'll need up to four every time you apply for a visa).

Access the Lonely Planet Web site (www .lonelyplanet.com.au) for more information.

British Visas Visa regulations are always subject to change, so it is essential to check the situation with your local British embassy, high commission or consulate before leaving home.

Currently, if you are a citizen of Australia, Canada, New Zealand, South Africa or the USA, you are given 'leave to enter' Britain at your place of arrival. Tourists from these countries are generally permitted to stay for up to six months, but are prohibited from working. To stay longer you need an entry clearance certificate: apply to the high commission.

Citizens of the European Union (EU) can live and work in Britain free of immigration control – you don't need a visa to enter the country.

The immigration authorities have always been tough and are getting tougher; dress neatly and carry proof that you have sufficient funds to support yourself. A credit card and/or an onward ticket will help. People have been refused entry because they happened to be carrying papers (like references) that suggested they intended to work.

No visas are required for Scotland if you arrive from England or Northern Ireland. If you arrive from the Republic of Ireland or any other country, normal British customs and immigration regulations apply.

Visa Extensions To extend your stay in the UK contact the Home Office, Immigration & Nationality Department (☎ 0181-686 0688, or, from June 1999, ☎ 020-8686 0688), Lunar House, Wellesley Rd, Croydon, London CR9 *before* your existing permit expires. You'll need to send your passport or ID card with your application.

Travel Insurance

This not only covers you for medical expenses, theft or loss, but also for cancellation of or delays in your travel arrangements. There's a variety of policies and your travel agent will have recommendations. The international student travel policies handled by STA Travel and other student travel organisations are usually good value.

Make sure the policy includes health care and medication in the countries you may visit to/from Scotland. Go for as much as you can afford, especially if you're also visiting the Channel Islands, the USA, Switzerland, Germany or Scandinavia, where medical costs are high.

Always read the small print carefully:

- Some policies specifically exclude 'dangerous activities' like scuba diving, motorcycling, skiing, mountaineering, even trekking.
- You may prefer a policy that pays doctors or hospitals directly rather than forcing you to pay on the spot and claim the money back later. If you have to claim later, make sure you keep all documentation. Some policies ask you to call back (reverse charges) to a centre in your home country where an immediate assessment of your problem is made.
- Not all policies cover ambulances, helicopter rescue or emergency flights home.
- Most policies exclude cover for pre-existing illnesses.

Driving Licence & Permits

Your normal driving licence is legal for 12 months from the date you last entered Britain; you can then apply for a British licence at post offices.

Ask your automobile association for a Card of Introduction. This entitles you to services offered by British sister organisations (touring maps and information, help with breakdowns, technical and legal advice etc), usually free of charge.

Hostel Cards

If you're travelling on a very tight budget, then membership of the Scottish Youth Hostel Association/Hostelling International (SYHA/HI) is a must (£10 over-18, £5 under-18). There are almost 80 hostels in Scotland and members are eligible for an impressive list of discounts.

Student & Youth Cards

The most useful is the plastic ID-style International Student Identity Card (ISIC), with your photograph. This can perform wonders, including producing discounts on many forms of transport. Even if you have your own transport, the card soon pays for itself through cheap or free admission to attractions, and cheap meals in some student restaurants.

There's a worldwide industry in fake student cards, and many places now stipulate a maximum age for student discounts or, more simply, substitute a 'youth discount' for a 'student discount'. If you're aged under 26 but not a student, you can apply for a Federation of International Youth Travel Organisations (FIYTO) card or a Euro26 Card which give much the same discounts. Your hostelling organisation should be able to help with this.

Both types of card are issued by student unions, hostelling organisations or student travel agencies. They don't automatically entitle you to discounts, but you won't find out until you flash the card.

International Health Card

You may need this yellow booklet if you're travelling onwards through parts of Asia, Africa and South America, where yellow fever is prevalent.

If you're a national of another EU country, Form E111 (available from post offices) entitles you to free or reduced-cost medical treatment in Britain.

Photocopies

It's wise to keep photocopies of all important documents (passport, air tickets, insurance policy, travellers cheque serial numbers) in a separate place in case of theft; stash £50 away with the photocopies just in case. Ideally, leave a second set of copies with someone responsible in your home country.

EMBASSIES & CONSULATES
UK Embassies & Consulates Abroad

Following are some of the countries where the UK has diplomatic representation:

Australia
    High Commission:
    (☎ 02-6270 6666)
    Commonwealth Ave, Yarralumla, Canberra, ACT 2600
Canada
    High Commission:
    (☎ 613-237 1530)
    80 Elgin St, Ottawa, Ontario K1P 5K7
France
    Consulate:
    (☎ 01 42 66 38 10)
    9 Ave Hoche, 8e, Paris
Germany
    Embassy:
    (☎ 0228-23 40 61)
    Friedrich-Ebert-Allee 77, 53113 Bonn
Japan
    Embassy:
    (☎ 03-3265 5511)
    1 Ichiban-cho, Chiyoda-ku, Tokyo
New Zealand
    High Commission:
    (☎ 04-472 6049)
    44 Hill St, Wellington 1
South Africa
    High Commission:
    (☎ 27-21-461 7220)
    91 Parliament St, Cape Town
USA
    Embassy:
    (☎ 202-462 1340)
    3100 Massachusetts Ave NW, Washington DC 20008

Consulates & High Commissions in Edinburgh

Most foreign diplomatic missions are in London, but some also have consulates or high commissions in or near Edinburgh:

Belgium
    (☎ 01968-679969)
    21B The Square, Penicuik, EH26 8LH
Denmark
    (☎ 556 4263)
    4 Royal Terrace, EH7 5AB
Canada
    (Map 6, ☎ 245 6013), 30 Lothian Rd, EH1 2DH
France
    (Map 6, ☎ 225 7954)
    11 Randolph Crescent, EH3 7TT
Germany
    (Map 3, ☎ 337 2323)
    16 Eglinton Crescent, EH12 5DG
Italy
    (☎ 226 3631)
    32 Melville St, EH3 7HA
Japan
    (☎ 225 4777)
    2 Melville Crescent, EH3 7HW
Netherlands
    (☎ 220 3226)
    53 George St, EH2 2HT
Spain
    (☎ 220 1843)
    63 North Castle St, EH2 3LJ
Sweden
    (☎ 554 6631)
    6 John's Place, Leith, EH6 7EP
Switzerland
    (☎ 226 5660)
    66 Hanover St, EH2 1HH
USA
    (Map 5, ☎ 556 8315)
    3 Regent Terrace, EH7 5BW

CUSTOMS

Entering Britain, if you have nothing to declare go through the green channel; if you have something to declare go through the red channel. For imported goods there's a two-tier system; the first for goods bought duty free, the second for goods bought in an EU country where tax and duty have been paid.

The second tier is relevant because a number of products (eg alcohol and cigarettes) are much cheaper on the continent.

Under single market rules, however, as long as tax and duty have been paid somewhere in the EU there is no prohibition on importing them within the EU provided they are for personal consumption. The result has been a thriving market for day trips to France where Brits can load up their cars with cheap beer, wine and cigarettes – the savings can more than pay for the trip.

Duty Free
If you purchase from a duty-free shop, you can import 200 cigarettes or 250g of tobacco, 2L of still wine plus 1L of spirits or another 2L of wine (sparkling or otherwise), 60cc of perfume, 250cc of toilet water, and other duty-free goods (eg cider and beer) to the value of £145.

Within the EU, duty free shopping is scheduled to be abolished on 30 June 1999. This will mean you can still take duty-free goods into an EU country from outside the EU (or conversely, buy duty-free goods in an EU country to take outside the EU) but you can't buy duty free goods in one EU country to take to another EU country.

Tax & Duty Paid
If you buy from a normal retail outlet, customs will nod through 800 cigarettes or 1kg of tobacco, 10L of spirits, 20L of fortified wine, 90L of wine (not more than 60L sparkling wine) and 110L of beer as legitimate personal imports.

MONEY
Currency
The British currency is the pound sterling (£), with 100 pence (p) to a pound. One and 2p coins are copper; 5p, 10p, 20p and 50p coins are silver; the £1 coin is gold-coloured; and the new £2 coin is gold and silver-coloured. Like its written counterpart the word pence is usually abbreviated and pronounced 'pee'.

Notes (bills) come in £5, £10, £20 and £50 denominations and vary in colour and size. Notes issued by several Scottish banks – the Clydesdale Bank, Royal Bank of Scotland and Bank of Scotland – including a £1 note are legal tender in other parts of the UK. You won't have any trouble changing them in shops etc immediately south of the border, but elsewhere it may be difficult. However, any bank will exchange them.

Exchange Rates

country	unit		pence
Australia	A$1	=	£0.34
Canada	C$1	=	£0.43
euro	€1	=	£0.71
France	FF1	=	£0.10
Germany	DM1	=	£0.35
Ireland	IR£1	=	£0.88
Japan	¥100	=	£0.42
New Zealand	NZ$1	=	£0.32
USA	US$1	=	£0.60

Exchanging Money
The TIC bureau de change opens the same hours as the TIC; it charges 2.5% commission with a minimum of £2.50. There's a bureau de change in the post office. American Express (Map 4, ☎ 0131-225 7881), 139 Princes St, opens Monday to Friday from 9 am to 5.30 pm, Saturday to 4 pm. Thomas Cook (Map 4, ☎ 0131-465 7700), 26-28 Frederick St, opens Monday to Saturday from 9 am to 5.30 pm.

Most banks also change money. The Royal Bank of Scotland (Map 4, ☎ 0131-556 8555) and the Bank of Scotland (Map 4, ☎ 0131-442 7777) both have branches in St Andrew Square.

Cash Nothing beats cash for convenience ... or risk. It's still a good idea, though, to travel with some local currency in cash, if only to tide you over until you get to an exchange facility. There's no problem if you arrive at Edinburgh airport which has several exchange counters open for incoming flights.

If you're travelling in several countries, some extra cash in US dollars is a good idea; it can be easier to change a small amount of cash (when leaving a country, for example) than a cheque.

Banks rarely accept foreign coins, although some airport foreign exchanges will.

Before you leave one country for the next, try to use up your change.

Travellers Cheques Travellers cheques offer some protection from theft. American Express or Thomas Cook cheques are widely accepted and have efficient replacement policies. Keep a record of the cheque numbers and the cheques you've cashed somewhere separate from the cheques themselves.

Although cheques are available in various currencies, there's little point using US$ cheques in Britain (unless you're travelling from the USA), since you'll lose on the exchange rate when you buy the cheques and again each time you cash one. Bring pounds sterling to avoid changing currencies twice. In Britain, travellers cheques are rarely accepted outside banks or used for everyday transactions; you need to cash them in advance.

Take most cheques in large denominations. It's only towards the end of a stay that you may want to change a small cheque to make sure you don't get left with too much local currency.

Plastic Cards & ATMs If you're not familiar with the options, ask your bank to explain the workings and relative merits of credit, credit/debit, debit and charge cards.

Plastic cards are ideal for major purchases and can allow you to withdraw cash from selected banks and automatic telling machines (ATMs – called cashpoints in Britain). ATMs are usually linked to international money systems such as Cirrus, Maestro or Plus, so you can insert your card, punch in a personal identification number (PIN) and get instant cash. But ATMs aren't fail-safe, especially if the card was issued outside Europe, and it's safer to go to a human teller – it can be a headache if an ATM swallows your card.

Credit cards usually aren't hooked up to ATM networks unless you specifically request a PIN number from your bank. You should also ask which ATMs abroad will accept your particular card. Cash cards, which you use at home to withdraw money from your bank account or savings account, are becoming more widely linked internationally – ask your bank at home for advice.

Charge cards like American Express and Diners Club don't have credit limits but may not be accepted in small establishments or off the beaten track. If you have an American Express card, you can cash up to £500 worth of personal cheques at American Express offices in any seven day period.

Credit and credit/debit cards like Visa and MasterCard (known as Access in Britain) are more widely accepted. If you have too low a credit limit to cover major expenses like car hire or airline tickets, you can pay money into your account so it's in credit when you leave home.

Visa, MasterCard, Access, American Express and Diners Club cards are widely recognised although some places make a charge for accepting them. B&Bs usually require cash. MasterCard is operated by the same organisation that issues Access and Eurocards and can be used wherever you see one or other of these signs.

You can use MasterCard in ATMs belonging to the Royal Bank of Scotland and Clydesdale Bank; with a Visa card you can use the Bank of Scotland, Royal Bank of Scotland, Clydesdale Bank and TSB; American Express card holders can use the Bank of Scotland.

If you have a UK bank account south of the border, then you can use a National Westminster or Midland cash card at the Clydesdale Bank, and a Lloyds or Barclays cash card at the Royal Bank of Scotland or Bank of Scotland.

Combine plastic and travellers cheques so you have something to fall back on if an ATM swallows your card or the local banks don't accept your card.

International Transfers You can instruct your home bank to send you a draft. Specify the city, the bank and the branch to which you want your money directed, or ask your home bank to tell you where there's a suitable one. The whole procedure will be easier if you've authorised someone back home to access your account.

Money sent by telegraphic transfer should reach you within a week; by mail, allow at least two weeks. When it arrives, it will most likely be converted into local currency – you can take it as it is or buy travellers cheques.

You can also transfer money by American Express or Thomas Cook. Americans can also use Western Union (☎ 0800 833833).

Security

Keep your money in a money belt or something similar, out of easy reach of thieves. You might want to stitch an inside pocket into your skirt or trousers to keep an emergency stash; keep about £50 apart from the rest of your cash in case of an emergency. Take care in crowded places, and never leave wallets sticking out of trouser pockets or daypacks.

Costs

Scotland is expensive, but backpacker accommodation is widely available, so backpackers will be able to keep their costs down. Edinburgh is more expensive than most other Scottish towns.

While in Edinburgh you'll need to budget £16 to £25 a day for bare survival. In a hostel, dormitory accommodation costs £8.50 to £14 a night, a one-day bus travel card is £2.20, and drinks and the most basic sustenance cost at least £6, with any sightseeing or nightlife costs on top. To enjoy some of the city's life, if possible add another £10 to £15.

Costs obviously rise if you stay in a central B&B or hotel and eat restaurant meals. B&B rates start at around £18 to £25 per person and a restaurant meal will be at least £8. Add a couple of pints of beer (around £2 each) and entry fees to a tourist attraction or nightclub and you could easily spend £50 per day – without being extravagant.

Tipping & Bargaining

In general, if you eat in a restaurant you should leave a tip of at least 10% unless the service was unsatisfactory. Waiting staff are often paid derisory wages on the assumption that the money will be supplemented by tips. If the bill already includes a service charge of 10 to 15%, you needn't add a further tip.

Taxi drivers expect to be tipped (about 10%). It's less usual to tip minicab drivers.

Bargaining is virtually unheard of, even at markets, although it's fine to ask if there are discounts for students, young people, or youth hostel members. Some 'negotiation' is also OK if you're buying an expensive item such as a car or motorcycle.

Taxes & Refunds

Value-added tax (VAT) is a 17.5% sales tax that is levied on all goods and services except food and books. Restaurant prices must by law include VAT.

It's sometimes possible to claim a refund of VAT paid on goods – a considerable saving. You're eligible if you've spent *less* than 365 days out of the two years prior to making the purchase living in Britain, and if you're leaving the EU within three months of making the purchase.

Not all shops participate in the VAT refund scheme, and different shops have different minimum-purchase conditions (normally around £40). On request, participating shops give you a special form/ invoice; they'll need to see your passport. This form must be presented with the goods and receipts to customs when you depart (VAT-free goods can't be posted or shipped home). After customs has certified the form, it should be returned to the shop for a refund less an administration fee.

Several companies offer a centralised refunding service to shops. Participating shops carry a sign in their window. You can avoid bank charges for cashing a sterling cheque by using a credit card for purchases and asking to have your VAT refund credited to your card account. Cash refunds are sometimes available at major airports.

POST & COMMUNICATIONS
Post

The main post office (☎ 0345-223344) is inconveniently tucked away inside the sprawling St James' Shopping Centre (Map 5), off Leith St. It's open Monday from 9 am to 5.30 pm, Tuesday to Friday from 8.30 am to 5.30 pm, and Saturday from 8.30 am to 6 pm. Items addressed to poste restante are automatically sent here and can be picked up from any counter. Most other post offices open weekdays from 9 am to 5.30 pm, and Saturday from 9 am to 12.30 pm.

First-class mail is quicker and more expensive (26p per letter) than 2nd-class mail (20p). Air-mail letters to EU countries are 30p, to the Americas and Australasia 43p (up to 10g) and 63p (up to 20g). An air-mail letter generally takes less than a week to get to the USA or Canada and around a week to Australia or New Zealand.

If you don't have a permanent address, mail can be sent to poste restante in the town or city where you're staying. American Express offices also hold card-holders' mail free.

Telephone

There are plenty of public telephones around Edinburgh, all of which have STD or international access. Although British Telecom (BT) is the largest of the telephone operators, with the most public phone booths, there are also several competing companies including Scottish Telecom.

Red phone booths survive in conservation areas. More usually you'll see glass cubicles of two types: one takes money (and doesn't give change), while the other uses prepaid, plastic debit cards and credit cards.

All phones come with reasonably clear instructions. If you're likely to make several calls (especially international) and don't want to be caught out, buy a BT phonecard. Ranging in values from £2 to £20, they're widely available from all sorts of retailers, including post offices and newsagents.

Some codes worth knowing about include:

☎ 0345	local call rates apply
☎ 0500	call is free to caller
☎ 0800	call is free to caller
☎ 0891	premium rates apply; 39p cheap rate, 49p at other times
☎ 0990	national call rate applies

Local & National Calls Local calls are charged by time; national calls are charged by time and distance. Daytime rates are from 8 am to 6 pm, Monday to Friday; the cheap rate is from 6 pm to 8 am, Monday to Friday, and the cheap weekend rate is from midnight Friday to midnight Sunday. The latter two rates offer substantial savings.

For directory inquiries call ☎ 192. These are free from public telephones but are charged at 25p from a private phone. To get the operator call ☎ 100.

International Calls Dial ☎ 155 for the international operator. To get an international line (for international direct dialling) dial 00, then the country code, area code (drop the first zero if there is one) and number. Direct dialling is cheaper, but some budget travellers prefer the operator-connected reverse-charges (collect) calls.

You can also use the Home Country Direct service to make a reverse-charge or credit card call via an operator in your home country which should avoid language problems. If you need to get a message overseas urgently, call ☎ 0800-190190.

For most countries (including Europe, USA and Canada) it's cheaper to phone overseas between 8 pm and 8 am Monday to

---

Telephone Code

The telephone area code for Edinburgh is ☎ 0131. Unless otherwise stated phone numbers in this book should be prefixed with this code if you're ringing from outside the city. You don't need to use this code if you're calling from within the city.

Friday and at weekends; for Australia and New Zealand, however, it's cheapest from 2.30 to 7.30 pm and from midnight to 7 am every day. The savings are considerable.

Emergency Dial ☎ 999 or ☎ 112 (free calls) for fire, police or ambulance.

Fax, Email & Internet Access

Most hotels have faxes and the larger ones also have email access. Some hostels, too, offer Internet access to their customers or you can try one of the cybercafés. Web 13 Internet Café (Map 6, ☎ 229 8883), 13 Bread St near the corner of Lothian Rd, offers online access for £5 per hour. It opens weekdays from 9 am to 10 pm, Saturday to 6 pm, and Sunday from noon to 6 pm. Cyberia Cyber Café (Map 4, ☎ 220 4403), 88 Hanover St, is similar.

Some shops also offer fax services, advertised by a sign in the window.

INTERNET RESOURCES

There are plenty of sites of interest to cyber travellers. In this guide, web sites are given with addresses where appropriate.

The Edinburgh & Lothians Tourist Board's web site is at www.edinburgh.org. It has information on accommodation, attractions, festivals etc in and around Edinburgh. For details of the city's changing program of exhibitions at museums and galleries check www.cac.org.uk. The Scottish Tourist Board has its own site (see Tourist Offices earlier), or if you'd like to find out about more of Scotland's museums go to www.museum.scotland.net. For details of things to see, art, music, theatre and other entertainment in and around Edinburgh check out www.eae.co.uk.

Lonely Planet's web site (www.lonely planet.com.au) offers a speedy link to numerous sites of interest to travellers to Britain.

BOOKS
Lonely Planet

If you're planning a wider journey than just Edinburgh, consider taking Lonely Planet's

Scotland guide. For travel elsewhere in Britain, Lonely Planet publishes a *Britain* guide as well as a *London* city guide. LP's *Walking in Britain* has two chapters on Scottish walking trails.

Guidebooks

Insight Guides' *Edinburgh* is an interesting collection of essays and photographs on various aspects of the city. For walkers there are a couple of useful books: *Edinburgh & Lothian – 25 Walks* by Roger Smith and *One Hundred Hill Walks Around Edinburgh* by John Chalmers & Derek Storey.

The List magazine publishes the *Edinburgh & Glasgow Eating & Drinking Guide*, a comprehensive review of cafés, restaurants and bars.

If you're bringing children get a copy of the City of Edinburgh council's publication, the *Child Friendly Guide to Edinburgh*, available free from libraries and leisure centres.

The *Cruelty Free Guide to Edinburgh* contains information on cafés, restaurants, shops and accommodation that provide goods and services without involving cruelty to animals. It's available around town or from Forthprint (☎ 229 8171), 30-32 Lochrin Buildings, Edinburgh EH3 9ND.

History

Edinburgh – Portrait of a City, by Charles McKean, gives a readable, succinct review of the city's past. *A Short History of Scotland*, by Richard Killeen, is a concise, up-to-date introduction to the country's history. More in-depth is Michael Lynch's large tome, *Scotland – A New History*, which provides a good historical background up to the early 1990s. Andrew Marr's *The Battle for Scotland*, is an interesting political history of Scotland from the 19th century to 1992.

General

Portrait of Edinburgh is one of a series of attractive photographic books on Scotland produced by Colin Baxter and Jim Crumley. *Arthur's Seat & Holyrood Park*, by CR

Wickham-Jones, contains photographs, descriptions, and historical and literary connections of these famous Edinburgh locations.

A useful companion to Charles McKean's history of the city is his *Edinburgh – an Illustrated Architectural Guide*, with information on many of the city's most notable buildings.

NEWSPAPERS & MAGAZINES

The Scots have published newspapers since the mid-17th century. Scotland's home-grown dailies include the *Scotsman*, a Liberal Democrat paper published in Edinburgh, and the popular tabloid *Daily Record*. The *Herald*, formerly the *Glasgow Herald* is the oldest daily newspaper in the English-speaking world having been founded in 1783. The *Evening News* is an Edinburgh daily containing news on the city and its environs. The *Sunday Post* is the country's best-selling Sunday paper with a circulation of over 2.5 million people.

Most papers sold elsewhere in Britain are available in Edinburgh, some designed specifically for Scottish readership (the *Scottish Daily Mail*, *The Scottish Express* etc).

The monthly *Scots Magazine*, with articles on all aspects of Scottish life, has been in circulation since the 18th century. *Scottish Memories* is a monthly magazine that highlights people and moments from Scottish history.

You can also buy many foreign-language papers and magazines in central Edinburgh, including the *International Herald Tribune*, *Time* and *Newsweek*.

RADIO & TV

Radio and TV stations are linked to the UK-wide networks.

Radio

The BBC caters for most tastes though much of the material comes from England. Its main pop music station, Radio 1 aims at a young audience; Radio 2 is mostly middle of the road but also plays music by 'dinosaur' bands like Status Quo; Radio 3

spins the classics; Radio 4 offers a mix of drama, news and current affairs for a mostly mature audience; Radio 5 Live intersperses sport with current affairs. The BBC World Service offers brilliant news coverage and quirky bits and pieces from around the world.

BBC Radio Scotland provides a mix of music, drama, news and sport from a Scottish point of view. It also oversees regional stations in Aberdeen, the Highlands, the Orkneys and the Shetlands and a Gaelic language channel, Radio nan Gaidheal.

UK-wide commercial stations can be picked up in Edinburgh. These include Classic FM (classical music), Virgin Radio (pop) and Talk Radio ('shock jock' chat and phone-ins).

Radio frequencies and programs are published in the daily press.

TV

Britain still turns out some of the world's best TV, although increasing competition as channels proliferate seems to be resulting in standards slipping. BBC1 and BBC2 are publicly funded by a TV licence and don't carry advertising; ITV and Channels 4 and 5 are commercial stations and do.

There are two Scotland-based commercial TV broadcasters. Scottish Television (STV) covers southern Scotland and some of the western Highlands and Grampian TV transmits to Fife northward to Shetland. Both include Gaelic-language programs. Border TV covers Dumfries & Galloway and the Borders as well as north-west England.

These channels are up against competition from Rupert Murdoch's satellite TV, BSkyB, and assorted cable channels. Cable churns out mostly missable rubbish but BSkyB is slowly monopolising sports coverage with pay-per-view screenings of the most popular events.

VIDEO SYSTEMS

With many tourist attractions selling videos as souvenirs it's worth bearing in mind that

Britain, like much of Europe, uses the Phase Alternative Line (PAL) system which isn't compatible with other standards (NTSC or SECAM) unless converted.

PHOTOGRAPHY & VIDEO
Film & Equipment
Although print film is widely available, slide film can be more elusive; if there's no specialist photographic shop around, Boots, the High St chemist chain, is the likeliest stockist. Thirty-six exposure print films cost from £4.30 for ISO 100 to £5 for ISO 400. With slide film it's usually cheapest to go for process-inclusive versions although these generally need to be developed in Britain: 36-exposure films cost from £7 for ISO 100 to £10.50 for ISO 400.

Technical Tips
With dull, overcast conditions common, high-speed film (ISO 200, or ISO 400) is useful. In summer, the best times of day for photography are usually early in the morning and late in the afternoon when the glare of the sun has passed.

Restrictions
Many tourist attractions either charge for taking photos or prohibit it altogether. Use of flash is frequently forbidden to protect delicate pictures and fabrics. Video cameras are often disallowed because of the inconvenience they can cause to other visitors.

Airport Security
You'll have to put your camera and film through the X-ray machine at Edinburgh airport. X-ray machines are supposed to be film-safe, but you may feel happier if you put exposed films in a lead-lined bag to protect them.

TIME
Wherever you are in the world, the time on your watch is measured in relation to Greenwich Mean Time (GMT) – although, strictly speaking, GMT is used only in air and sea navigation, and is otherwise referred to as Universal Time Coordinated (UTC).

Daylight-saving time (DST) muddies the water so that even Britain itself is ahead of GMT from late March to late October. But to give you an idea, during that period San Francisco is eight hours and New York five hours behind GMT, while Sydney is nine hours ahead. Phone the international operator on ☎ 155 for the exact difference.

Most public transport timetables use the 24-hour clock.

ELECTRICITY
The standard voltage in Scotland, as in the rest of Britain, is 240V AC, 50Hz. Plugs have three square pins and adaptors are widely available.

WEIGHTS & MEASURES
In theory Britain has moved to metric weights and measures although non-metric equivalents are still used by much of the population. Most distances continue to be given in miles. This book uses miles to indicate distance although the heights of mountains are given in metres and feet.

Most liquids other than milk and beer are sold in litres. For conversion tables, see the inside back cover.

LAUNDRY
For those staying in Pilrig St, there's the Bendix Launderette & Dry Cleaners (Map 2, ☎ 554 2180) just round the corner (toward Leith) on Leith Walk at No 342-46. Canonmills Dry Cleaners & Launderette (Map 2, ☎ 556 3199), 7 Huntly St, is convenient for people staying in Eyre Place; a service wash (where someone does the washing for you) costs £3.60.

The pick of the laundrettes is Sundial Launderette (Map 2, ☎ 556 2743), at the junction of Broughton and East London Sts in New Town. It's bright, clean and has an adjacent café. The laundrette opens daily and charges £2.80 for a wash.

South of the centre in Bruntsfield is Tarvit Launderette (Map 6, ☎ 229 6382) on Tarvit St opposite Gilmore Place.

TOILETS

Although some city-centre facilities can be grim those at Waverley train station, St Andrew Square bus station and the main visitor attractions are good, usually with facilities for disabled people and those with young children. Some busy public toilets, like the ones at Waverley station and at Edinburgh Castle charge 20p to use their facilities.

Many disabled toilets can only be opened with a special key which can be obtained from the TIC or by sending a cheque or postal order for £2.50 to RADAR (see Disabled Travellers), together with a brief description of your disability.

LEFT LUGGAGE

Left-luggage facilities are available at Waverley train station (from £2.50 all day) opposite the Edinburgh Rail Travel Centre. It's open Monday to Saturday from 8.30 am to 5.30 pm, and Sunday from 9 am to 5 pm. At St Andrew Square bus station, the left-luggage department is in the ticket office building and charges £1 to £2 depending on size. Both also have left-luggage lockers for £4 per day.

HEALTH

How healthy you are while travelling largely depends on predeparture preparations, day-to-day health care and how you handle any medical problem or emergency that does develop.

Dial ☎ 999 or ☎ 112 for an ambulance or ☎ 0800-665544 for the address of the nearest doctor or hospital (see the end of this section for the names and addresses of specific hospitals in Edinburgh).

Predeparture Planning

Make sure that you have adequate health insurance; see Travel Insurance earlier for details. No immunisations are necessary to visit Scotland.

Make sure you're healthy before you start travelling. If you're going on a long

trip make sure your teeth are OK. If you wear glasses take a spare pair and your prescription.

If you require a particular medication take an adequate supply, as it may not be available locally. Take part of the packaging showing the generic name, rather than the brand, which will make getting replacements easier. It's a good idea to have a legible prescription or letter from your doctor to show that you legally use the medication to avoid any problems.

Reciprocal arrangements with Britain allow Australians, New Zealanders and several other nationalities to receive free emergency medical treatment and subsidised dental care through the National Health Service (NHS); you can use hospital emergency departments, general practitioners (GPs) and dentists (check the Yellow Pages phone book).

EU nationals can obtain free emergency treatment on presentation of an E111 form. Inquire about this at your national health service, post office or travel agent. However, travel insurance is advisable because it offers greater flexibility over where and how you're treated, and covers expenses for ambulance and repatriation that won't be picked up by the NHS. Regardless of nationality, anyone should receive free emergency treatment if it's a simple matter like bandaging a cut.

Basic Rules

Care in what you eat and drink is the most important health rule; stomach upsets are the most likely travel health problem (between 30% and 50% of travellers in a two-week stay experience this) but the majority of these upsets are relatively minor. Unfortunately, food poisoning is not unknown so it doesn't pay to be complacent.

Water Tap water is always safe unless there's a sign to the contrary (eg on trains). Don't drink straight from a stream – you can never be certain there are no people or cattle upstream.

Medical Problems & Treatment

Sunburn Even in Scotland, and even when there's cloud cover, it's possible to get sunburnt surprisingly quickly – especially if you're on water, snow or ice. Use 15+ sunscreen, wear a hat and cover up with a long-sleeved shirt and pants.

Heat Exhaustion Dehydration or salt deficiency can cause heat exhaustion. In hot conditions and if you're exerting yourself make sure you get sufficient nonalcoholic liquids. Salt deficiency is characterised by fatigue, lethargy, headaches, giddiness and muscle cramps. Vomiting or diarrhoea can rapidly deplete your liquid and salt levels.

Fungal Infections To prevent fungal infections, wear loose, comfortable clothes, wash frequently and dry carefully. Always wear thongs (flip-flops) in shared bathrooms. If you get an infection, consult a chemist. Try to expose the infected area to air or sunlight as much as possible and wash all towels and underwear in hot water as well as changing them often.

Cold Hypothermia can occur when the body loses heat faster than it can produce it and the body's core temperature falls. It's surprisingly easy to progress from very cold to dangerously cold through a combination of wind, wet clothing, fatigue and hunger, even if the air temperature is above freezing.

Walkers in Scotland should always be prepared for difficult conditions. It's best to dress in layers, and a hat is important as a lot of heat is lost through the head. A strong, waterproof outer layer is essential. Carry basic supplies, including food that contains simple sugars to generate heat quickly.

Symptoms of hypothermia are exhaustion, numb skin (particularly toes and fingers), shivering, slurred speech, irrational or violent behaviour, lethargy, stumbling, dizzy spells, muscle cramps and violent bursts of energy.

To treat it, get the person out of wind and rain, remove wet clothing and replace it with dry, warm clothing. Give them hot liquids – not alcohol – and some high-calorie, easily digestible food. Do not rub victims; instead, allow them to warm themselves. This should be enough to treat the early stages of hypothermia.

Diarrhoea A change of water, food or climate can cause the runs; diarrhoea caused by contaminated food or water is more serious.

Dehydration is the main danger with any diarrhoea, particularly in children or the elderly, and it can occur quite quickly. *Fluid replacement* (at least equal to the volume being lost) is the most important thing to remember. Weak black tea with a little sugar, soda water, or soft drinks allowed to go flat and diluted 50% with clean water are all good. With severe diarrhoea a rehydrating solution is preferable to replace minerals and salts lost. Keep drinking small amounts often and stick to a bland diet as you recover.

Motion Sickness Eating lightly before and during a trip will reduce the chances of motion sickness. If you are prone to motion sickness try to find a place that minimises disturbance – near the wings on aircraft, close to midships on boats, near the centre on buses. Fresh air usually helps; reading and cigarette smoke don't. Commercial motion-sickness preparations, which can cause drowsiness, have to be taken before the trip commences; when you're feeling sick it's too late. Ginger (available in capsule form) and peppermint (including mint-flavoured sweets) are natural preventatives.

HIV & AIDS The Human Immunodeficiency Virus (HIV) develops into Acquired Immune Deficiency Syndrome (AIDS), which is fatal. Any exposure to blood, blood products or body fluids may put the individual at risk. The disease is often transmitted through sexual contact or dirty needles – vaccinations, acupuncture, tattooing and body piercing can be potentially as dangerous as intravenous drug use. HIV/

AIDS can also be spread through infected blood transfusions, but in Scotland these are screened and safe.

Sexually Transmitted Diseases Gonorrhoea, herpes and syphilis are among these diseases; sores, blisters or rashes around the genitals, discharges or pain when urinating are common symptoms. In some sexually transmitted diseases (STDs), such as chlamydia, symptoms may be less marked or not observed at all especially in women. Syphilis symptoms eventually disappear completely, but the disease continues and can cause severe problems in later years. While abstinence from sexual contact is the only 100% effective prevention, using conoms is also effective. The treatment of gonorrhoea and syphilis is with antibiotics. Each individual STD requires specific antibiotics. There is no cure for herpes or AIDS.

Insect Bites & Stings Bee and wasp stings are usually painful rather than dangerous. However, in people who are allergic to them severe breathing difficulties may occur and require urgent medical care. Calamine lotion or Stingose spray will give relief and ice packs will reduce the pain and swelling.

Midges – small blood-sucking flies – are a major problem in the Highlands and Islands during summer. Bring mosquito repellent and some antihistamine if you plan to visit those areas.

Women's Health

Gynaecological Problems Antibiotic use, synthetic underwear, sweating and contraceptive pills can lead to fungal vaginal infections. Fungal infections, characterised by a rash, itch and discharge, can be treated with a vinegar or lemon-juice douche, or with yoghurt. Nystatin, miconazole or clotrimazole pessaries or vaginal cream are the usual treatment.

STDs are a major cause of vaginal problems. Symptoms include a smelly discharge, painful intercourse and sometimes a burning sensation when urinating. Male sexual partners must also be treated. Medical attention should be sought. Remember that in addition to these diseases HIV or hepatitis B may also be acquired during exposure. Besides abstinence, the best thing is to practise safe sex using condoms.

Medical Services

Chemists can advise you on minor ailments. At least one local chemist opens round the clock and other chemists post details of this in their window. Alternatively, look in the local newspaper or in the Yellow Pages. Boots (☎ 225 6757), 48 Shandwick Place (the extension of Princes St in the West End), opens Monday to Saturday, from 8 am to 9 pm, and Sunday from 10 am to 5 pm. Medications are readily available either over the counter or on prescription, so there's no need to stock up.

Not all hospitals have an accident and emergency department; look for red signs with an 'H', followed by 'A&E' (Accident & Emergency). The Royal Infirmary of Edinburgh, 1 Lauriston Place south of Grassmarket, has a 24-hour accident and emergency department (Map 6, ☎ 536 4000). It also has its own dental hospital (☎ 536 4900). On Crewe Rd South in the city's north, the Western General Hospital's minor injuries unit (Map 2, ☎ 537 1330/1331) opens daily from 9 am to 9 pm.

The Western General Hospital operates an emergency dental service (☎ 537 1338) weekday evenings from 7 to 9 pm, weekends from 10 am to noon and from 7 to 9 pm. There's a casualty dental clinic (☎ 543 4903) at the Edinburgh Dental Hospital, 31 Chambers St off South Bridge.

For those with HIV/AIDS, help, advice and support are available from the National AIDS Helpline (☎ 0800 567123, 24 hours).

WOMEN TRAVELLERS

Women are unlikely to have too many problems provided they take the usual big-city precautions.

Attitudes Towards Women

The occasional wolf-whistle and groper aside, women will find Scotland reasonably enlightened. There's nothing to stop women going into pubs alone, although not everyone likes doing this; pairs or groups of women blend more naturally into the wallpaper. Some restaurants persist in assigning the table by the toilet to lone female diners, but fortunately such places are becoming fewer.

Safety Precautions

Solo travellers should have few problems, although common-sense caution should be observed, especially at night.

Condoms are increasingly sold in women's toilets. Otherwise, chemists and many service stations stock them. The contraceptive pill is available only on prescription, as is the 'morning-after' pill (effective for up to 72 hours after unprotected sexual intercourse).

It can help to go on a women's self-defence course before setting out on your travels, if only for the increased feeling of confidence it's likely to give you.

Organisations

Edinburgh's Well Woman Clinic (☎ 343 6243) is at the Dean Terrace Centre, 18 Dean Terrace, Stockbridge. This is the place to come to for advice on general health issues, contraception and pregnancy.

If worst comes to worst contact the Rape Crisis Centre (☎ 556 9437), which can offer support after an attack.

GAY & LESBIAN TRAVELLERS

Edinburgh has a small but flourishing gay scene. In general, Scotland is fairly tolerant of homosexuality. That said, there remain pockets of hostility and overt displays of affection aren't necessarily wise away from acknowledged 'gay' venues or districts. The British parliament has voted to reduce the age of homosexual consent from 18 to 16.

Good sources of information for gays, lesbians and bisexuals are the newspapers *Gay Scotland* and *Scotsgay*. Also useful is *The List*, the Edinburgh and Glasgow listings magazine. The main centre for information on gay, lesbian and bisexual issues is at 58A Broughton St (☎ 557 2625) in the New Town. The Gay Switchboard (☎ 556 4049) or the Lesbian Line (☎ 557 0751) can help with most general inquiries.

DISABLED TRAVELLERS

For many disabled travellers, Scotland is a mix of user-friendliness and unfriendliness. Few new buildings aren't accessible to wheelchair users, so large, new hotels and modern tourist attractions are usually fine. However, most B&Bs and guesthouses are in hard-to-adapt older buildings. This means that travellers with mobility problems may pay more for accommodation than their more able-bodied fellows.

It's a similar story with public transport. Newer buses sometimes have steps that lower for easier access, as do trains, but it's always wise to check before setting out. Tourist attractions sometimes reserve parking spaces near the entrance for disabled drivers.

Many ticket offices, banks etc are fitted with hearing loops to assist the hearing impaired; look for the symbol of a large ear. A few tourist attractions, such as cathedrals have braille guides or scented gardens for the visually impaired.

Information & Organisations

If you have a physical disability, get in touch with your national support organisation (preferably the travel officer if there is one). These often have complete libraries devoted to travel, and can put you in touch with travel agents who specialise in tours for the disabled.

The STB produces a guide, *Accessible Scotland*, for disabled travellers and the TIC will have accessibility details for Edinburgh and the Lothians. For more information, including specialist tour operators, contact Disability Scotland (☎ 229 8632), Princes House, 5 Shandwicke Place, Edinburgh EH2 4RG.

The National Trust for Scotland (see Useful Organisations) publishes a free leaflet on disabled facilities at its properties.

The Royal Association for Disability & Rehabilitation (RADAR) publishes a guide on travelling in the UK which gives a good overview of facilities. Contact RADAR (☎ 0171-250 3222, or, from June 1999, ☎ 020-7250 3222), Unit 12, City Forum, 250 City Rd, London EC1V 8AF. The Holiday Care Service (☎ 01293-774535), 2 Old Bank Chambers, Station Rd, Horley, Surrey RH6 9HW, also publishes a guide to accessible accommodation and travel in Britain and can offer general advice.

Rail companies offer a Disabled Persons' Railcard.

SENIOR TRAVELLERS

Senior citizens are entitled to discounts on such things as public transport and museum admission fees, provided they show proof of their age. Sometimes they need a special pass. The minimum qualifying age is generally 60 to 65 for men, 55 to 65 for women.

In your home country, a lower age may entitle you to special travel packages and discounts (on car hire, for instance) through organisations and travel agents that cater to senior travellers. Start hunting at your local senior citizens advice bureau.

In Scotland, rail companies offer a Senior Citizens Railcard for people of 60 and over, giving 33% discounts.

EDINBURGH FOR CHILDREN

Successful travel with young children requires effort but can certainly be done. Try not to overdo things and consider using self-catering accommodation. Children under a certain age can often stay free with their parents in hotels, but be prepared for hotels and B&Bs that won't accept children. Modern, purpose-built hotels can usually provide a cot.

Include children in the planning process; if they've helped to work out where you'll be going, they'll be more interested when they get there. Include a range of activities – balance a visit to Edinburgh Castle with one to the Museum of Childhood or Edinburgh Zoo.

There's no reason why children shouldn't enjoy their visit to Edinburgh, too

The free *Child Friendly Guide to Edinburgh*, published by the city council, has lots of info on things to do with your children. *The List* magazine has a section on children's activities and events in and around Edinburgh; also check the local newspapers.

The Children's Library is on George IV Bridge (see Libraries).

Cyberia Cyber Café (Map 4, ☎ 220 4403), 88 Hanover St, provides a children's club on Saturday morning when kids can play computer games or research school projects.

USEFUL ORGANISATIONS

Membership of Historic Scotland (HS) and the National Trust for Scotland (NTS) is worth considering, especially if you're going to be in Scotland for a while. Both are non-profit organisations dedicated to the preservation of the environment, and both care for hundreds of spectacular sites.

Historic Scotland

Historic Scotland (HS, Map 3, ☎ 668 8800), Longmore House, Salisbury Place, Edinburgh EH9 1SH, manages more than 330 historic sites in Scotland, including top attractions like Edinburgh and Stirling castles. A year's membership costs £22/16 for an adult/child, giving free entry to HS sites and half-price entry to English Heritage properties in England, and Cadw properties in Wales. It also offers short-term 'Explorer' membership – seven/14 days for £12.50/17.

There are standard HS opening times. From April to September properties open daily from 9.30 am to 6.30 pm. From October to March they close two hours earlier. Last entry is 30 minutes before closing time.

In this book, the initials HS indicate a Historic Scotland property – and, unless indicated otherwise, standard opening times apply.

National Trust for Scotland

The National Trust for Scotland (NTS, Map 4, ☎ 226 5922), 5 Charlotte Square, Edinburgh EH2 4DU, is separate from the National Trust (England, Wales and Northern Ireland), although there are reciprocal membership agreements. The NTS cares for over 100 properties and 185,000 acres of countryside.

A year's membership of the NTS costing £25 (£10 if you're aged under 26) offers free access to all NTS and NT properties. Short-term membership (touring ticket) costs £16/24 for one/two weeks. HI/SYHA members and student-card holders get half-price entry to NTS properties.

In this book, the letters NTS indicate a National Trust for Scotland property.

LIBRARIES

The Central Library (Map 6, ☎ 225 5584), George IV Bridge, has a room devoted to Edinburgh, another to all things Scottish. It opens Monday to Thursday from 10 am to 8 pm, Friday to 5 pm, and Saturday from 9 am to 1 pm. Next to the Central Library is the Children's Library open Monday and Wednesday from 1 to 8 pm, Tuesday,

Thursday and Friday from 10 am to 5 pm, and Saturday from 9 am to 1 pm.

The National Library of Scotland (Map 6, ☎ 226 4531, www.nls.uk), opposite the Central Library, houses a reference-only, general reading room. It was undergoing major refurbishment at the time of research, but will be open by the time you read this. It opens weekdays from 9.30 am to 8.30 pm (from 10 am Wednesday), and Saturday from 9.30 am to 1 pm. There's a branch south of the city in Newington (Map 3), at 33 Salisbury Place on the corner of Causewayside, which contains the Scottish science library, the Scottish business information service and a map room. It's open Monday, Tuesday, Thursday and Friday from 9.30 am to 5 pm, and Wednesday from 10 am to 8.30 pm.

UNIVERSITIES

Edinburgh has three universities. The oldest and most prestigious is the University of Edinburgh. Its information centre (Map 7, ☎ 650 1000) on Nicolson St (the southern extension of South Bridge) next to the Edinburgh Festival Theatre, opens weekdays from 9.15 am to 5 pm.

Napier University (Map 3, ☎ 444 2266), 219 Colinton Rd, is in Craiglockhart, southwest of Bruntsfield. Heriot-Watt University (Map 7, ☎ 449 5111) is mainly south-west of town at the Riccarton Campus in Currie, but it has city centre sites in the Mountbatten Building (Map 6) on Grassmarket, and on Cowgate.

CULTURAL CENTRES

The British Council promotes cultural, educational and technical cooperation between Britain and other countries. Its Scottish headquarters (Map 3, ☎ 447 4716, fax 452 8487) is at 3 Bruntsfield Crescent, Bruntsfield.

The Institut Français d'Écosse (Map 6, ☎ 225 5366, fax 220 0648), 13 Randolph Crescent, offers French language lessons and courses in aspects of French culture.

DANGERS & ANNOYANCES

Rose St and the west end of Princes St at the junction with Shandwick Place and Queensberry and Hope Sts, can get a bit rowdy on Friday and Saturday nights after people have been drinking. Calton Hill offers good views during the day, but is probably best avoided at night.

Crime

Edinburgh is safer than most cities of a similar size, but it has its share of crime (often drug related), so the normal big city precautions apply. Pickpockets and bag snatchers operate in crowded public places, although this isn't a big problem. To make it harder for them, place your wallet in a front pocket or carry your daypack in front of you.

Carry valuables next to your skin or in a sturdy pouch on your belt. Carry your own padlock for hostel lockers. Be careful even in hotels; don't leave your valuables lying around in your room. Never leave valuables in a car, and remove all luggage overnight. Report thefts to the police and ask for a statement, or your travel insurance won't pay out; thefts from cars are often excluded anyway.

Beggars

Edinburgh has its share of beggars. If you give money, don't wave a full wallet around – carry some change in a separate pocket. If you don't want to give money, but would like to help the homeless and long-term unemployed, you could buy a copy of the magazine *The Big Issue* (80p) from homeless street vendors who benefit directly from sales. Also, consider giving to Shelter Scotland (☎ 313 1550), 8 Hampton Terrace, a charity that helps the homeless and gratefully accepts donations.

Lost Property

If you lose anything check with the lost property department (Map 2, ☎ 311 3141) at the police headquarters on Fettes Ave

north of the centre near the Western General Hospital. The lost property office (☎ 554 4494) of the LRT bus company, 1-4 Shrub Place on Leith Walk, opens Monday to Friday from 10 am to 1.30 pm.

LEGAL MATTERS

The 1707 Act of Union preserved a Scottish legal system separate from England and Wales, although there has been considerable mergence since then.

A barrister in Scotland is called an advocate and the Scottish Bar is known as the Faculty of Advocates. Scottish law places more importance on principle than precedence and doesn't separate equity (jurisprudence based on principles of natural justice and fair conduct) and law. The court system is also different. The criminal courts in Scotland are the High Court of Justiciary (the supreme criminal court), the Sheriff Court and District Court. The two main civil courts are the Court of Session and the Sheriff Court. Most crimes and offences may be prosecuted only by the Lord Advocate, the chief law officer in Scotland.

In Scotland you only need to be 16 years of age to marry without parental consent; in the rest of the UK it's 18.

If you need legal assistance contact the Scottish Legal Aid Board (☎ 226 7061, fax 220 5133), 44 Drumsheugh Gardens, Edinburgh.

Drugs

The importation of illegal drugs is prohibited and could result in prison. Possession of small quantities of cannabis usually attracts a fine (still a criminal conviction) or a warning; harder drugs are treated more seriously.

Driving Offences

The legal drinking age is 18. You're allowed to have a maximum blood-alcohol level of 35mg/100ml when driving, but the safest approach is not to drink at all.

Traffic offences (illegal parking, speeding etc) usually incur a fine for which you're usually allowed 30 days to pay.

BUSINESS HOURS

Offices generally open weekdays from 9 am to 5 pm. Shops may open longer hours, and most open on Saturday from 9 am to 5 pm. An increasing number of shops also open on Sunday, often from 10 am to 4 pm. Late-night shopping is usually on Thursday or Friday.

Bank hours vary, but you'll be safe if you visit weekdays from 9.30 am to 4 pm. Friday afternoons get very busy. Some banks open later on Wednesday and Thursday, and on Saturday from 9.30 am to 12.30 pm.

PUBLIC HOLIDAYS & SPECIAL EVENTS

Public Holidays

Although 'bank holidays' are general public holidays in the rest of the UK, in Scotland they only apply to banks and some other commercial offices. Bank holidays occur at the start of January, the first weekend in March, the first and last weekend in May, the first weekend in August and Christmas Day and Boxing Day.

Christmas Day, New Year's Day and 2 January are also general public holidays. Edinburgh also has its own local holiday in mid-September.

Special Events

Edinburgh hosts diverse events throughout the year, but August is far and away the busiest month. You'll find up-to-date details in the STB's *Events in Scotland* brochure, published twice a year and available free from the TIC.

December/January

Hogmanay
A range of indoor and outdoor celebrations held across the city to greet the New Year, and includes a huge street party (☎ 557-1700).

Burns Night
Suppers are held all over the country celebrating Robbie Burns, 25 January.

March/April

Edinburgh International Science Festival
A huge two week festival with exhibitions, shows, lectures and hands-on activities for adults and children (☎ 220 6220).

April

Edinburgh Folk Festival
Specialises in Scottish music but also attracts international performers; held for one week early in the month (☎ 0585-559870).

May

Scottish International Children's Festival
One week of music, drama and dance for youngsters in late May (☎ 553 7700).

June

Royal Highland Show
A huge agricultural fair showcasing Scottish produce, with craft and antique fairs, showjumping etc; held at the Royal Highland Showground (☎ 333 2444) in Ingliston near Edinburgh airport.

Pride Scotland March & Festival
This gay and lesbian event takes place every two years and alternates with Glasgow.

Late July/August

Edinburgh International Highland Games
Traditional games, pipe bands and highland dancing held on three separate days spread over a month at Stewarts Melville Playing Fields, Ferry Rd (☎ 319 2005).

August

Edinburgh Military Tattoo
Pageantry and military displays which run for three weeks (☎ 225 1188).

Edinburgh International Jazz & Blues Festival
A week-long series of gigs around the city (☎ 668 2019).

Edinburgh Book Festival
Two weeks of readings, workshops and discussions in Charlotte Square Gardens (☎ 228 5444).

Edinburgh Festival Fringe
Major international fringe performing arts festival; runs for three weeks (☎ 226 5257).

Edinburgh International Festival
Premier international performing arts festival; runs for three weeks (☎ 473 2001).

Edinburgh International Film Festival
World's oldest film festival; runs for two weeks (☎ 228 4051).

Mid September

Festival of the Environment
One week of displays and workshops that begins in the Meadows (☎ 469 5427).

FACTS FOR THE VISITOR

Edinburgh's Festivals

Following its inception in 1947 as a counterpoint to the austerity and problems of reconstruction after WWII, the Edinburgh International Festival has grown into the world's largest, most important arts festival. It attracts top performers in 'serious' music, dance and drama who play to capacity audiences.

The Fringe Festival began unofficially at the same time and grew in tandem to become the largest such event in the world. It showcases wannabe stars, and over 500 amateur and professional groups present every possible kind of avant-garde performance in venues all around the city.

A separate event but a major attraction in its own right, the Edinburgh Military Tattoo is held in the same period and takes place on the Esplanade of Edinburgh Castle. The show is an extravaganza of daredevil displays, regimental posturing and swirling bagpipes and ends with a single piper playing a lament on the battlements.

To make sure that every B&B and hotel room for over 40 miles is full, several other festivals take place at roughly the same time. The nine-day Edinburgh International Jazz & Blues Festival attracts top musicians from around the world who perform at various venues in early August. The two-week Edinburgh International Film Festival, dating from 1947, is Britain's chief film festival. Authors and literary enthusiasts gather in Charlotte Square during the Edinburgh Book Festival. These latter two festivals occur during the second half of the month.

The festival period is a great time to be in Edinburgh. The city is at its best, and the Fringe isn't at all elitist. In most cases the performers and front of house people are friendly and relaxed – they're grateful to have an audience – so there's no need to feel intimidated. Just be prepared to take the bad with the good ...

The International Festival runs from mid-August to early September. If you're more interested in this festival the last week is a good time to go, because the Fringe and Tattoo finish at the end of August, reducing the number of visitors. If you want to attend the International Festival, it's best to book ahead; the program is published in April and is available from the Edinburgh Festival Office (Map 4, ☎ 226 4001, 473 2000, www.goedinburgh.co.uk), 21 Market St, EH1 1BW. Prices are generally reasonable, and any unsold tickets are sold half-price on the day of performance (1 to 5 pm) from the venue one hour before each performance or from the Festival Box Office in Market St. (The box office is scheduled to move to the Highland Tolbooth Kirk on the Royal Mile; check with the TIC.)

The Fringe is less formal, and many performances have empty seats left at the last moment. It's still worth booking for well-known names, or if the production has good reviews. Programs are available, from June, from the Festival Fringe Society (Map 5, ☎ 226 5257, www.edfringe.com), 180 High St, EH1 1QS.

To book for the Military Tattoo contact the Tattoo Office (Map 4, ☎ 225 1188, fax 225 8627, www.edintattoo.co.uk), 33-34 Market St, EH1 1QS.

Hogmanay, the Scottish celebration of the New Year, is another major fixture in Edinburgh's festival calendar with concerts, street parties and a massive bonfire on Calton Hill. Plans are under way to celebrate the year 2000 with the mother of all street parties. For details contact Unique Events (Map 5, ☎ 557 3390, fax 557 8566), 17-23 Calton Rd, Edinburgh EH8 8DL.

For all these festivals, booking accommodation months ahead is strongly advised.

Half Moon Battery, Edinburgh Castle

Scott Monument, National Gallery & Edinburgh Castle

Cycling past Arthur's Seat and Nether Hill

A city bus in Old Town's narrow streets

TOM SMALLMAN

Patisserie Florentin, St Giles Street

TOM SMALLMAN

Women's drum band, Hunter Square, Royal Mile

TOM SMALLMAN

Calton Hill from Leith Street, with foot sculpture in foreground

DOING BUSINESS

Edinburgh is the second most important business centre in the UK after London and one of the largest financial centres in the European Union. Two Scottish banks, and several insurance companies and other financial bodies are headquartered here. The city has a highly developed public transport network and is easily accessible by air, rail and road. With three universities and five colleges, the city has a highly educated professional workforce. Many of the educational institutions themselves have business divisions to provide better communication between business and education.

The annual *Edinburgh Business Directory*, published jointly by the City of Edinburgh Council and the Edinburgh Chamber of Commerce & Enterprise, has much useful information on the city and its business economy. The directory can be viewed in the Edinburgh Room of the Central Library. The Newington branch of the National Library has an information service on business in Scotland. See Libraries earlier.

The pink-coloured daily *Financial Times* and *The Economist*, published weekly, are the foremost publications on business and finance in the UK.

Most of Edinburgh's top and higher mid-range hotels provide business facilities including conference rooms, secretarial services, fax and photocopying services, ISDN lines and use of computer and private office space.

Some language schools provide translation and interpreting services as well as training in English and other languages. These include:

Edinburgh Language Centre
(☎/fax 343 6596), 10B Oxford Terrace, Edinburgh EH4

Institute for Applied Language Studies
(☎ 650 6200), University of Edinburgh, 21 Hill Place, Edinburgh EH8 9DP

Conferences

Edinburgh is high in the world league table of cities hosting business conferences. The Edinburgh Convention Bureau (☎ 473 3666), 4 Rothesay Terrace, Edinburgh EH3 7RY, is responsible for promoting Edinburgh as a conference destination and offers information and support in planning. There's a range of conference venues, but the main one is the Edinburgh International Conference Centre (☎ 300 3000), Morrison St, The Exchange, Edinburgh EH3 8EE, which can hold up to 1200 people. The bureau can advise on smaller, more intimate locations.

Useful Organisations

Edinburgh has a number of development and business support organisations.

The City of Edinburgh Council's Development Department (☎ 529 3595/4625), 1 Cockburn St, Edinburgh EH1 1BP, is responsible for integrating transport, town planning and economic development. It promotes local economic regeneration, investment and vocational training. An arm of the Council, Edinburgh Development & Investment (EDI, ☎ 220 4424), Dolphin House, 4 Hunter Square, Edinburgh EH1 1QW, manages development of and investment in the city's property.

The Edinburgh Chamber of Commerce & Enterprise (☎ 477 7000) is at Conference House, The Exchange, 152 Morrison St, Edinburgh EH3 8EB. It provides a wide range of business support services including information technology, start up and development advice and financial help. It works with the council's Development Department under the banner of the Edinburgh Business Support Partnership whose role is to support business growth and the creation of new jobs.

Lothian & Edinburgh Enterprise Limited (LEEL, ☎ 313 4000), Apex House, 99 Haymarket Terrace, Edinburgh EH12 5HD, is part of the Scottish Enterprise Network (SEN). Its role is to promote economic development in Edinburgh and the Lothians. It provides support to new and existing business and improves access to jobs.

Other useful addresses are:

Edinburgh Business Development
(☎ 477 8000), Conference House, The Exchange, 152 Morrison St, Edinburgh EH3 8EB
Edinburgh International Trade
(☎ 01506-497667), Export House, Quarrywood Court, Livingston EH54 6AX
Edinburgh Business Training
(☎ 225 4796), 3 Randolph Crescent, Edinburgh EH3 7UD
Invest in Lothian
(☎ 313 6206), Apex House, 99 Haymarket Terrace, Edinburgh EH12 5HD
Scottish Financial Enterprises
(☎ 225 6990), 91 George St, Edinburgh EH2 3ES

WORK

Despite the fact that large numbers of locals are jobless, if you're prepared to do anything and work long hours for poor pay, you'll probably find work. Lowly paid seasonal work is available in the tourist industry, usually in restaurants and pubs which advertise for staff in their windows. Hostel noticeboards sometimes advertise casual work and hostels themselves sometimes employ travellers to staff the reception, clean up etc. Without skills, though, it's difficult to find a job that pays well enough to save money. Those with computer skills will find IT jobs advertised on the Internet at www.recruitment.scotland.net.

Whatever your skills, it's worth registering with a number of employment agencies. Job-centres (government employment offices) are scattered around and open Monday to Thursday from 9 am to 4.30 pm, Friday from 9.30 am to 3.30 pm. They're listed in the telephone book and the most central ones are at: 24-26 Torpichen St (☎ 229 9321), 11-13 South St Andrew St (☎ 556 9211) and 20 High Riggs (☎ 229 7551).

EU citizens can work in Scotland without a work permit. Citizens of Commonwealth countries aged 17 to 27 can apply for a Working Holiday Entry Certificate that allows them to spend up to two years in the UK and to take work that is 'incidental' to a holiday. Commonwealth citizens with a UK-born parent may be eligible for a Certificate of Entitlement to the Right of Abode, which entitles them to live and work in the UK free of immigration control.

Commonwealth citizens with a UK-born grandparent, or a grandparent born before 31 March 1922 in what's now the Republic of Ireland, may qualify for a UK Ancestry-Employment Certificate, allowing them to work full time for up to four years in the UK.

Visiting full-time US students aged 18 and over can get a six-month work permit through the Council on International Educational Exchange (☎ 212-822 2600; www.ciee.org), 205 East 42nd St, New York, NY 10017. British Universities North America Club (BUNAC; ☎ 203-264 0901, www.BUNAC.org), PO Box 49, South Britain CT 06487 can also help organise a permit and find work.

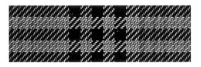

Getting There & Away

Whichever way you're travelling, make sure you take out travel insurance. (See Documents in the Facts for the Visitor chapter.)

For travel to/from Europe or other parts of the UK, buses are the cheapest and most exhausting method of transport, although discount rail tickets are competitive, and budget flights can be good value. Bear in mind a small saving on the fare may not adequately compensate you for time spent travelling that leaves you exhausted.

Travelling from Europe you'll often be best off flying to London, then taking the train or bus north. Flying time from London to Edinburgh is about one hour, but once you add the time taken to get between the airports and the city centres, and boarding time, the four hour centre-to-centre rail trip takes only about an hour more than flying in actual travelling time.

And when making an assessment, don't forget the hidden expenses: getting to/from airports, departure taxes, and food and drink consumed en route.

AIR

Edinburgh's international airport (☎ 333 1000) has frequent direct flights to Europe, Ireland and other parts of the UK and a limited number of services to Africa, the Middle East and Asia. There are no direct air services from North America.

Buying Tickets

The plane ticket may be the single most expensive item in your budget, and buying it can be an intimidating business. There's a multitude of travel agents hoping to separate you from your money, and it's always worth researching the current state of the market. Start early – some of the cheapest tickets have to be bought months in advance, and some popular flights sell out early.

Cheap tickets are available in two distinct categories; official and unofficial. Official ones are advance-purchase tickets, budget fares, Apex, super-Apex, or whatever other brand name airlines care to use.

Unofficial tickets are discounted ones that airlines release through selected travel agents. Airlines can supply information on routes and timetables, and their low-season, student and senior citizens' fares can be competitive, but they don't sell discounted tickets. Remember that normal, full-fare airline tickets sometimes include one or more side trips to Europe free of charge, and/or fly-drive packages, which can make them good value.

Return tickets usually work out cheaper than two one-ways – often *much* cheaper. In some cases, a return ticket can even be cheaper than a one-way. Round-the-World (RTW) tickets can also be great bargains, sometimes cheaper than an ordinary return ticket. RTW prices start at about UK£900, A$2000 or US$1900 depending on the season. An RTW might take you directly to Edinburgh or Glasgow or as a side trip from London.

Official RTW tickets are usually put together by two airlines, and permit you to fly anywhere on their route systems so long as you don't backtrack. There may be restrictions on how many stops you are permitted, and on the length of time the ticket remains valid. Travel agents put together unofficial RTW tickets by combining a number of discounted tickets.

Discounted tickets are usually available at prices as low as or lower than the official Apex or budget tickets. When you phone around, find out the fare, the route, the duration of the journey, the stopovers allowed and any restrictions on the ticket (see the Air Travel Glossary), and ask about cancellation penalties.

You're likely to discover that the cheapest flights are 'fully booked, but we have another one that costs a bit more'. Or the flight is on an airline notorious for its poor

Air Travel Glossary

Baggage Allowance This will be written on your ticket and usually includes one 20kg item to go in the hold, plus one item of hand luggage.

Bucket Shops These are unbonded travel agencies specialising in discounted airline tickets.

Bumped Just because you have a confirmed seat doesn't mean you're going to get on the plane (see Overbooking).

Cancellation Penalties If you have to cancel or change a discounted ticket, there are often heavy penalties involved; insurance can sometimes be taken out against these penalties. Some airlines impose penalties on regular tickets as well, particularly against 'no-show' passengers.

Check-In Airlines ask you to check in a certain time ahead of the flight departure (usually one to two hours on international flights). If you fail to check in on time and the flight is overbooked, the airline can cancel your booking and give your seat to somebody else.

Confirmation Having a ticket written out with the flight and date you want doesn't mean you have a seat until the agent has checked with the airline that your status is 'OK' or confirmed. Meanwhile you could just be 'on request'.

Courier Fares Businesses often need to send urgent documents or freight securely and quickly. Courier companies hire people to accompany the package through customs and, in return, offer a discount ticket which is sometimes a phenomenal bargain. In effect, what the companies do is ship their freight as your luggage on regular commercial flights. This is a legitimate operation, but there are two shortcomings - the short turnaround time of the ticket (usually not longer than a month) and the limitation on your luggage allowance. You may have to surrender all your allowance and take only carry-on luggage.

Full Fares Airlines traditionally offer 1st class (coded F), business class (coded J) and economy class (coded Y) tickets. These days there are so many promotional and discounted fares available that few passengers pay full economy fare.

ITX An ITX, or 'independent inclusive tour excursion', is often available on tickets to popular holiday destinations. Officially it's a package deal combined with hotel accommodation, but many agents will sell you one of these for the flight only and give you phoney hotel vouchers in the unlikely event that you're challenged at the airport.

Lost Tickets If you lose your airline ticket an airline will usually treat it like a travellers cheque and, after inquiries, issue you with another one. Legally, however, an airline is entitled to treat it like cash and if you lose it then it's gone forever. Take good care of your tickets.

MCO An MCO, or 'miscellaneous charge order', is a voucher that looks like an airline ticket but carries no destination or date. It can be exchanged through any International Association of Travel Agents (IATA) airline for a ticket on a specific flight. It's a useful alternative to an onward ticket in those countries that demand one, and is more flexible than an ordinary ticket if you're unsure of your route.

No-Shows No-shows are passengers who fail to show up for their flight. Full-fare passengers who fail to turn up are sometimes entitled to travel on a later flight. The rest are penalised (see Cancellation Penalties).

On Request This is an unconfirmed booking for a flight.

Air Travel Glossary

Onward Tickets An entry requirement for many countries is that you have a ticket out of the country. If you're unsure of your next move, the easiest solution is to buy the cheapest onward ticket to a neighbouring country or a ticket from a reliable airline which can later be refunded if you do not use it.

Open Jaw Tickets These are return tickets where you fly out to one place but return from another. If available, this can save you backtracking to your arrival point.

Overbooking Airlines hate to fly empty seats and since every flight has some passengers who fail to show up, airlines often book more passengers than they have seats. Usually excess passengers make up for the no-shows, but occasionally somebody gets bumped. Guess who it is most likely to be? The passengers who check in late.

Point-to-Point Tickets These are discount tickets that can be bought on some routes in return for passengers waiving their rights to a stopover.

Promotional Fares These are officially discounted fares, available from travel agencies or direct from the airline.

Reconfirmation At least 72 hours prior to departure time of an onward or return flight, you must contact the airline and 'reconfirm' that you intend to be on the flight. If you don't do this the airline can delete your name from the passenger list and you could lose your seat.

Restrictions Discounted tickets often have various restrictions on them - such as needing to be paid for in advance and incurring a penalty to be altered. Others are restrictions on the minimum and maximum period you must be away, such as a minimum of 14 days or a maximum of one year.

Round-the-World Tickets RTW tickets give you a limited period (usually a year) in which to circumnavigate the globe. You can go anywhere the carrying airlines go, as long as you don't backtrack. The number of stopovers or total number of separate flights is decided before you set off and they usually cost a bit more than a basic return flight.

Stand-by This is a discounted ticket where you only fly if there is a seat free at the last moment. Stand-by fares are usually available only on domestic routes.

Travel Agencies Travel agencies vary widely and you should choose one that suits your needs. Some simply handle tours, while full-services agencies handle everything from tours and tickets to car rental and hotel bookings. If all you want is a ticket at the lowest possible price, then go to an agency specialising in discounted tickets.

Transferred Tickets Airline tickets cannot be transferred from one person to another. Travellers sometimes try to sell the return half of their ticket, but officials can ask you to prove that you are the person named on the ticket. This is less likely to happen on domestic flights, but on an international flight tickets are compared with passports.

Travel Periods Ticket prices vary with the time of year. There is a low (off-peak) season and a high (peak) season, and often a low-shoulder season and a high-shoulder season as well. Usually the fare depends on your outward flight - if you depart in the high season and return in the low season, you pay the high-season fare.

safety standards and liable to leave you confined in the world's least favourite airport for 14 hours in mid-journey. Or the agent claims to have the last two seats available, which they'll hold for you for a maximum of two hours. Don't panic – keep ringing around.

If you're travelling from the USA or South-East Asia, or leaving Britain, you'll probably find that the cheapest flights are advertised by small, obscure agencies. Most are honest and solvent, but a few rogue ones will take your money and disappear. If you feel suspicious about a firm, leave a deposit (no more than 20%) and pay the balance when you get the ticket. You could phone the airline direct to check you actually have a booking before picking up the ticket. If the travel agent insists on cash in advance, go somewhere else or be prepared to take a very big risk.

You may decide to pay more than the rock-bottom fare by opting for the safety of a better known travel agent. Firms like STA Travel, which has offices worldwide, Council Travel in the USA, Travel CUTS in Canada and Trailfinders in London offer good prices to most destinations, and are competitive and reliable.

Use the fares quoted in this book as a guide only. They're likely to have changed by the time you read this.

Travellers with Special Needs

If you have special needs – you've broken a leg, you require a special diet, you're taking the baby, or whatever – let the airline people know as soon as possible so that they can make arrangements. Remind them when you reconfirm your booking and again when you check in at the airport.

Children aged under two travel for 10% of the standard fare (or free on some airlines) if they don't occupy a seat, but they don't get a baggage allowance either. 'Skycots', baby food and nappies (diapers) should be provided if requested in advance. Children aged between two and 12 usually get a seat for half to two-thirds of the full fare, and do get a baggage allowance.

Departure Tax

People taking flights from Britain pay an Air Passenger Duty, which is built into the price of an air ticket. Those flying to countries in the European Union (EU) pay £10; those flying beyond pay £20. See Money in the Facts for the Visitor chapter for details on how to reclaim value-added tax when you depart.

Other Parts of Scotland

Flying is a pricey way to get round relatively short distances. Unless you're going to the outer reaches of Scotland, in particular the northern Highlands and islands, planes are only marginally quicker than trains if you include the time it takes to get to/from airports. It's also worth checking whether any passes are available.

The British Airports Authority (BAA) publishes a free *Scheduled Flight Guide* to Scotland with information on flight schedules and carriers and on Aberdeen, Edinburgh and Glasgow airports.

Several carriers, including British Airways/Logan Air (☎ 0345-222111; www .british-airways.com), British Midland (☎ 0345-554554; www.iflybritishmidland .com) and Gillair (☎ 0191-214 6666), connect Edinburgh with the Western Isles, Orkney and Shetland.

An Apex fare to Kirkwall in the Orkneys on British Airways costs around £126. The full return economy fare to Sumburgh in the Shetlands is £261.

England & Wales

Trailfinders (☎ 0171-938 3939, or, from June 1999 ☎ 020-7938 3939), 194 Kensington High St, London W8 6FT, produces a brochure which includes air fares. STA Travel (☎ 0171-361 6262, or, from June 1999 ☎ 020-7361 6262), 86 Old Brompton Rd, London SW7, has a number of branches in the UK.

The London listings magazine *Time Out*, the Sunday papers and the *Evening Standard* carry ads for cheap fares. Also look out for free magazines like *TNT Magazine* which you can often pick up outside main train and tube stations.

Make sure the agent you use is a member of a traveller-protection scheme, such as that offered by the Association of British Travel Agents (ABTA). If you've paid an ABTA-registered agent for your flight and it goes out of business, ABTA guarantees a refund or an alternative. Unregistered bucket shops are riskier but sometimes cheaper.

The Globetrotters Club (BCM Roving, London WC1N 3XX) publishes the *Globe* newsletter which can help in finding travelling companions.

British Airways has flights from London's Heathrow, Gatwick and Stansted, and from Birmingham, Manchester and Cardiff; British Midland flies from Heathrow, Manchester, the East Midlands and Leeds, KLM UK flies from Stansted; EasyJet flies from London's Luton airport.

Most airlines offer a range of tickets including full fare (very expensive but flexible), Apex (for which you must book at least 14 days in advance) and special offers on some services (British Airways calls these Seat Sale or World Offer fares). There are also youth fares (for under 25s) but Apex and special-offer fares are usually cheaper.

Prices vary enormously. The standard economy return ticket from London to Edinburgh on British Airways costs £266; British Airways' and British Midlands' lowest return fare is £59 but there are restrictions. EasyJet and KLM UK offer no-frills flights for £29 one-way between London (Luton/Stansted) and Edinburgh.

Ireland

The Union of Students in Ireland (USIT) (☎ 01-679 8833, 677 8117), 19 Aston Quay, O'Connell Bridge, Dublin 2, the Irish youth and student travel association, has offices in most major cities in Ireland.

Aer Lingus (☎ 0645-737747) is the main operator between Ireland and Scotland. It flies from Dublin, Cork, Donegal and Shannon to Edinburgh; British Airways flies from Dublin, Belfast and Derry to Edinburgh. The one way fare between Edinburgh and Dublin is from around £80.

Continental Europe

Discount charter flights are often available to full-time students aged under 30 and all young travellers aged under 26 (you need an ISIC or official youth card) and are available through the large student travel agencies.

Edinburgh is connected with major cities and some regional centres in Europe. Discount return fares from Edinburgh to Amsterdam cost £137, to Rome £234. Official tickets with carriers like British Airways can cost a great deal more.

The USA & Canada

Flights from North America put down in Glasgow and Aberdeen, but because competition on flights to London is much fiercer, it's generally cheaper to fly to London first.

As well as British Airways, major airlines operating across the North Atlantic to Scotland are Air Canada (☎ 0990-247226), American Airlines (☎ 0345-789789) and Continental Airlines (☎ 0800-776464). They connect Glasgow directly with many cities including Boston, Calgary, Chicago, Denver, Las Vegas, Los Angeles, Miami, Montreal, New Orleans, New York City, Philadelphia, San Francisco, Seattle, Toronto, Vancouver and Washington. The return fare from New York City to Glasgow is around US$600 (£390).

British Airways connects Aberdeen with New York and Toronto.

Check the Sunday travel sections of papers like the *New York Times*, the *LA Times*, the *Chicago Tribune*, the *San Francisco Chronicle* and the *San Francisco Examiner* for the latest fares. The *Globe & Mail*, *Montreal Gazette*, *Toronto Star* and *Vancouver Sun* have similar details from Canada. Offices of Council Travel and STA Travel in the USA or Travel CUTS in Canada are good sources of reliable discounted tickets.

The *Travel Unlimited* newsletter, PO Box 1058, Allston, MA 02134, USA, publishes monthly details of the cheapest airfares and courier possibilities for destinations all over the world from the USA and other countries.

Australia & New Zealand

Flights from Australia and New Zealand arrive via London.

STA Travel and Flight Centres International are major dealers in discounted airfares from Australia and New Zealand. Check the travel agents' ads and ring around.

The Saturday travel sections of the *Sydney Morning Herald* and Melbourne's *The Age* newspapers have ads offering cheap fares to London, but don't be surprised if they happen to be sold out when you contact the agents – they're usually low-season fares on obscure airlines with conditions attached.

Discounted return fares on mainstream airlines through a reputable agent like STA Travel cost between A$1800 (low season) and A$3000 (high season). Flights to/from Perth are a couple of hundred dollars cheaper. A Britannia charter service also operates between Britain and Australia/New Zealand. November to March, prices can drop as low as £499 return from London to Sydney and £698 return from Sydney to London. Contact UK Flight Shop (☎ 02-9247 4833), 7 Maquarie Place, Sydney, or, in the UK, Austravel (☎ 0171-838 1011, or, from June 1999 ☎ 020-7838 1011), 152 Brompton Rd, Knightsbridge, London SW3 1HX.

The cheapest fares from New Zealand will probably take the eastbound route via the USA, but a Round-the-World ticket may be cheaper than a return.

Africa

There are direct flights from Edinburgh to Cairo, Johannesburg and Nairobi. Nairobi, Kenya, is probably the best place in Africa to buy tickets to Britain, thanks to the many bucket shops and the strong competition between them. A typical one-way/return fare to Scotland would be about US$750/

950. If you're thinking of flying from Cairo, it's often cheaper to fly to Athens and to proceed with a budget bus or train from there.

Two travel agents in South Africa with keen prices are Student Travel, Rosebank, Johannesburg (☎ 011-447 5551; Cape Town, 021-418 6570) and The Africa Travel Centre (☎ 021-235555), on the corner of Military Rd and New Church St, Tamboerskloof, Cape Town.

Asia

There are direct flights from Edinburgh to Singapore; most other flights arrive via London.

Ask the advice of other travellers before buying a ticket in Asia. Many of the cheapest fares from South-East Asia to Europe and Britain are offered by Eastern European carriers. STA Travel has branches in Tokyo, Singapore, Bangkok and Kuala Lumpur.

To/from India, the cheapest flights tend to be with Eastern European carriers like LOT and Aeroflot, or with Middle Eastern airlines such as Syrian Arab Airlines and Iran Air. Bombay is the air transport hub, with many transit options to/from South-East Asia, but tickets are slightly cheaper in Delhi.

Airlines

The main operators into Edinburgh are British Airways (☎ 0345-222111, www .british-airways.com), British Midland (☎ 0345-554554, www.iflybritishmidland .com) and KLM UK (☎ 0990-074074, www.klmuk.com). Some of the other airlines can be contacted on the following numbers:

Aer Lingus	☎ 0645-737747
Air Canada	☎ 0990-247226
Air France	☎ 0345-581393
American Airlines	☎ 0345-789789
Continental Airlines	☎ 0800-776464
EasyJet	☎ 01582-445566
EuroScot Express	☎ 0870-607 0809
Gillair	☎ 01292-678000
Jersey European	☎ 01392-360777
Sabena	☎ 0345-256256
SAS	☎ 0345-090900

GETTING THERE & AWAY

BUS

Long-distance buses (coaches) are usually the cheapest method of getting to Edinburgh. The main operator is Scottish Citylink (☎ 0990-505050), part of the Britain-wide National Express (☎ 0990-808080; www.nationalexpress.co.uk).

Buses and coaches leave from St Andrew Square bus station (Map 4) where Scottish Citylink has an inquiry and ticket counter.

Passes & Discounts

The National Express Explorer Pass allows unlimited coach travel within a specified period. It's available to all overseas visitors but must be bought outside Britain. You'll be given a travel voucher which can be exchanged at any of the larger National Express agencies. For adults/concessions they cost £59/45 for three days travel within five consecutive days, £110/80 for seven days in a 21-day period and £170/130 for 14 days in a 30-day period.

National Express Tourist Trail Passes are available to UK and overseas citizens. They provide unlimited travel on all services for two days travel within three consecutive days (£49/39 for an adult/discount cardholder), any five days travel within 10 consecutive days (£85/69), any seven days travel within 21 consecutive days (£120/94) and any 14 days travel within 30 consecutive days (£187/143). The passes can be bought overseas, or at any National Express agent in the UK.

Citylink also honours European under-26 cards, including the Young Scot card (£7), which provides discounts all over Scotland and Europe.

If they don't have one of these cards, full-time students and people aged under 26 can buy a Smart Card. On presentation of proof of age, or student status (an NUS or ISIC card), a passport photo and a £8 fee, you get the Smart Card to add to your collection. It entitles you to a 30% discount, so chances are you'll be ahead after buying your first ticket.

Other Parts of Scotland

Scottish Citylink has buses to virtually every major town in Scotland. Most west coast towns are reached via Glasgow. There are numerous buses to Glasgow, with peak/off-peak returns for £7/5, and to St Andrews, Aberdeen and Inverness.

Hop on, Hop off Buses From June to September, Haggis Backpackers (Map 7, ☎ 557 9393), 6 Blackfriars St, Edinburgh, runs a daily service on a circuit between hostels in Edinburgh, Perth, Pitlochry, Aviemore, Inverness, Loch Ness, Isle of Skye, Fort William, Glencoe, Oban, Inverary, Loch Lomond and Glasgow (although there's no obligation to stay in the hostels). You can hop on and off the minibus wherever and whenever you like, booking up to 24 hours in advance. There's no fixed time for completing the circuit, but you can only cover each section of the route once. It costs £85.

Go Blue Banana (Map 5, ☎ 0131-556 2000), 16 High St, Edinburgh, also runs a jump-on, jump-off service on the same circuit.

England & Wales

Scottish Citylink has numerous regular services from London and other departure points in England and Wales. Buses from London are very competitive and you may be able to get cheap promotional tickets. The fare with Scottish Citylink is £18/28 one way/return. Smaller operators sometimes undercut Scottish Citylink on this route, but their services are less frequent. Other cities include Newcastle (2¾ hours, £8 one way) and York (5½ hours, £20.25 one way).

The budget bus company Slowcoach (☎ 0171-373 7737, or, from June 1999, ☎ 020-7373 7737; www.straytravel.com) operates between youth hostels in England and ventures into Scotland as far as Edinburgh, Glasgow and Stirling. You can get on and off the bus where you like (and there's no compulsion to stay at a hostel). Buses leave London three times a week throughout the year; the price (£119) includes some activities and visits en route.

GETTING THERE & AWAY

TRAIN

The main train station is Waverley in the heart of the city, although most trains also stop at Haymarket station, convenient for the West End. Edinburgh Rail Travel Centre at Waverley station opens Monday to Saturday from 8 am to 11 pm, Sunday from 9 am to 8 pm. For rail inquires, phone ☎ 0345-484950.

ScotRail operates most train services, but a separate company, Railtrack, owns and maintains the tracks and stations. You can make ScotRail bookings by credit card on ☎ 0345-550033. Phone the general inquiry line (☎ 0345-484950, open 24 hours) for timetables and fares; or try the web site www.rail.co.uk for rail services. For short journeys, it's not really necessary to purchase tickets or make seat reservations in advance. Just buy them at the station before you go.

ScotRail has two northern lines from Edinburgh: one that cuts across the Grampians to Inverness (3½ hours) and on to Thurso, and another that follows the coast to Aberdeen (three hours) and on to Inverness. There are numerous trains to Glasgow (50 minutes, £7.10). The trains south first head east to North Berwick, Dunbar and Eyemouth on the coast before arriving in Berwick-upon-Tweed in England.

Frequent InterCity services can whisk you from London's King's Cross to Edinburgh in as little as four hours; apart from Apex fares they're expensive, but they're quicker and more comfortable than buses. The cheapest adult return ticket is the SuperApex, which costs only £35. Numerous restrictions apply to these tickets, which must be purchased 14 days in advance and are difficult to get hold of in summer. Apex tickets (£49 return) must be bought seven days in advance and are more readily available.

Train Passes

Unfortunately, Eurail passes are not recognised in Britain. There are local equivalents, but they in turn aren't recognised in the rest of Europe. The BritRail pass, which includes travel in Scotland, must be bought outside Britain. ScotRail's Freedom of Scotland Travelpass and Regional Rover tickets can be bought in Britain, including from most train stations in Scotland.

The Highland Rover ticket covers the West Highlands and Inverness–Kyle line (£42 for four out of eight consecutive days). The Festival Cities Rover covers the central area (£26 for three out of seven consecutive days).

The ScotRail Rover covers all the ScotRail network and costs £60 for four out of eight consecutive days, £88 for eight consecutive days, or £115 for 12 out of 15 consecutive days. Holders of either the Young Person's or Senior Citizen's Railcard get a 30% discount.

Reservations for bicycles (£3.50) are compulsory on many services.

Railcards

You can get discounts of up to 33% on most off-peak fares if you're aged 16 to 25 or over 60, or studying full-time, or disabled – but you must first buy the appropriate railcard. There is also a railcard for families.

The cards are valid for one year and most are available from major stations. You'll need two passport photos, and proof of age (birth certificate or passport) or student status.

Young Person's Railcard Costs £18 and gives you 33% off most tickets and some ferry services; you must be aged 16 to 25, or be a student of any age studying full-time in the UK.

Senior Railcard Available to anyone over 60, this card costs £18 and gives a 33% discount.

Disabled Person's Railcard Costs £16 and gives a 33% discount to a disabled person and one person accompanying them; pick up an application form from a station and then send it to Disabled Person's Railcard Office, PO Box 1YT, Newcastle-upon-Tyne, NE99 1YT; it can take up to three weeks to process this card so you should apply early.

Family Railcard Costs £20 and allows discounts of 33% (20% for some tickets) for up to four adults travelling together, providing a card-holder is a member of the party; up to four accompanying children pay a flat fare of £2 each. A couple of journeys can pay for the card.

Tickets

If the various train passes and railcards aren't complicated enough, try making sense of the different tickets.

Children under five years old travel free; aged between five and 15 they pay half-price for most tickets. However, when travelling with children it is almost always worth buying a Family Railcard (see above).

Single ticket Valid for a single (ie one-way) journey at any time on the day specified; expensive.

Day Return ticket Valid for a return journey at any time on the day specified; relatively expensive.

Cheap Day Return ticket Valid for a return journey on the day specified on the ticket, but there are time restrictions and it is usually only available for short journeys; often about the same price as a single; you're not usually allowed to travel on a train that leaves before 9.30 am.

Open Return For outward travel on a stated day and return on any day within a month.

Apex One of the cheapest return fares; usually for distances of more than 100 miles; you must book at least 48 hours in advance, but seats are limited so book ASAP.

SuperSaver The cheapest ticket where advance purchase isn't necessary; can't be used on Fridays after 2.30 pm, Saturdays in July and August or on Bank Holidays, or on days after these before 2.30 pm. The return journey must be within one calendar month.

SuperAdvance Similarly priced to the Super-Saver but fewer time/day restrictions; however, tickets must be bought before 2 pm on the day before travel and both the outward and return journey times must be specified; limited availability so book ASAP.

Saver Higher priced than the SuperSaver, but can be used any day and there are fewer time restrictions.

Rail Classes

There are two classes of rail travel: 1st, and what is now officially referred to as standard (although in class-conscious Britain this will always be called 2nd class). First class costs 30 to 50% more than 2nd and, except on very crowded trains, isn't really worth the extra money. On overnight trains there are sleeping compartments, with one berth in 1st and two in 2nd. These cost extra and must be reserved in advance.

CAR & MOTORCYCLE

Travelling by private car or motorcycle enables you to travel quickly, independently and flexibly. Unfortunately, however, the independence you enjoy tends to isolate you and cars can be inconvenient in Edinburgh's centre.

Glasgow is 46 miles west of Edinburgh on the M8 motorway. North-westward the M9 runs to Stirling (35 miles) along the southern banks of the Firth of Forth. North from Edinburgh the A90 crosses the Firth of Forth on the Forth Rd Bridge into Fife from where it continues to Perth as the M90. The A1 runs east to the coast near Dunbar then follows it south to Eyemouth, Berwick-upon-Tweed and Newcastle upon Tyne.

The A68 heads south through the Lothians and the Borders to Darlington in north-eastern England. The other main road due south, the A7, passes through Midlothian and the central Borders and skirts eastern Dumfries & Galloway before arriving in Carlisle in north-west England. The A71 heads south-west from Edinburgh to Kilmarnock.

Edinburgh is 373 miles north of London; allow eight hours for the trip. It makes more sense to break the journey en route, perhaps in York or Chester, or in the Lake District.

BICYCLE

Travelling by bicycle to Edinburgh is straightforward. Bikes aren't allowed on motorways, but you can cycle on all other roads (on the left!) unless the road is marked 'private'. A roads tend to be busy and are best avoided. B roads are usually quieter and many are pleasant for cycling. The best roads are the unclassified roads, or country lanes linking small villages together; they're not numbered, you simply follow the signposts. Lanes are clearly shown on Ordnance Survey (OS) maps.

Bicycles can be transported by bus provided there's enough room in the luggage compartment and that they're folded or dismantled and boxed. On most long distance rail routes it's necessary to make a reservation for your bike. Some trains carry only one or two bikes so make your reservation (and get your ticket) at least 24 hours before travelling.

HITCHING

Hitching is never entirely safe and we can't recommend it as a way of getting to Edinburgh. That said, if you're determined to risk it, you can minimise the likelihood of problems by hitching with someone else and making sure someone knows where you're going and when you expect to arrive.

It's against the law to hitch on motorways or the immediate slip roads; make a sign and use approach roads, nearby roundabouts, or the service stations. If you don't like the look of someone who stops for you, don't get in the car. Likewise, if you're a driver, take care over who you pick up.

It's easy enough to hitch to Edinburgh along the A7, or A696 and A697 which become the A68. The coastal route (A1) to Edinburgh is slow.

TRAVEL AGENTS

Two travel agencies specialise in budget and student travel. Campus Travel (Map 6, ☎ 225 6111), 53 Forrest Rd, opens Monday to Friday, from 9 am to 5.30 pm, Saturday from 10 am to 5 pm; it's often busy. Close to the university campus, Edinburgh Travel Centre (☎ 668 2221), 3 Bristo Square, opens Monday to Friday from 9 am to 5.30 pm; it issues ISIC cards.

American Express and Thomas Cook have offices in the city (see Money in the Facts for the Visitor chapter). Going Places (☎ 225 5373), 30 George St on the corner of Hanover St, is a general travel agent which opens on Sunday.

ORGANISED TOURS

There are many companies offering tours of Scotland which include Edinburgh in their itinerary. See your travel agent, check the small ads in newspaper travel pages, or contact the nearest branch of the British Tourist Authority or Scottish Tourist Board for the names of tour operators (see Tourist Offices in the Facts for the Visitor chapter).

Pitched at a young crowd is Outback UK (☎ 01327-704115, fax 01327-703883), The

Cottage, Church Green, Badby, Northants, NN11 3AS. It offers two to 14-day tours round Britain with departures every Saturday (March to November) from London, though it's possible to join at any point. See also Slowcoach under Buses earlier.

Shearings Holidays (☎ 01942-824824), Miry Lane, Wigan, Lancashire, WN3 4AG, has a wide range of four to 12-day coach tours. It also offers Club 55 holidays for the more mature holiday-maker.

For the over 60s, Saga Holidays (☎ 0800-300500), Saga Building, Middleburg Square, Folkestone, Kent CT20 1AZ, offers cheap coach tours and resort holidays around Britain. Saga also operates in the USA (☎ 617-262 2262), 222 Berkeley St, Boston, MA 02116, and in Australia (☎ 02-9957 4266), Level 1, 10-14 Paul St, Milsons Point, Sydney, NSW 2061.

Warning

The information in this chapter is particularly vulnerable to change: prices for international travel are volatile, routes are introduced and cancelled, schedules change, special deals come and go, and rules and visa requirements are amended. Airlines and governments seem to take a perverse pleasure in making price structures and regulations as complicated as possible. You should check directly with the airline or a travel agent to make sure you understand how a fare (and ticket you may buy) works. In addition, the travel industry is highly competitive and there are many lurks and perks.

The upshot of this is that you should get opinions, quotes and advice from as many airlines and travel agents as possible before you part with your hard-earned cash. The details given in this chapter should be regarded as pointers and are not a substitute for your own careful, up-to-date research.

Getting Around

THE AIRPORT

Edinburgh airport (☎ 333 1000) is 8 miles west of the city centre along the A8 Edinburgh–Glasgow road. It's currently undergoing a massive redevelopment program to help it handle an expected 5.5 million passengers a year by 2002. All facilities will be available while this is going on, but some locations may change and you may experience some congestion and disruption as you pass through.

The airport is divided into five zones, A to E. The airport information desk is in zone D, the TIC with information on the city and Scotland is in zone E. Rental cars including Alamo (☎ 333 5100), Avis (☎ 333 1866), Europcar (☎ 333 2588) and Hertz (☎ 333 1019) are in zone A. In zone B, the Thomas Cook (☎ 333 5119) accommodation booking service opens from 8.30 am to 9.30 pm. There are several *bureaux de change* throughout the terminal.

TO/FROM THE AIRPORT

Frequent LRT Airline buses run from Waverley Bridge near the train station to Haymarket and the airport, taking 35 minutes and costing £3.20/5 one way/return. Guide Friday's (☎ 556 2244) Air Bus Express provides a similar service. A taxi costs around £14 one way.

BUS

Bus services are frequent and cheap, and most leave from either St Andrew Square bus station or Waverley Bridge near the train station. Two main companies, Lothian Regional Transport (LRT; ☎ 555 6363) and Scottish Motor Traction (SMT; ☎ 556 8464), compete on some services and their tickets aren't interchangeable. SMT operates much of the service between Edinburgh and the Lothians. LRT is the main operator within Edinburgh, but also runs buses to East Lothian. You can buy tickets when you board buses, but on LRT buses you must have exact change.

For short trips on LRT, fares are 50p to 65p. A Day Saver (£2.20), available from bus drivers when you board, covers a whole day's travel. If you're staying a week or longer, Ridacards give unlimited travel on LRT buses; one week costs £10. After midnight there are special night buses from Waverley Bridge; these cost a flat £1.50.

Tickets and information for LRT buses are available from its Travelshops: at 27 Hanover St (Map 4, ☎ 554 4494), open Monday to Saturday from 8.30 am to 6 pm, and Waverley Bridge (Map 4, ☎ 555 6363), open May to October, Monday to Saturday, from 8 am to 7.15, Sunday from 9 am to 4.30 pm, and November to April, Tuesday to Saturday, from 9 am to 4.30 pm.

SMT has a Bus Shop (☎ 663 9233) at St Andrew Square bus station (Map 4) open Monday, Tuesday and Thursday to Saturday, from 8.40 am to 5 pm, Wednesday from 9 am to 5 pm.

Greenways

The Greenways scheme has been a big success. The city council and LRT have introduced low-emission buses and bus-priority lanes on a number of routes in order to reduce the number of cars (and pollution) on Edinburgh's roads and to improve movement along the main traffic corridors. In its first six months the scheme was initially used on two heavily used routes – from Leith and Maybury to the centre. It resulted in faster journey times and a big rise in the number of passengers (estimated to be the equivalent of 200,000 car journeys). These were expanded to other routes – from the centre to Wester Hailes, Slateford and Tollcross. More routes are under consideration.

The free *Edinburgh Travelmap* shows the most important services. It's available from the TIC, or during weekdays (8.30 am to 4.30 pm) from Traveline (Map 4, ☎ 225 3858, 0800 232323), 2 Cockburn St, which has information on all of Edinburgh's public transport.

TRAIN

Edinburgh doesn't have its own separate rail network. Those running through the city are part of the national rail system. Trains heading west and north link Waverley station with Haymarket, but it's cheaper to catch a bus down Princes St. There are regular trains west to Dalmeny near South Queensferry. Trains east to North Berwick stop at Musselburgh and Prestonpans.

Phone the general inquiry line (☎ 0345-484950, 24 hours) for timetables and fares.

CAR & MOTORCYCLE

Though useful for day trips beyond the city, a car in central Edinburgh is as much a millstone as a convenience. There is restricted access on Princes St, George St and Shandwicke Place and a number of streets are one-way. Queen's Drive around Holyrood Park is closed to motorised traffic on Sunday.

Road Rules

Anyone using the roads should get hold of the *Highway Code* (99p), which is often available in TICs. A foreign driving licence is valid in Britain for up to 12 months from the time of your last entry into the country. If you're bringing a car from Europe make sure you're adequately insured.

Briefly, vehicles drive on the left-hand side of the road; front seat belts are compulsory and if seat belts are fitted in the back they must be worn; the speed limit is 30 mph (48 kph) in built-up areas, 60 mph (96 kph) on single carriageways, and 70 mph (112 kph) on dual or triple carriageways; you give way to your right at roundabouts (traffic already on the roundabout has the right of way); and motorcyclists must wear helmets.

See Legal Matters in Facts for the Visitor for information on drink-driving rules.

Parking

There's no parking on main roads into the city Monday to Saturday from 8 am to 6 pm. On-street parking is limited – Monday to Friday from 8.30 am to 5.30 pm, Saturday from 8.30 am to 1.30 pm – and meters are expensive. Cars parked illegally may be towed away. There are 'short-stay' and 'long-stay' car parks. Prices are often the same for stays of up to two or three hours, but for lengthier stays the short-stay car parks rapidly become much more expensive. The long-stay car parks may be slightly less convenient but they're much cheaper. The TIC has a map of off-street car parks.

Motorcycles can be parked for free at designated areas in the city centre.

A yellow line painted along the edge of the road indicates there are parking restrictions. The only way to establish the exact restrictions is to find the nearby sign that spells them out. A double line means no parking at any time; a single line means no parking for at least an eight-hour period somewhere between 7 am and 7 pm; and a broken line means there are some restrictions. Red lines mean no stopping or parking.

Rental

In addition to the big national operators, the TIC has details of reputable local car rental companies. Some rental companies with offices in the city include:

Avis
   (☎ 337 6363), 100 Dalry Rd
Europcar
   (☎ 557 3456), 24 East London St
Hertz
   (☎ 557 5273), Waverley station
Melville's
   (☎ 337 5333), 9 Clifton Terrace, Haymarket
Practical Car & Van Rental
   (☎ 346 4545), 23 Roseburn St

Practical Car & Van Rental is one of the cheaper ones with weekly rates of £70 (plus insurance) for its smallest cars, including unlimited mileage.

TAXI

Hailing a cab on the street should present no problems and there are numerous central taxi ranks including at Waverley station. The flagfall starts at £1.20 for the first 340 yards, then 20p for every subsequent 240 yards; about £6 will get you to most places in the city centre. Local companies include Capital Taxis (☎ 228 2555), Central Radio Taxis (☎ 229 2468), City (☎ 228 1211) and Radiocabs (☎ 225 9000).

BICYCLE

Although there are plenty of steep hills to negotiate, Edinburgh is ideal for cycling – nothing is more than half an hour away, there are signposted cycle routes and outside the centre the traffic is fairly tolerable.

Edinburgh Cycle Hire (Map 7, ☎ 556 5560), 29 Blackfriars St, hires out city bikes for £5 a day, and mountain and hybrid bikes for £10 to £15 a day, or £50 a week. It also hires out tents and touring equipment, and arranges cycling tours of the city. It sells used bikes and buys them back, the price depending on the state they come back in.

Mountain Magic Cycle Hire (Map 6, ☎ 225 7855), Cowgatehead, has mountain bikes from £10 per day.

Central Cycle Hire (Map 6, ☎ 228 6333), Lochrin Place off Home St, near Tollcross, operates from the Bike Trax shop and has touring/mountain bikes for £10/15 per day.

ORGANISED TOURS
Walking Tours

There are lots of organised walks of Edinburgh, many of them related to ghosts, witches and torture – and with appropriately dressed guides. Mercat Tours (☎ 661 4541) has a Ghost Hunter Tour of the Old Town's underground vaulted chambers which starts at 9.30 pm, lasts 1½ hours and costs £5. Other companies offering similar walks are Robin's Tours (☎ 661 0125), Auld Reekie Tours (☎ 557 4700) and Witchery Tours (☎ 225 6745). Mercat Tours and Robin's Tours also do straightforward historical guided walks of the Royal Mile.

One of the most popular tours is the Macallan Edinburgh Literary Pub Tour (☎ 226 6665) in which actors take you to the pubs frequented by Burns, Scott, Stevenson et al and give you a light-hearted lesson in Scottish literature. Tours leave from the Beehive Inn (Map 6) in Grassmarket and cost £6.

Bus Tours

Open-topped buses leave from Waverley Bridge outside the main train station and offer hop-on, hop-off tours of the main sights. Guide Friday (☎ 556 2244) charges £7.50 and LRT's (☎ 555 6363) Edinburgh Classic Tour costs £5.50. They're a good way of getting your bearings – although with a bus map and a Day Saver bus ticket (£2.20) you could do the same thing, without a commentary.

Scotline Tours (☎ 557 0162) does four-hour tours of the city for £4, leaving Waverley Bridge daily at 9 am. It also offers tours further afield to St Andrews, the Borders and Loch Ness.

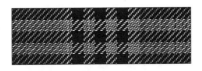

Things to See & Do

HIGHLIGHTS

- Enjoying the views from Arthur's Seat and Salisbury Craigs
- And then enjoying more views from Calton Hill
- Walking or cycling in Holyrood Park
- Being entertained throughout The Fringe Festival
- Experiencing ghost walks along the underground passages
- Strolling the Royal Mile
- Taking a cruise on the Firth of Forth to Inchcolm Island
- Visiting Hopetoun House and Gladstone's Land
- Relaxing in the pubs

WALKING TOUR

One of the simplest walking tours is to follow the Royal Mile in the Old Town from Castle Hill in front of Edinburgh Castle down to the Palace of Holyroodhouse. The Royal Mile walk is described in detail later in the chapter.

The following Edinburgh walking tour is to help you get acquainted with parts of the Old and New Towns; it's about 3 miles in length and takes 1½ to two hours. The number in brackets beside the item corresponds to the number in the key of the Edinburgh Walking Tour & The Royal Mile map.

Starting from in front of the TIC (1) on Princes St cross north over the road and walk up Andrew St. On your right you come to **Dundas House** (2), the head office of the Royal Bank of Scotland. Turn left and cross over to the south side of **St Andrew Square** (3), then turn right onto St David St and left onto **George St**, the centre of Edinburgh's finance industry. Head west

along George St to Charlotte Square. On the way you pass **St Andrew & St George Church** (4) and **Castle St** where, at No 39, Sir Walter Scott lived for 24 years.

Charlotte Square was designed by Robert Adam and is a superb example of Georgian architecture. On the north side is the restored **Georgian House** (5), at No 7, now a museum. Turn left onto South Charlotte St, cross over to the southern side of the square, then turn left onto Hope St. Heading south this brings you to the **West End**, where Hope St converges with several other streets including Princes St. Turn left then cross over Princes St to the corner of Lothian Rd where you'll find the Gothic **St John's Church** (6) and below it, **St Cuthbert's Church** (7). To the left (east) is **Princes St Gardens**.

Continue south on Lothian Rd; then turn left onto King's Stables Rd, which curves south then east in the shadow of **Edinburgh Castle** under King's Bridge to **Grassmarket** (8), where there are some good pubs and restaurants. Head east on Grassmarket to **West Bow**, which leads into curving **Victoria St** with its interesting collection of shops. Follow Victoria St up to the junction with George IV Bridge. To the right is the **Central Library** (9) and opposite, the **National Library** (10). Turn left onto George IV Bridge and continue over the Royal Mile to Bank St. Ahead, the building with the dome and the Scottish national flags flying is a branch of the **Royal Bank of Scotland** (11).

Follow Bank St round to the left as far as the start of **The Mound**, the road that connects the Old and New Towns. From here there are views north over Princes St Gardens. To the left is Mound Place, where you can see the main entrance to the **Assembly Rooms** (12) of the Church of Scotland. As you head down The Mound, you pass first the classical **National Gallery of Scotland** (13) then the **Royal Scottish Academy** (RSA) (14) before arriving back on Princes St.

Edinburgh Festival Theatre, Nicolson Street

Monument to Greyfriars Bobby, Greyfriars Kirkyard

RL Stevenson, Scottish National Portrait Gallery

Stone carving, Greyfriars Kirkyard cemetery

Street sign, Royal Mile

Edinburgh Festival Box Office, Market Street

Haggis, Scotland's culinary delight

Charlotte Square, New Town, has excellent examples of Georgian architecture

Turning right here leads you to the tall Gothic **Sir Walter Scott Monument** (15), then to Waverley Bridge from where sight-seeing and other buses depart. Continuing east a little farther brings you back to the piazza above **Waverley Market** shopping centre and the TIC.

EDINBURGH CASTLE

Edinburgh Castle dominates the city centre, sitting astride the core of an extinct volcano, its three sides scoured almost vertical by glacial action. The castle is overrun with tourists, and although the views are great, you may decide it's more impressive from the outside looking in.

The castle (☎ 225 9846, HS) opens April to September, daily from 9.30 am to 6 pm (5 pm in winter). The admission price of £6/1.50 includes provision of an audio tape commentary.

History

There was a settlement here as early as 850 BC, although the first historical references date from the 6th century when the Northumbrian king, Edwin, rebuilt a fortress here as a defence against the Picts.

A favoured royal residence from the 11th to the 16th centuries, Edinburgh only became Scotland's capital at the end of the Middle Ages. The oldest surviving part of the castle is St Margaret's Chapel.

Although it looks impregnable, the castle often changed hands between the Scots and English. It last saw action in 1745, when Bonnie Prince Charlie's army tried but failed to breach its walls.

During the Wars of Independence (1174 to 1356), the English captured it several times. In 1313 it was demolished by the Scots as part of Robert the Bruce's scorched earth policies and wasn't rebuilt until 1371

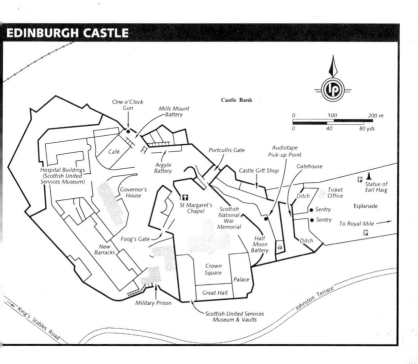

EDINBURGH CASTLE

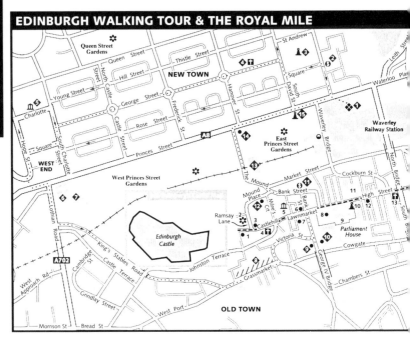

EDINBURGH WALKING TOUR & THE ROYAL MILE

by David II. Little of this work survives, however, because the castle was strengthened and renovated in the 16th, 17th and 18th centuries.

From the 16th century the royal family built more comfortable domestic accommodation at places like Holyrood, and the castle developed as a seat of government and military power. However, in 1566 Mary Queen of Scots underlined its continuing symbolic importance when she chose to give birth to her son in the castle. In 1573 much of it was destroyed when loyalists attempted to hold it for Mary; the oldest substantial work – including the Half Moon Battery and Portcullis Gate – survives from the subsequent rebuilding.

The castle was then taken in turn by the Covenanters (in 1640), Cromwell (in 1650) and King William and Queen Mary (the last true siege, in 1689). In 1715 and 1745 the Stuarts tried unsuccessfully to recapture it. In the gaps between sieges more defences were added, and (apart from some 19th and 20th century additions) by the mid-18th century the castle looked much as it does today.

Partly thanks to Sir Walter Scott, in the 19th century the castle began to recover its importance as a Scottish symbol. Efforts were made to improve its appearance and to restore important buildings.

The Castle

Visitors enter from the **Esplanade**, a parade ground where the Military Tattoo takes place each August. The changing of the guard occurs on the hour, and on summer evenings a piper plays here. On the right as you enter the Esplanade is a statue of Field Marshall Earl Haig on horseback. Haig was commander-in-chief of British forces during WWI and was responsible for the

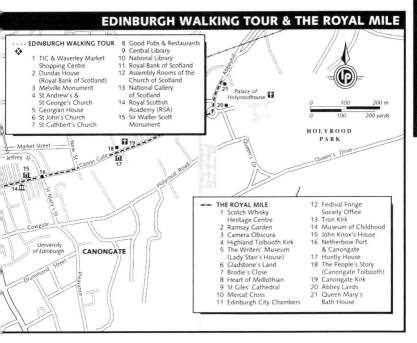

EDINBURGH WALKING TOUR & THE ROYAL MILE

···· EDINBURGH WALKING TOUR

1 TIC & Waverley Market
   Shopping Centre
2 Dundas House
   (Royal Bank of Scotland)
3 Melville Monument
4 St Andrew's &
   St George's Church
5 Georgian House
6 St John's Church
7 St Cuthbert's Church
8 Good Pubs & Restaurants
9 Central Library
10 National Library
11 Royal Bank of Scotland
12 Assembly Rooms of the
   Church of Scotland
13 National Gallery
   of Scotland
14 Royal Scottish
   Academy (RSA)
15 Sir Walter Scott
   Monument

── THE ROYAL MILE
1 Scotch Whisky
   Heritage Centre
2 Ramsay Garden
3 Camera Obscura
4 Highland Tolbooth Kirk
5 The Writers' Museum
   (Lady Stair's House)
6 Gladstone's Land
7 Brodie's Close
8 Heart of Midlothian
9 St Giles' Cathedral
10 Mercat Cross
11 Edinburgh City Chambers
12 Festival Fringe
   Society Office
13 Tron Kirk
14 Museum of Childhood
15 John Knox's House
16 Netherbow Port
   & Canongate
17 Huntly House
18 The People's Story
   (Canongate Tolbooth)
19 Canongate Kirk
20 Abbey Lairds
21 Queen Mary's
   Bath House

policy of attrition in the trench warfare that killed thousands of troops. He later founded the Royal British Legion.

After entering the castle proper through the **Gatehouse** (added in the late 19th century) with its drawbridge, the pathway curves round to the right. It passes through the 16th century **Portcullis Gate**, whose upper section was added in 1886-87, before coming to **Argyle Battery** then **Mills Mount Battery**. There are good views to the north from both batteries and at Mills Mount the weekday 1 pm gun salute takes place.

Continuing round, you pass the **Governor's House** and the **New Barracks**, both dating from the 18th century, but which aren't open to the public. Behind the Governor's House, in the old hospital buildings, is an annexe of the Scottish United Services Museum. In the **Military Prison** (1842) you

can view the cells where recalcitrant soldiers were held in solitary confinement.

You enter the central defensive area through **Foog's Gate**. Here you'll find the small Norman **St Margaret's Chapel**, the oldest building in Edinburgh. It's a simple stone edifice that was probably built by David I or Alexander I in memory of their mother sometime around 1130. Following Cromwell's capture of the castle in 1650 it was used to store ammunition until Queen Victoria had it restored; it was rededicated in 1934.

On the eastern end of Crown Square is the **Palace** built between the 15th and 16th centuries. Among the royal apartments is the bedchamber where Mary Queen of Scots gave birth to her son James, who was to unite the crowns of Scotland and England. Another room is used to house the Scottish crown jewels, made up of sceptre,

The Stone of Destiny

Alleged to have accompanied the Scots in all their mythical journeyings, the original Stone of Destiny (the Fatal Stone) was a carved block of sandstone on which the Scottish monarchs placed their feet during the coronation.

Stolen by Edward I in 1296, this venerable talisman was incorporated into the Coronation Chair, used by English (and later British) monarchs, in London's Westminster Abbey. Apart from being taken to Gloucester during air raids in WWII, the Stone lay undisturbed for centuries.

On Christmas Eve 1950, however, a plucky band of Scottish students drove down from Glasgow, jemmied the door of Westminster Abbey and made off with the Stone. English officialdom was outraged. The border roads had roadblocks on them for the first time in 400 years, but while Scots living in London jeered the English police as they searched the Serpentine Lake and the River Thames, the Stone was smuggled back to Scotland.

King George VI was 'sorely troubled about the loss', but the students issued a petition affirming their loyalty to him, stating that they would give back the Stone as long as it could remain on Scottish soil. The authorities refused to negotiate and, three months after it was stolen, the Stone turned up on the altar of the ruined Abbey of Arbroath. It was here, in 1320, that the Arbroath Declaration had been signed, reaffirming the right of Scots to self-rule and independence from England. Before the public were aware that the Stone had even been found, it was back in London. No charges were brought and Ian Hamilton, the student who led this jolly caper, published his story in *The Taking of the Stone of Destiny*.

Many Scots, however, hold that the original Stone is safely hidden somewhere in Scotland, and that Edward I was fobbed off with a shoddy imitation. This is possibly true, for descriptions of the original state that it was decorated with carvings, not that it was a plain block of sandstone. Given that Scottish nationalism is running high, this powerful symbol of Scotland would surely have been brought out by now if it hadn't been quite so safely hidden.

Imitation or not, the Scottish Secretary and Conservative MP, Michael Forsyth, arranged for the return of the sandstone block to Edinburgh Castle, with much pomp and circumstance, in 1996. If it was an attempt to boost his flagging political standing, it failed dismally: Forsyth lost his seat in the House of Commons in the May 1997 general election.

---

sword and crown; with them now lies the Stone of Destiny (see boxed text).

Adjacent to the Palace is the **Great Hall**, built for James IV as a ceremonial hall and used as a meeting place for the Scottish Parliament until 1639. In former barracks opposite, the massive, sombre **Scottish National War Memorial** was added to the castle complex in the 1920s and is a memorial to the Scots dead of WWI.

At the western end of the square in the Queen Anne Building, the **Scottish United Services Museum** houses displays on the history of Scottish regiments as well as the air force and navy. From this end of the square you can descend into the dark, dank **Vaults**, a former prison for foreigners. One of its rooms contains **Mons Meg**, a huge 15th century siege cannon.

ROYAL MILE

Following a ridge that runs from Edinburgh Castle to the Palace of Holyroodhouse, the Royal Mile is one of the world's most fascinating streets. From the west end you can see beyond craggy Arthur's Seat and over the waters of the Firth of Forth, with tantalising glimpses of the Old and New Towns through the *closes* (entrances) and *wynds* (alleyways) on either side. Although there are tourists and shops stuffed with tacky Scottish souvenirs aplenty, the street still feels a real part of a thriving city. It's lined with extraordinary buildings, including multistoreyed *lands* (tenements) dating from the 15th century.

To see the numerous sites would take several days, but even with limited time, it's worth ducking through a *pend* (arched gateway) or close to explore the narrow wynds and courts beyond.

The map reference in brackets beside each item corresponds to the map on which the item is found, while the number beside it corresponds to the number in the key of the Edinburgh Walking Tour & The Royal Mile map.

Scotch Whisky Heritage Centre (Maps 1 & 6)

If you'd like to know how whisky is manufactured the Scotch Whisky Heritage Centre (☎ 220 0441), Castle Hill, offers a tour with several audiovisual presentations followed by a ride in a car past a tableau explaining the history of the 'water of life'. You can take the ride only (15 minutes) for £3.80/2, but it's not really worth it. It's better value to do the full tour or put the money toward the purchase of one (or more) of the hundreds of different brands of whisky sold in the shop. The centre opens daily from 10 am to 5.30 pm; the full experience including a tasting costs £4.95/2.50.

Ramsay Garden (Maps 2 & 6)

Constructed around the mid-18th century home of the poet Alan Ramsay, the attractive apartments here overlook The Esplanade and the small garden from which they get their name. They were designed in the 1890s by an early town planner, Patrick Geddes, in an attempt to revitalise the Old Town. They're now very expensive, very wonderful private apartments.

Camera Obscura (Maps 3 & 6)

Just beyond Ramsay Lane, the Camera Obscura (☎ 226 3709) offers great views over the city. The 'camera' itself is a curious device (originally dating from the 1850s, although improved in 1945) a bit like a periscope, which uses lenses and mirrors to throw a 'live' image onto a large interior bowl. The accompanying 'guided tour' is entertaining, and the whole exercise has a quirky charm. It's open Monday to Friday from 9.30 am to 6 pm, weekends from 10 am; admission is £3.85/1.95, family £11.50.

Highland Tolbooth Kirk (Maps 4 & 6)

With the tallest spire (71.7m, 239 feet) on one of Edinburgh's highest points, the Highland Tolbooth Kirk is an important feature of the skyline. It was built in the 1840s by James Graham and Augustus Pugin (architect of the London Houses of Parliament).

It gets its name from the Gaelic services that were held here for Edinburgh's Highland congregations (which now occur at Greyfriars Kirk). It's being refurbished and will eventually be the home of the Edinburgh Festival office.

Opposite the kirk are the **Assembly Rooms** of the Church of Scotland, which are the temporary home of the new Scottish Parliament.

The Writers' Museum (Maps 4 & 5)

The Writers' Museum (☎ 529 4901) is in Lady Stair's House, built in 1622, and contains manuscripts and memorabilia belonging to Robert Burns, Sir Walter Scott and Robert Louis Stevenson.

The static displays will only entertain enthusiasts of these writers but it's open Monday to Saturday from 10 am to 5 pm and, during the Edinburgh Festival, on Sunday from 2 to 5 pm; admission is free.

Gladstone's Land (Map 6)

Gladstone's Land (☎ 226 5856; NTS), 477 Lawnmarket, gives a fascinating glimpse of the Old Town's past. The house was built in about the mid-16th century and extended around 1617 by wealthy merchant Thomas

Gledstanes. Its comfortable interior contains fine painted ceilings, walls and beams and some splendid furniture from the 17th and 18th centuries. It's open April to October, Monday to Saturday from 10 am to 5 pm, Sunday from 2 to 5 pm; admission is £2.80/1.90.

Brodie's Close (Maps 6 & 7)

Brodie's Close is named after the father of the notorious William Brodie, a deacon and respected citizen by day, a burglar by night. William Brodie was the inspiration for Robert Louis Stevenson's *Dr Jekyll and Mr Hyde* and, some would say, a dramatic reflection of Edinburgh's darker undercurrents. He met his end on the gallows in 1788.

Parliament Square (Map 6)

Lawnmarket ends at the crossroads of Bank St and George IV Bridge; at the south-east corner, brass strips set in the road mark the site of the scaffold where public hangings took place until 1864. From there the Royal Mile continues as High St.

Parliament Square, largely filled by St Giles' Cathedral (see below), the High Kirk of St Giles, is on the north side. This was the heart of Edinburgh until the 18th century, and a cobblestone **Heart of Midlothian** (8) is set in the paving. Passers-by traditionally spit on it for luck. This was the site of the entrance to the Tolbooth, originally built to collect tolls, but subsequently a meeting place for parliament, the town council and the General Assembly of the Reformed Kirk, then law courts and, finally, a prison and place of execution.

The 19th century **Mercat Cross** (10) replaced the original 1365 cross and marks the spot where merchants and traders met to transact business and Royal Proclamations were read.

The square's southern side is flanked by **Parliament House**, the meeting place of the Scottish Parliament from 1639; its neoclassical façade was added in the early 19th century. After the Act of Union in 1707 the building became the centre for the Scottish

legal system – the Court of Session and High Court – which retained its independence. The most interesting feature is **Parliament Hall**, where the parliament actually met, which is now used by lawyers and their clients as a meeting place.

St Giles' Cathedral (Maps 6 & 9)

There has been a church on this site since the 9th century. A Norman-style church was built in 1126, but this was burnt by the English in 1385; the only substantial remains are the central piers that support the tower. The present church was then built in stages, with the crown spire completed in 1495.

Inside, near the entrance is a life-size statue of John Knox, minister from 1559 to 1572; from here he preached his uncompromising Calvinist message and launched the Scottish Reformation. The new austerity this ushered in led to changes in the building's interior – decorations, stained glass, altars and the relics of St Giles were thrown into the Nor Loch.

The High Kirk of St Giles was at the heart of Edinburgh's struggle against episcopacy (the rule of the church by bishops). In 1637 when Charles I attempted to re-establish episcopacy and made the kirk a cathedral, he provoked a possibly apocryphal outburst by Jenny Geddes which, according to popular belief, led to the signing of the National Covenant at Greyfriars the following year. Jenny hurled a stool at the dean who was using the English prayer book (a symbol of episcopacy); a tablet marks the spot and a copy of the National Covenant is displayed on the wall.

One of the most interesting corners of the kirk is the Thistle Chapel built 1909-11 for the Knights of the Most Ancient & Most Noble Order of the Thistle. The carved Gothic-style stalls have canopies topped with the helms and arms of the 16 knights.

Entry to the kirk is free, but a £1 donation is requested.

Edinburgh City Chambers (Maps 5 & 11)

The City Chambers were originally built by John Adam (brother of Robert) in 1761 to replace the Mercat Cross and serve as a Royal Exchange. However, the merchants continued to prefer the street, and the building was taken over by the town council which has been using it since 1811.

Tron Kirk (Maps 5 & 13)

At the south-western corner of the intersection with South Bridge, Tron Kirk owes its name to a salt *tron* or public weighbridge that stood on the site. It was built in 1637 on top of Marlin's Wynd which has been excavated to reveal a cobbled street with cellars and shops on either side. Run by the Edinburgh Old Town Renewal Trust (☎ 225 8818), the church acts as a visitor centre for the Old Town. It's open early April to mid June, Thursday to Monday from 10 am to 5 pm, and mid June to early September daily from 10 am to 7 pm.

Museum of Childhood (Maps 5 & 14)

This museum (☎ 529 4142), 42 High St, attempts to cover the serious issues related to childhood – health, education, upbringing and so on – but more enjoyable is the enormous collection of toys, dolls, games and books which fascinate children and, for adults, brings childhood memories back. It includes a video history of the various Gerry Anderson puppet TV series, like *Thunderbirds*, made in the 1960s. The museum opens Monday to Saturday from 10 am to 5 pm, and, during the Edinburgh Festival only, Sunday from 2 to 5 pm; admission is free.

John Knox's House (Maps 5 & 15)

Perhaps the most extraordinary building on the Royal Mile, John Knox's House (☎ 556 9579), 43-45 High St, dates from around 1490. The outside staircase, overhanging upper floors and crow-stepped gables are all typical of a 15th century town house. John Knox is thought to have occupied the 2nd

floor from 1561 to 1572. The labyrinthine interior has an interesting display on his life including a recording of his interview with Mary Queen of Scots, whose mother was a target of his diatribe *First Blast of the Trumpet Against the Monstrous Regiment of Women*. It's open Monday to Saturday, from 10 am to 4.30 pm; admission is £1.95/75p.

Netherbow Port & Canongate (Maps 5 & 16)

High St ends at the intersection with St Mary's and Jeffrey Sts, where the city's eastern gate, Netherbow Port, part of the Flodden Wall, once stood. Though it no longer exists, it's commemorated by brass strips set in the road.

The next stretch of the Mile, Canongate, takes its name from the canons (priests) of Holyrood Abbey. From the 16th century, it was home to aristocrats attracted to the Palace of Holyroodhouse. Originally governed by the canons, it remained an independent burgh until 1856.

Huntly House (Maps 5 & 17)

Huntly House, built in 1570, is a good example of the luxurious accommodation that aristocrats built for themselves along Canongate; the projecting upper floors of plastered timber are typical of the time. It now contains a local history museum (☎ 529 4143) with some interesting displays, including a copy of the National Covenant of 1638 signed in protest against Charles I's attempt to re-establish episcopacy and the English prayer book. It opens Monday to Saturday, from 10 am to 5 pm, and, during the Edinburgh Festival only, Sunday from 2 to 5 pm; admission is free.

The People's Story (Maps 5 & 18)

Canongate Tolbooth, with its picturesque turrets and projecting clock, is an interesting example of 16th century architecture. Built in 1591, it served successively as a collection point for tolls (taxes), a council house, a courtroom and a jail. It now houses a fascinating museum (☎ 331 5545) telling the story of the life, work and pastimes of ordinary Edinburgh folk from the 18th century to the present day. It opens Monday to Saturday, from 10 am to 5 pm, and, during the Edinburgh Festival only, Sunday from 2 to 5 pm; admission is free.

Canongate Kirk (Maps 5 & 19)

Attractive Canongate Kirk was built in 1688. In 1745 Prince Charles Stuart (Bonnie Prince Charlie, the Young Pretender) used it to hold prisoners taken at the Battle of Prestonpans. The churchyard has good views and several famous people are buried there. These include the economist Adam Smith, author of *The Wealth of Nations*, who lived nearby in Panmure Close, and the 18th century poet Robert Fergusson.

Abbey Lairds (Maps 5 & 20)

On the north side of Abbey Strand, flanking the entrance to the Palace of Holyroodhouse, the Abbey Lairds provided sanctuary for aristocratic debtors from 1128 to 1880. It was one of a number of hovels, most of which were pulled down when Queen Victoria occupied the palace. The debtors or 'lairds' could avoid prison as long as they remained within the palace and Holyrood Park, although they were allowed out on Sunday.

Queen Mary's Bath House (Maps 5 & 21)

According to legend, Mary Queen of Scots used to bathe in white wine and goat's milk in this small, 16th century turreted lodge – but only twice a year! More likely, it was a dovecote or summer house.

PALACE OF HOLYROODHOUSE & HOLYROOD ABBEY (MAP 5)

The Palace of Holyroodhouse developed from a guesthouse attached to medieval Holyrood Abbey. It was a royal residence at various times from the 16th century, and is still the Queen's official residence in Scotland, so access is very restricted. You're only allowed to view a few apartments, walk around part of the grounds and visit the abbey ruins.

The abbey was founded by David I in 1128, and was probably named after a fragment of the Cross (*rood* is an old word for cross) said to have belonged to his mother St Margaret. As it lay outside the city walls it was particularly vulnerable to English attacks, but the church was always rebuilt and survived as Canongate parish church until it collapsed in 1768. Most of the surviving ruins date from the 12th and 13th centuries, although a doorway in the far south-eastern corner has survived from the original Norman church.

King James IV extended the abbey guesthouse in 1501 to create more comfortable living quarters than were possible in bleak and windy Edinburgh Castle; the oldest surviving section of the building, the north-west tower, was built in 1529 as a royal apartment. Mary Queen of Scots spent 16 eventful years living in the tower. During this time she married Darnley (in the abbey) and Bothwell (in what is now the Picture Gallery), and this is where she debated with John Knox and witnessed the murder of her secretary Rizzio.

Although Holyrood was never again a permanent royal residence after Mary's son James VI departed for London, it was further extended during Charles II's reign.

Although you're carefully shepherded through a limited part of the palace, there's a certain fascination to following in Mary's footsteps and seeing the room where Rizzio was cut down.

Opening hours are normally April to October, daily from 9.30 am to 5.15 pm; November to March, daily from 9.30 am to 3.45 pm. Entry is £5.30/2.60. However, the complex is sometimes closed for state functions or when the Queen is in residence, usually in mid-May, and mid-June to around early July; phone ☎ 556 7371 to check.

Close to Holyroodhouse construction is under way for the new purpose-built **Scottish Parliament** and the **Dynamic Earth** exhibition presenting the geological story of the planet.

HOLYROOD PARK & ARTHUR'S SEAT

In Holyrood Park, Edinburgh is blessed in having a real wilderness on its doorstep. The former hunting grounds of Scottish monarchs, it covers 650 acres of varied landscape, including hills, moorland, lochs and fields. The highest point is the 251m (823 feet) extinct volcano, Arthur's Seat.

The park can be circumnavigated along Queen's Drive by car or bike, but it's closed to motorised traffic on Sunday. There are several excellent walks. Opposite the palace's southern gate, a footpath named Radical Road runs up immediately along the base of the Salisbury Craigs, but is partly blocked off because of danger from falling rocks. A fairly easy half-hour walk leads from Dunsapie Loch to the summit of Arthur's Seat. There are magnificent views of the city to the Pentland Hills and across the Firth of Forth.

To the south, **Duddingston Loch** is a natural lake and a bird sanctuary.

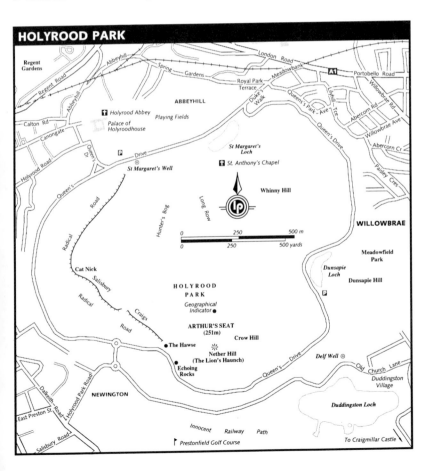

HOLYROOD PARK

Arthur's Seat

Arthur's Seat, the eroded stump of a lava flow that erupted around 325 million years ago, sits in Holyrood Park, the ancient hunting ground of Scottish kings. It forms part of a volcano that includes Calton Hill and Castle Rock.

It's not certain where the name derives from. There's no evidence to connect it with the King Arthur of Camelot and round table fame. It may have been named after the 6th century Arthur of Strathclyde. Alternatively, it may come from the Gaelic *Ard-na-Saighead*, which means 'Height of Arrows'.

SOUTH OF THE ROYAL MILE

The area south of the Royal Mile includes some of the oldest, most crowded and atmospheric parts of the Old Town at the foot of Castle Rock and the Mile. Around the university and the beautiful Meadow Park it opens up to run into sturdy Victorian suburbs like Bruntsfield, Marchmont and Grange.

One of the city's main traffic arteries (carrying traffic to/from the A68 and A7), with many shops, restaurants and guesthouses, runs down the eastern side – beginning as North Bridge and becoming successively South Bridge, Nicolson St, Clerk St, Newington Rd, Minto St, Mayfield Gardens and Craigmillar Park.

Grassmarket

Grassmarket is one of Edinburgh's nightlife centres, with numerous restaurants and pubs, including the White Hart Inn which was patronised by Robert Burns. An open area hedged by tall tenements and dominated by the looming castle, it can be approached from George IV Bridge, via Victoria St, an unusual two-tiered street clinging to the ridge below the Royal Mile, with some excellent shops.

The site of a market from at least 1477 to the start of the 20th century, Grassmarket was always a focal point for the Old Town. This was the main place for executions and over 100 hanged Covenanters are commemorated with a cross at the east end. The notorious murderers Burke and Hare operated from a now vanished close off the west end. In around 1827 they enticed at least 18 victims here, suffocated them and sold the bodies to Edinburgh's medical schools.

Leading off from the south-east corner, Candlemaker Row climbs back up to the George IV Bridge and Chambers St with the Royal Museum of Scotland and the University of Edinburgh's Old College.

Cowgate

Cowgate, which runs off the eastern end of Grassmarket parallel to the Royal Mile, is less a canyon than a bleak tunnel, thanks to the bridges that were built above it. Once a fashionable place to live, it now has a couple of Fringe Festival venues and one or two good pubs.

Royal Museum of Scotland

The Royal Museum of Scotland (☎ 225 7534), Chambers St, is a Victorian building whose grey, solid exterior contrasts with its large, bright, galleried entrance hall of slim wrought-iron columns and glass roof. The museum houses an eclectic, comprehensive series of exhibitions. These range from the natural world (evolution, mammals, geology, fossils etc) to scientific and industrial technological development, with one section featuring the world's oldest steam locomotive, *Wylam Dilly* (1813) and to the decorative arts of ancient Egypt, Islam, China, Japan, Korea and the west.

The adjacent **Museum of Scotland**, opened in 1998, houses archaeological artefacts from the old Museum of Antiquities. It shows the history of Scotland in chronological order starting with the country's earliest history in the basement.

The museums open Monday to Saturday from 10 am to 5 pm (to 8 pm Tuesday), and

Sunday from noon to 5 pm. Entry is £3 (free on Tuesday from 5 to 8 pm), children free.

University of Edinburgh

The University of Edinburgh is one of Britain's oldest, biggest and best universities: founded in 1583, it now has around 17,000 undergraduates. The students make a major contribution to the lively atmosphere of Grassmarket, Cowgate, and the nearby restaurants and pubs. The university sprawls for some distance, but the centre is the **Old College** (also called Old Quad), at the junction of South Bridge and Chambers St, a Robert Adam masterpiece designed in 1789, but not completed till 1834.

Inside the Old College is the **Talbot Rice Art Gallery** (Map 7, ☎ 650 2210) which houses a permanent, small collection of old masters, plus regular exhibitions of new work.

Greyfriars Kirk & Kirkyard (Map 6)

At the bottom of a stone canyon made up of tenements, churches, volcanic cliffs and the castle, Greyfriars Kirkyard is one of Edinburgh's most evocative spots – a peaceful oasis dotted with memorials and surrounded by Edinburgh's dramatic skyline.

The kirk was built on the site of a Franciscan friary and opened for worship on Christmas Day 1620. In 1638, the National Covenant was signed inside near the pulpit. The covenant rejected Charles I's attempts to reintroduce episcopacy and a new English prayer book, and affirmed the independence of the Scottish church. Many who signed were later executed in Grassmarket and, in 1679, 1200 Covenanters were held prisoner in terrible conditions in an enclosure in the yard. There's a small exhibition inside.

Tour groups, however, come to pay homage to a tiny statue of Greyfriars Bobby (Map 6) in front of the nearby pub. Bobby was a Skye terrier who maintained a vigil over the grave of his master, an Edinburgh police officer, from 1858 to 1872. The story was immortalised (and distorted) in a novel by Eleanor Atkinson in 1912 and later turned into a film. In the kirk you can buy *Greyfriars Bobby – The Real Story at Last* (£3.50), Forbes Macgregor's debunking of some of the myths. Bobby's grave is just inside the entrance to the kirkyard.

CALTON HILL (MAP 5)

Calton Hill, at the east end of Princes St, is another distinctive component of Edinburgh's skyline, 100m (333 feet) high and scattered with grandiose memorials mostly dating from the first half of the 19th century. Here you get one of the best views of Edinburgh, taking in the entire panorama – the castle, Holyrood, Arthur's Seat, the Firth of Forth, the New Town and Princes St.

Approaching from Waterloo Place, you pass the imposing **Royal High School**, Regent Rd, dating from 1829 and modelled on the Temple of Theseus in Athens. Former pupils include Robert Adam, Alexander Graham Bell and Sir Walter Scott. Now called St Andrew's House, it was at one time cited as a potential home for the new Scottish parliament, and houses part of the Scottish Office. To the east, on the other side of Regent Rd, is the **Burns Monument** (1830), a Greek-style memorial to Robert Burns. It was designed by Thomas Hamilton, another former pupil of the school.

The largest structure is the **National Monument**, an over-ambitious attempt to replicate the Parthenon, in honour of Scotland's dead in the Napoleonic Wars. Construction began in 1822, but funds ran dry when only 12 columns were complete.

The design of the **City Observatory** (1818) was based on the Greek Temple of the Winds. Here you'll find the **Edinburgh Experience** (☎ 556 4365), a 20 minute, 3-D audio-visual portrayal of Edinburgh's history. It's open April to October, daily from 10 am to 5 pm; admission is £2/1.20.

Looking a bit like an upturned telescope, the **Nelson Monument** was built to commemorate Nelson's victory at Trafalgar. It's open (for great views) April to September, Monday from 1 to 6 pm, Tuesday to Saturday from 10 am to 6 pm; October to March,

Monday to Saturday from 10 am to 3 pm; admission is £2.

There's also the small, circular **Monument to Dugald Stewart** (1753-1828), an obscure professor of philosophy.

NEW TOWN

The New Town, dating from the 18th century, lies north of the Old Town, separated from it by Princes St Gardens and occupying a ridge that runs below, but parallel to, the Royal Mile. It's in complete contrast to the chaotic tangle of streets and buildings that evolved in the Old Town, and typifies the values of the Scottish Enlightenment.

Despite being confined behind city walls, the Old Town was periodically sacked by the English or torn by civil wars and disputes. The overcrowding and numerous domestic chimneys gave it its nickname, Auld Reekie (Old Smokey). So when the Act of Union in 1707 brought the prospect of long-term stability, aristocrats were keen to find healthier, more spacious surroundings. Cowgate was bridged to open up the south, Nor Loch at the northern foot of Castle Rock was drained and the North Bridge constructed.

In 1767, 23-year-old James Craig won a competition to design a New Town. His plan was brilliant in its simplicity. George St followed the line of the ridge between Charlotte and St Andrew Squares. Building was restricted to one side of Princes St and Queen St only, so the town opened onto the Firth of Forth to the north, and to the castle and Old Town to the south.

The New Town continued to sprout squares, circuses, parks and terraces, and some of its finest neoclassical architecture was designed by Robert Adam. Today, the New Town is the world's most complete and unspoilt example of Georgian town planning and architecture.

Princes St

Princes St was originally envisaged as the back of the New Town, as it was literally and figuratively turning away from its Jacobite past. However, the transport links and stunning outlook soon led to its development as Edinburgh's principal thoroughfare.

The main train station at the east end is now overshadowed by the uninspiring **Waverley Market** (Map 5) shopping centre. The entrance to the TIC is via the street level piazza which is frequently used by buskers and other street performers.

The street's north side is lined with standard High St shops, and few 18th century buildings survive. One exception is the beautiful **Register House** (1788) (Map 5), designed by Robert Adam, at the eastern end of Princes St, with the statue of the Duke of Wellington on horseback in front. It's home to the Scottish Record Office.

Back on the south side, about halfway along, the massive Gothic spire of the **Sir Walter Scott Monument** (Map 4), built by public subscription after his death in 1832, testifies to a popularity largely inspired by his role in rebuilding pride in Scottish identity. At the time of research it was closed for refurbishment (costing about £2 million), but when it reopens you'll be able to climb the 287 steps to the top.

Behind the monument are the **Princes St Gardens** (Map 4) a public park which stretch east to west from Waverley Bridge to Lothian Rd, and up the hillside to the castle. The Princes St Gardens are cut by **The Mound** (Map 4), a pile of earth dumped during the construction of the New Town to provide it with a road link to Old Town. It was completed in 1830. The Royal Scottish Academy and the National Gallery of Scotland are also here (see later).

St John's Church (Map 4), at the west end of Princes St on the corner of Lothian Rd, stands above some interesting shops and is worth visiting for its fine Gothic Revival interior. It overlooks **St Cuthbert's Church** (Map 4) below, off Lothian Rd, which has a watch tower in the graveyard – a reminder of the Burke and Hare days when graves had to be guarded against robbers. Inside are ornate furnishings and many murals.

Royal Scottish Academy (RSA) (Map 4)

The RSA (☎ 225 6671), fronting Princes St, was designed by William Playfair and built in Grecian style in 1826, with its fluted Doric columns added later. It contains artwork by academy members and hosts temporary exhibitions throughout the year. It's open Monday to Saturday from 10 am to 5 pm, Sunday from 2 to 5 pm; admission is free (although there are charges for some exhibitions).

National Gallery of Scotland (Map 4)

Also designed by William Playfair, the National Gallery (☎ 556 8921) behind the RSA at the foot of The Mound, is an imposing classical building dating from the 1850s. It houses an important collection of European art from the 15th century Renaissance to 19th century postimpressionism. There are paintings by Verrocchio (Leonardo da Vinci's teacher), Tintoretto, Titian, Holbein, Rubens, van Dyck, Vermeer, El Greco, Poussin, Rembrandt, Gainsborough, Turner, Constable, Monet, Pissaro, Gauguin and Cezanne.

The USA is also represented by the works of Frederick Church, John Singer Sargent and Benjamin West. The section specifically on Scottish art, in the basement, includes portraits by Allan Ramsay and Sir Henry Raeburn, rural scenes by Sir David Wilkie and impressionistic landscapes by William MacTaggart.

Antonio Canova's statue of the Three Graces (room X) is owned jointly with London's Victoria & Albert Museum. In Greek mythology the Three Graces – Aglaia, Euphrosyne and Thalia – daughters of Zeus and Euryonome, embodied beauty, gracefulness and youth.

The gallery opens Monday to Saturday from 10 am to 5 pm, Sunday from 2 to 5 pm; admission is free.

St Andrew Square & George St (Map 4)

Dominated by the fluted Doric column of the Melville Monument, St Andrew Square isn't particularly architecturally distinguished (partly thanks to the bus station at the northeast corner). On the eastern side, however, is the impressive Palladian-style **Dundas House** which has a spectacular dome, best seen from the interior banking hall, and frieze. It's the head office of the Royal Bank of Scotland, which has been there since 1825.

George St, parallel to Princes St and connecting St Andrew Square with Charlotte Square, was originally envisaged as the main thoroughfare of the residential New Town. It's now Scotland's Wall St, home to highly successful Scottish financial institutions which control billions of pounds. **St Andrew & St George Church**, built in 1784, boasts a wonderful oval plaster ceiling, and was where the Church of Scotland split in two in 1843.

Charlotte Square (Map 4)

At the western end of George St, Charlotte Square, designed in 1791 by Robert Adam shortly before his death, is regarded as the architectural jewel of the New Town. On Hope St, the west side of Charlotte Square, St George's Church (1811) is now **West Register House**, an annexe to Register House in Princes St. It houses part of Scotland's official records which appear in occasional exhibitions in the entrance hall.

The north side of Charlotte Square is a Robert Adam's masterpiece, and one of the finest examples of Georgian architecture anywhere. **Bute House**, at No 6, is the office of the Secretary of State for Scotland. Next door at No 7, the **Georgian House** (☎ 225 2160; NTS), has been beautifully restored and refurnished to show (albeit in idealised form) how Edinburgh's wealthy elite lived at the end of the 18th century. The walls are decorated with paintings by Allan Ramsay, Henry Raeburn and Sir Joshua Reynolds. A 35 minute video brings it all to life rather well. It's open April to October, Monday to Saturday from 10 am to 5 pm, Sunday from 2 to 5 pm; admission is £4.20/2.80, family £11.20.

Scottish National Portrait Gallery (Map 4)

The gallery (☎ 556 8921), at the junction of St Andrew and Queen Sts, is in a large, red sandstone, Italian-Gothic building dating from 1882. It records Scottish history through portraits and sculptures. Although the subjects are probably the main source of interest, some portraits are also fine paintings.

The entrance hall is decorated with a frieze showing the chief protagonists in Scottish history and the balcony with frescoes of important moments in Scottish history painted by William Hole in 1897. The collection's subjects range from the kings, queens and nobles of earlier times to modern-day Scots from various walks of life.

There's a good café (see the Places to Eat chapter). The gallery opens Monday to Saturday, from 10 am to 5 pm, Sunday from 2 to 5 pm; admission is free.

WEST END

The last part to be built, the West End is an extension of the New Town. Huge **St Mary's Episcopal Cathedral** (Map 3), Palmerston Place, built in the 1870s, was Sir George Gilbert Scott's last major work.

If you follow Palmerston Place north over the Water of Leith, you come to **Dean Village** ('dean' means deep valley), an odd corner of Edinburgh. Once a milling community, it has been restored and taken over by yuppies. A pleasant walk begins by the Water of Leith at Belford Bridge. The footpath takes you up onto Dean Path, then onto Dean Bridge, from where you can look down on the village. You can continue on the south bank of the Leith, north-east through Stockbridge, then detour to the Royal Botanic Garden.

Scottish National Gallery of Modern Art (Map 2)

West of Dean Village, the Scottish National Gallery of Modern Art (☎ 556 8921), off Belford Rd, repays the effort of getting there (walk from Belford Bridge or take bus No 13 from George St). It's in an impressive classical Greek-style building that's surrounded by a sculpture park, which features work by Henry Moore and Barbara Hepworth among others.

Inside, the collection concentrates on 20th century art, with various European art movements represented by the likes of Matisse, Picasso, Kirchner, Magritte, Miro, Mondrian and Giacometti. American and English artists are also represented, but most space is given to Scottish painters – from the Scottish colourists early in the 20th century to contemporary artists. The gallery is small enough not to overwhelm and opens Monday to Saturday from 10 am to 5 pm, Sunday from 2 to 5 pm; admission is free.

NORTH OF THE NEW TOWN

The New Town's Georgian architecture extends north to Stockbridge and the Water of Leith, a rewarding area to explore since it's well off the tourist trail. **Stockbridge** is a trendy area with its own distinct identity, some interesting shops, and a good choice of pubs and restaurants. The painter, Sir Henry Raeburn, was born in Stockbridge, and he helped develop part of the area, most notably **Ann St**, one of the most exclusive addresses in Edinburgh.

Just north of Stockbridge is the lovely **Royal Botanic Garden** (Map 2, ☎ 552 7171) on Inverleith Row. It's worth visiting for the different perspective you get on the Edinburgh skyline from the Terrace Café. The garden opens daily November to January from 10 am to 4 pm; February and October to 5 pm; March and September to 6 pm; April to August to 7 pm; admission is free. Bus Nos 8, 19, 23, 27 and 37 will get you there.

GREATER EDINBURGH

Outside the centre there are some worthwhile attractions in the suburbs and beyond.

Craigmillar Castle

Edinburgh's suburbs are beginning to surround the castle, and the approach road, Craigmillar Castle Rd, is strewn with litter. Nevertheless, massive Craigmillar Castle (☎ 244 3101; HS), about 2½ miles south of the city centre off the A68 to Dalkeith, is still impressive.

Dating from the 15th century, the tower house rises above two sets of walls that enclose an area of 1½ acres. Mary Queen of Scots took refuge here after the murder of Rizzio; it was here too that plans to murder her husband Darnley were laid. Look for

Art Galleries

You shouldn't miss the National Gallery of Scotland, the Royal Scottish Academy (RSA), the Scottish National Portrait Gallery or the Scottish National Gallery of Modern Art. But there are also many other smaller galleries.

The Edinburgh Gallery Guide is a free monthly booklet available around town containing an index of current exhibitions and venues. *The List* magazine and *The Scotsman* also provide a list of what's on. You can find out more at the web site www.scottish-gallery.co.uk.

Some of the galleries are:

Calton Gallery (Map 5)
(☎ 556 1010), 10 Royal Terrace, displays paintings, watercolours and sculpture by British and European artists from 1750 to 1940; open Monday to Friday from 10 am to 6 pm, Saturday from 10 am to 1 pm.
City Art Centre (Map 5)
(☎ 529 3993), 2 Market St, the largest of the smaller galleries, it comprises six floors of exhibitions with a variety of themes, including an extensive collection of Scottish art; open Monday to Saturday from 10 am to 5.30 pm, Sunday from noon to 5 pm.
Collective Gallery (Map 4)
(☎ 220 1260), 22-24 Cockburn St, an artist-run gallery with exhibitions by contemporary, innovative Scottish and other artists; open Tuesday to Saturday from 11 am to 5.30 pm.
Edinburgh Printmakers' Workshop & Gallery (Map 5)
(☎ 557 2479), 23 Union St off Leith Walk; workshops and courses on the ground floor, exhibitions of lithographs, screenprints etc by local artists on the 1st floor; open Tuesday to Saturday from 10 am to 6 pm.
Fruitmarket Gallery (Map 5)
(☎ 225 2383), 29 Market St, showcases contemporary Scottish and international artists; open Tuesday to Saturday from 10.30 am to 5.30 pm, Sunday from noon to 5 pm.
The Leith Gallery
(☎ 553 5255), 65 The Shore, has exhibitions on young Scottish artists; open Tuesday to Friday from 11 am to 6 pm, Saturday from 11 am to 4 pm.
Portfolio Gallery (Map 6)
(☎ 220 1911), 43 Candlemaker Row, a photographic gallery with the emphasis on local and Scottish themes; open Tuesday to Saturday from noon to 5.30 pm.
The Scottish Gallery (Map 4)
(☎ 558 1200), 16 Dundas St (the northern extension of Hanover St), has exhibitions on both contemporary artists and past masters, including crafts as well as paintings; open Monday to Friday from 10 am to 6 pm, Saturday from 10 am to 4 pm.
Stills Gallery (Map 4)
(☎ 225 9876), 23 Cockburn St, refurbished photographic gallery; open Tuesday to Saturday from 11 am to 5 pm.

the prison cell complete with built-in sanitation, something some 'modern' British prisons only finally managed in 1996.

It's open daily April to September from 9.30 am to 6.30 pm; October to March, Monday to Saturday from 9.30 am to 4.30 pm, and Sunday from 2 to 4.30 pm; admission is £1.80/75p. Bus Nos 14, 21, C3 and C33 pass by.

Royal Observatory (Map 3)

Directly south of the centre on Blackford Hill, the observatory (☎ 668 8100) was moved here from Calton Hill in 1896. In the visitor centre there's a multimedia gallery with computers and CD ROMS on astronomy and there are terrific views of Edinburgh from the rooftop. It's open Monday to Saturday from 10 am to 5 pm, Sunday from noon to 5 pm. Entry costs £2.50/1.50. Take bus No 40 or 41 from the Mound to Blackford Ave.

Leith

Leith is and was Edinburgh's main port, although it remained an independent burgh until the 1920s. It's still among Britain's busiest ports, but in the 1960s and 70s it fell into decay. Since the 1980s a revival has been taking place and the area is now noted for its interesting eateries and pubs. It's a popular stopping-off point for cruise ships, and the former royal yacht *Britannia* is permanently docked here.

Parts are still rough, but it's a distinctive corner of Edinburgh and the prettiest area is around The Shore. From here a footpath follows the Water of Leith south-west through Edinburgh to Balerno, a distance of about 10 miles.

Take bus No 87, 88 or 88A from St Andrew Square. See the Leith map for references.

Britannia (Map 2) You'll find the former royal yacht *Britannia* (☎ 555 5566 for ticket reservation) moored in Leith harbour, just off Ocean Drive (the ship will be relocated at the new Ocean Terminal, also in Leith, in 2001). She's well worth visiting and you'll

learn some surprising things in the visitors centre and on board. Allow at least 1½ hours to look around, and note that the use of cameras on board is prohibited.

After a four minute introductory video, you enter the visitors centre. Take care to have a good look around – you can't get back in once you've boarded the ship. Among other things, you'll discover that the Queen travelled with five tonnes of luggage when making state visits, shouting by officers and crew was forbidden, and a three month deployment required 2200 toilet rolls.

The ship was launched by the Queen at John Brown's shipyard, Clydebank, on 16 April 1953, then sailed 1.1 million miles over the next 44 years, calling at nearly every Commonwealth country and making 25 state visits. After decommissioning at Portsmouth on 11 December 1997 the final voyage took *Britannia* to Leith.

On leaving the visitors centre, you'll embark on a self-guided 23-stop audio tour of the ship (also available in French, German, Italian and Spanish). You'll see that the ship does not have her name on the hull, and the well-appointed but certainly not lavish royal apartments for the Queen and the Duke of Edinburgh are equipped with single beds. The silver pantry has an impressive array of Edwardian silver. The grand royal dining room, which can accommodate 52 guests, has a mahogany dining table, and the drawing room (with its anteroom) can hold up to 250 guests. Visitors have included Nelson Mandela, Bill Clinton and Indira Gandhi.

Britannia is open daily, except Christmas Day, from 10.30 am to 6 pm (last admission at 4.30 pm). Entry to the visitors centre and the ship costs £7.50/5.75/3.75 for adults/seniors/children and there's an £18 family ticket for two adults and two children. Tickets should be reserved in advance by telephone or purchased from the Tattoo Office, 32 Market St.

Portobello

About 2¼ miles south-east of Leith along the coast, the suburb of Portobello has been

Edinburgh's seaside resort since the late 19th century. Although its heyday has long passed, its promenade and beach still attract crowds on warm summer days. Famous music-hall entertainer, Sir Harry Lauder (1870-1950) was born on Bridge St.

Take bus No 15, 20, 26, 42 or 46 from the centre.

Newhaven

Immediately west of Leith is Newhaven, once a small, distinctive fishing community, now absorbed into the Edinburgh conurbation. The old fish-market building has a **Heritage Centre** which is worth a visit. A 15 minute video reveals the astonishingly tribal lifestyle that survived here until the 1950s when overfishing put paid to the traditional source of income. In a matriarchal society, women in distinctive dress dominated the fish market and life in the home. The centre opens daily from noon to 5 pm; admission free.

Most people come here, however, to taste the delights of the enormously popular Harry Ramsden's (☎ 551 5566), purveyor of fish and chips, next to the centre.

Take bus No 7 or 11 from Princes St.

Edinburgh Zoo

Parents of young children will be relieved to know there's a zoo (☎ 334 9171), 3 miles west of the centre on the A8, offering an alternative to the museums. What will delight kids most are the zoo's penguins, especially when they (the penguins) are allowed out of their enclosure to go walkabout. The zoo also takes care of some rare and endangered animals such as the snow leopard, pygmy hippo and red panda.

It's open April to September, Monday to Saturday from 9 am to 6 pm, October and March to 5 pm, November to February to 4.30 pm (it opens Sunday at 9.30 am). Admission costs £6/3.20. Bus Nos 2, 26, 31, 69, 85 and 86 pass by.

Lauriston Castle

Three miles north-west of the centre, Lauriston Castle (☎ 336 2060), Cramond Rd South,

Sir Harry Lauder

These days not everyone will have heard of the Scottish music hall entertainer Sir Harry Lauder (1870-1950), but they almost certainly will have heard one or more of his songs.

Born in Portobello, he worked as a flax spinner in Arbroath while still at school, then in his teens as a pitboy in a Lanarkshire coal mine. He travelled around entering and winning talent competitions before achieving professional success in Glasgow. When he moved to London he was an immediate hit, and he then went on to wow them in the USA and around the world.

Two of his most famous songs are 'Roamin' in the Gloamin'' and 'I Love a Lassie', both written for his wife. Another, 'Keep Right on to the End of the Road' was written after their only son was killed in battle in WWI. Although he continued to perform he never fully recovered from this tragedy.

Sometimes derided for his stage persona of a stereotypical bekilted Scot, he was enormously talented and his musical legacy endures.

started life in the 16th century as a tower house. It was built by Archibald Napier, whose son, John, invented logarithms. The castle was extended and 'modernised' in 19th century baronial style and now contains a collection of fine art and furniture. It's set in peaceful grounds and allows great views north across the Firth of Forth to Fife.

There are 40-minute guided tours of the castle April to October, Saturday to Thursday, from 11 am to 5 pm; November to March, weekends only, 2 to 4 pm; £4/3. Bus Nos 40 and 41 from Hanover St pass by.

South Queensferry & the Forth Bridges

South Queensferry lies on the south bank of the Firth of Forth, at its narrowest point. From early times it was a ferry port, but ferries no longer operate and it's now overshadowed by two bridges.

The magnificent Forth Rail Bridge is one of the finest Victorian engineering achievements. Completed in 1890 after seven years work and the deaths of 58 men, it's over a mile long and the 50,000 tons of girders take three years to paint. The Forth Road Bridge wasn't completed until 1964 and is a graceful suspension bridge.

In the pretty High St there are several places to eat and the small **South Queensferry Museum** (☎ 331 5545) contains some interesting background information on the bridges. The prize exhibit is a model of the Furry Man; on the first Friday of August, some hapless male still has to spend nine hours roaming the streets covered from head to toe in burrs and clutching two floral staves in memory of a medieval tradition. It's open Thursday to Saturday from 10 am to 1 pm and from 2.15 to 5 pm, Sunday from noon to 5 pm; admission is free.

The *Maid of the Forth* (☎ 331 4857) leaves from Hawes Pier and cruises under the bridges to Inchcolm Island (see following section) and Deep Sea World (☎ 01383-411411), the huge aquarium in North Queensferry. There are daily sailings mid-July to early September (weekends

only April to June and October). In summer, evening cruises with jazz or folk music cost £9.50 a head.

Inchcolm Island & Abbey Inchcolm Island has one of Scotland's best preserved medieval abbeys which was founded for Augustinian priors in 1123. In well-tended grounds stand remains of a 13th century church and a remarkably well-preserved octagonal chapter house with stone roof.

It's half an hour to Inchcolm, and you're allowed 1½ hours ashore. Admission to the abbey is £2.30/1, included in the £7.50/3.60 ferry cost (HS members should show their cards for reduction); non-landing tickets cost £5.20/2.60 and allow you to see the island's grey seals, puffins and other seabirds.

Getting There & Away From St Andrew Square numerous buses (Nos 43, X43, 47, 47A) run to South Queensferry. From Edinburgh there are frequent trains to Dalmeny station (15 minutes).

Hopetoun House

Two miles west of South Queensferry, Hopetoun House (☎ 331 2451), one of Scotland's finest stately homes, has a superb location in lovely grounds beside the Firth of Forth. There are two parts, the older built to Sir William Bruce's plans between 1699 and 1702 and dominated by a splendid stairwell, the newer designed between 1720 and 1750 by three members of the Adam family, William and sons Robert and John.

The rooms have splendid furnishings and staff are on hand to make sure you don't miss details like the revolving oyster stand for two people to share. The Hope family supplied a Viceroy of India and a Governor-General of Australia so the upstairs museum displays interesting reminders of the colonial life of the ruling class. Even further up there's a viewing point on the roof, ideal for photos.

It's open April to September daily from

10 am to 5.30 pm; admission is £4.70/2.60 (for the grounds only it's £2.60/1.60).

Hopetoun House can be approached from South Queensferry, or from Edinburgh turn off the A90 onto the A904 just before the Forth Bridge Toll and follow the signs.

Edinburgh Canal Centre

The Edinburgh Canal Centre (☎ 333 1320) is beside the Union Canal in **Ratho**, 8 miles south-west of Edinburgh. The centre offers 1½-hour sightseeing barge trips on the canal for £4.50/2.50 April to October. Take bus No 37 from St Andrew Square. By car, follow the Calder Rd (A71), then turn right (north) onto Dalmeny Rd.

ACTIVITIES

Edinburgh offers numerous opportunities for recreational activities and the TIC can provide particular details. Favourite outdoor venues are Holyrood Park, Meadow Park and Bruntsfield Links.

There are plenty of good walks. Following the Water of Leith offers a relaxed stroll through the city, while more strenuous climbs to Arthur's Seat or along the Radical Rd in Holyrood Park are rewarded with great views. For longer hill-walking head for the Pentland Hills in the south.

Edinburgh has a network of signposted cycle paths that can get you around the city and out into the surrounding countryside.

Tracing Your Ancestors

For visitors with Scottish ancestors a trip here is a good chance to find out more about them and their lives; you may even discover relatives you never knew about.

You should first go to the General Register Office (GRO, Map 5, ☎ 334 0380), New Register House, 3 West Register St, Edinburgh EH1 3YT. This office holds birth, marriage and death records since 1855, the census records and old parochial registers. Contact the GRO for leaflets giving details of its records and fees. The office opens weekdays from 9 am to 4.30 pm. Before you go, contact the office to reserve a search-room seat, particularly if you have limited time.

Next door is part of the Scottish Record Office (☎ 535 1314), HM General Register House, 2 Princes St, Edinburgh EH1 3YY. There are two search rooms: the historical search room, where you should go to research ancestors (no charge); and the legal search room, where you can see records for legal purposes (a fee is payable). Staff answer simple inquiries, by correspondence, if you give precise details. If you want more research done for you (perhaps before you come), the office will send a list of professional searchers. All correspondence should be addressed to The Keeper of the Records of Scotland, Scottish Record Office, and sent to the above address.

The other place to try is the Scottish Genealogy Society (☎ 220 3677), 15 Victoria Terrace (above Victoria St), Edinburgh EH1, which has a library, microfiche, books for sale and helpful staff.

Visiting graveyards may seem morbid but it's something many tourists do as part of tracing their ancestors (and paying their respects). This address is useful: Anne King, Scottish Ancestral Research (email aking53104@aol.com), Tigh Righ, 4 Esplanade Terrace, Joppa, Edinburgh EH15 2ES.

If you're serious about ancestry research, it may be worth buying one or more of the following: *Tracing Your Scottish Ancestors* (Stationery Office) by Cecil Sinclair; *Tracing Your Scottish Ancestry* (Polygon, Edinburgh) by Kathleen B Cory; *My Ain Folk – an easy guide to Scottish family history*, by Graham S Holton & Jack Wind; and *Surnames of Scotland* by George F Black and published by the New York Library.

THINGS TO SEE & DO

Queen's Drive, that circles Holyrood Park, is popular especially on Sunday when it's closed to motorised traffic. The Innocent Railway Path from Holyrood Park takes you through Duddingston village to Craigmillar and Musselburgh.

Not surprisingly, golf is a favourite pastime and there are lots of courses around Edinburgh. Many people practise their golf stroke on Bruntsfield Links; others head for Braid Hills public course (Map 3) or the nearby floodlit driving range at Braid Hills Golf Centre (☎ 658 1755), 91 Liberton Drive. Some private courses also welcome visitors including Craigmillar Park Golf Club (☎ 667 0047), Observatory Rd, near the Royal Observatory.

Alien Rock (Map 2, ☎ 552 7211), Old St Andrew's Church, 8 Pier Place, Newhaven, is an indoor climbing centre open daily. Training courses are available. It costs £5 per session plus £3 for boots and harness hire.

On the southern boundary of the city off the A702 the Midlothian Ski Centre (☎ 445 4433), Hill End, is a large artificial ski area, open daily year round. Take bus No 4 from the city centre. The Edinburgh Ski Club (☎ 220 3121), 2 Howe St, Edinburgh EH3 6TD offers lessons, day trips, discounts to ski areas and equipment hire. For cross-country skiing contact the Edinburgh Nordic Ski Club (☎ 220 4371), c/o 60A Palmerston Place, Edinburgh, EH12 5AY.

Canoeing and sailing in the Firth of Forth are available from Port Edgar Marina & Sailing School (☎ 331 3330), in South Queensferry west of Edinburgh.

Good indoor sports centres providing swimming, squash, badminton etc include Meadowbank Sports Centre (☎ 661 5351), 139 London Rd, off Leith Walk, and the Royal Commonwealth Pool (Map 3, ☎ 667 7211), 21 Dalkeith Rd, Newington.

LANGUAGE COURSES

Given Edinburgh's high standard in education and Scotland's significant contribution to English literature, it's not surprising that the city is a good place to learn English (as well as other languages). Schools usually offer a range of programs including intensive courses, summer schools, weekend workshops and specialised-English courses (eg for business or tourism). Below are some of the schools where you could start making inquiries; also check the Yellow Pages under 'Language Courses & Schools'.

Edinburgh Language Centre
(☎/fax 343 6596), 10B Oxford Terrace, Edinburgh EH4

Edinburgh School of English
(☎ 557 9200, fax 557 9192), 271 Canongate, Edinburgh EH8 8BQ

English Language Institute
(☎ 447 2398, fax 447 7131), 69 Nile Grove, Edinburgh EH10

International Language Academy
(☎ 220 4278, fax 220 1107), 11 Great Stuart St, Edinburgh EH3 7T8

Institute for Applied Language Studies
(☎ 650 6200), University of Edinburgh, 21 Hill Place, Edinburgh EH8 9DP

Those interested in learning about French language and culture should contact the Institut Français d'Écosse (Map 6, ☎ 225 5366, fax 220 0648), 13 Randolph Crescent, just west of the centre.

If you're interested in learning more about Gaelic contact the Celtic department (Map 7, ☎ 650 1000) of the University of Edinburgh, David Hume Tower, George Square, Edinburgh EH8 9JX.

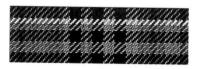

Places to Stay

Edinburgh has masses of accommodation, but the city can still fill up quickly over the New Year, at Easter and between mid-May and mid-September, especially while the festivals are in full swing. Book in advance if at all possible, or use an accommodation booking service.

The TIC's accommodation reservation service (☎ 473 3855) charges a steep £4 fee for booking accommodation. If you have the time, get its free accommodation brochure, the *Edinburgh Holiday Guide*, and ring round yourself.

For £5, three branches of Thomas Cook also make hotel reservations: the Edinburgh airport office (☎ 333 5119); the office (☎ 557 0905) in Waverley Steps near the TIC; and the office (☎ 557 0034) on Platform One of Waverley train station.

CAMPING

Edinburgh has two well-equipped campsites reasonably close to the centre. *Edinburgh Caravan Club Site* (☎ 312 6874, Marine Drive) overlooks the Firth of Forth, 3 miles north-west of the centre, and has full facilities and tent sites for £3. From North Bridge take bus No 8A, 9A or 14A. *Mortonhall Caravan Park* (☎ 664 1533, 38 Mortonhall Gate), off Frogston Rd East, Mortonhall, is 5 miles south-east of the centre. Sites are £8 to £12 and it's open March to October. Take bus No 11 from North Bridge.

HOSTELS & COLLEGES

If you're travelling on a budget, the numerous hostels offer cheap accommodation and are great centres for meeting fellow travellers. Hostels have facilities for self-catering and some provide cheap meals. From May to September and on public holidays, hostels can be heavily booked but so are most other places. Advance booking is advisable.

SYHA Hostels

The office of the Scottish Youth Hostels Association (SYHA, Map 3, ☎ 229 8660, fax 229 2456, www.shya.org.uk) is at 161 Warrender Park Rd in Bruntsfield. The SYHA produces a handbook (£1.50) giving details on around 80 hostels in Scotland, including transport links. Below, higher hostel prices for seniors are given first, followed by the reduced price for juniors.

There are four good SYHA hostels. *Eglinton Youth Hostel* (Map 3, ☎ 337 1120, 18 Eglinton Crescent) is about 1 mile west of the city near Haymarket train station; beds cost £12.50/9.95. To get there, walk down Princes St and continue on Shandwick Place which becomes West Maitland St; veer right at the Haymarket along Haymarket Terrace, then turn right into Coates Gardens which runs into Eglinton Crescent.

Bruntsfield Youth Hostel (Map 3, ☎ 447 2994, 7 Bruntsfield Crescent) has an attractive location overlooking Bruntsfield Links about 2½ miles from Waverley train station. Catch bus No 11 or 16 from the garden side of Princes St and alight at Forbes Rd. It's closed in January and rates are £8.60/7.10 (£9.60/8.10 in July and August).

The other two are summer only (late June to early September): *Central Youth Hostel* (Map 7, ☎ 337 1120, Robertson Close/College Wynd, Cowgate); and *Pleasance Youth Hostel* (Map 7, ☎ 337 1120, New Arthur Place).

Independent Hostels

There's a growing number of independent backpackers' hostels, some of them right in the centre. The long-established, well equipped *High St Hostel* (Map 5, ☎ 557 3984, 8 Blackfriars St) is popular although some have found it noisy. Beds cost £9.50 per night in a 10 bed dorm. It's opposite the Haggis Backpackers tour-booking office.

Not far away is *Royal Mile Backpackers* (Map 5, ☎ 557 6120, 105 High St), which

PLACES TO STAY

PLACES TO STAY

charges £9.90 for beds in dorms of up to 10 beds. *Edinburgh Backpackers Hostel* (*Map 5*, ☎ 220 1717, 65 Cockburn St) is close to the action; dorm beds cost from £10 and doubles are £35; a continental breakfast is available for £1.75.

Princes St Backpackers (*Map 4*, ☎ 556 6894, 5 West Register St) is well positioned, behind Princes St and close to the bus station. It's a fun place, but you do have to negotiate 77 exhausting steps to reach reception. Dorm beds cost £9.50, doubles £24. A full breakfast costs just £2, and Sunday night dinner is free!

Princes St West Backpackers (*Map 4*, ☎ 226 2939, 3-4 Queensferry St) is close to the nightlife. Rates are £10 for a dorm bed or £13 per person in a double; the seventh night is free, and there's a free meal on Sunday.

Belford Youth Hostel (*Map 2*, ☎ 225 6209, 6 Douglas Gardens) is in a converted church and although some people have complained of noise, it's well run and cheerful with good facilities. Dorm beds cost £8.50.

Quiet *Palmerston Lodge* (*Map 3*, ☎ 220 5141, 25 Palmerston Place), on the corner of Chester St, is in a listed building. There are no bunks, only single beds, and showers and toilets on every floor. The rates, which include a continental breakfast, start at £10 for a dorm bed; singles/doubles with bathroom are £30/40.

Women and married couples are welcome at the *Kinnaird Christian Hostel* (*Map 3*, ☎ 225 3608, 13-14 Coates Crescent), where beds in a Georgian house cost from £14. Singles/doubles cost £20/34.

Colleges

Edinburgh has a large student population and during vacations colleges and universities offer accommodation on their campuses, though most are a fair way from the centre and cost as much as lower-end, more central B&Bs. Most rooms are comfortable, functional single bedrooms with shared bathroom. Increasingly, however, there are

rooms with private bathroom, twin and family units, self-contained flats and shared houses. Full-board, half-board, B&B and self-catering options are available. Rooms are usually available from late June to late September.

Closest is *Pollock Halls of Residence* (*Map 3*, ☎ 667 0662, 18 Holyrood Park Rd), which has Arthur's Seat as a backdrop. Modern (often noisy) single rooms cost from £23.90 per person including breakfast. *Napier University* (☎ 455 4291, Colinton Rd off Bruntsfield Place) in Craiglockhart offers B&B in summer from £18 per person. *Queen Margaret College* (☎ 317 3310, 36 Clerwood Terrace) is 3 miles west in Corstorphine near Edinburgh Zoo. From June to September, B&B with shared bathroom costs from £17.50.

B&BS & GUESTHOUSES

On a tight budget the best bet is a private house; get the TIC's free accommodation guide and phone around. At the bottom end you get a bedroom in a private house, a shared bathroom and an enormous cooked breakfast (juice, cereal, bacon, eggs, sausage, baked beans and toast). Small B&Bs may only have one room to let. More upmarket B&Bs have private bathrooms and TVs in each room. Guesthouses, often large converted houses with half a dozen rooms, are just an extension of the B&B concept.

Outside festival time you should get something for around £18, although it'll probably be a bus ride away in the suburbs. Places in the centre aren't always good value if you have a car, since parking is restricted; when booking check whether the establishment has off-street parking. Guesthouses are generally two or three pounds more expensive, and to get a private bathroom you'll have to pay around £25.

The main concentrations are around Pilrig St, Pilrig; Minto St (a southern continuation of North Bridge), Newington; and Gilmore Place and Leamington Terrace, Bruntsfield.

North of the New Town

Pilrig St, left off Leith Walk, has lots of guesthouses, all within about a mile of the centre. Take bus No 11 from Princes St or walk north from the east end of the street.

Balmoral Guest House (*Map 2, ☎ 554 1857, 32 Pilrig St*) is a comfortable terraced house with beds from £17 to £20 per person. Similar is the **Barrosa** (*Map 2, ☎ 554 3700, 21 Pilrig St*), where B&B costs from £19.50/ 23.50 without/with bath. The attractive, detached, two-crown **Balquhidder Guest House** (*Map 2, ☎ 554 3377, 94 Pilrig St*) provides neat rooms with bath from £18 to £30 a head. Next door, the larger **Balfour House** (*Map 2, ☎ 554 2106, 92 Pilrig St*) has 19 mostly *en suite* rooms for £20/23 per person without/with bathroom.

There are several elegant places in Eyre Place, near Stockbridge and the Water of Leith, 1 mile from the centre. **Ardenlee Guest House** (*Map 2, ☎ 556 2838, 9 Eyre Place*) is a terraced Victorian townhouse with beds from £22 to £26 per person (£2 more for a private bath). The friendly, Georgian **Dene Guest House** (*Map 2, ☎ 556 2700, 7 Eyre Place*) has 10 rooms with B&B from £19.50/37 a single/double. If these are full try **Blairhaven Guest House** (*Map 2, ☎ 556 3025, 5 Eyre Place*), which does B&B from £18.

Newington

There are lots of guesthouses on and around Minto St/Mayfield Gardens in Newington. It's south of the city centre and university on either side of the continuation of North/South Bridge, with plenty of buses to the centre. This is the main traffic artery from the south and carries traffic from the A7 and A68 (both routes are signposted). The best places are in the streets on either side of the main road.

Salisbury Guest House (*Map 3, ☎ 667 1264, 45 Salisbury Rd*), just east of Newington Rd and 10 minutes from the centre by bus, is quiet, comfortable and non-smoking. Rooms with private bath cost from £23 to £30 per person.

The welcoming, red sandstone **Avondale**

Guest House (*Map 3, ☎ 667 6779, 10 South Gray St*), just west of Minto St, is a comfortable, traditional B&B with singles/ doubles from £19/32.

In a quiet street, **Fairholme Guest House** (*Map 3, ☎ 667 8645, 13 Moston Terrace*), just west of Mayfield Gardens, is a pleasant Victorian villa with free parking. The range of rooms includes a single from £15.

Grange Guest House (*Map 3, ☎ 667 2125, 2 Minto St*), near the corner of Salisbury Rd, is a two storey, terrace house convenient for the centre, but only provides a continental breakfast. Rooms with shared bathroom cost £16/28 a single/double. One of the better guesthouses on Minto St is **Sherwood Guest House** (*Map 3, ☎ 667 1200*), No 42, a refurbished Georgian villa with off-road parking. B&B costs £25/40, or £40/64 with bathroom.

Millfield Guest House (*Map 3, ☎ 667 4428, 12 Marchhall Rd*), east of Dalkeith Rd past Pollock Halls of Residence, is a pleasant, two-storey, Victorian house with singles/doubles from £18/33.

Further south, Kilmaurs Rd also east of Dalkeith Rd, has several B&Bs. The spacious **Casa Buzzo** (*Map 3, ☎ 667 8998*), No 8, has two doubles for £16 per person with shared bathroom. If you prefer private facilities the nearby **Kenvie Guest House** (*Map 3, ☎ 668 1964*), No 16, has a couple of *en suite* rooms for £26/46 a single/double.

Bruntsfield

Bruntsfield is less than a mile south-west of the centre; most places are on Gilmore Place and Leamington Terrace. Bus Nos 10 and 10A run to Gilmore Place from Princes St.

On Gilmore Place, busy **Averon Guest House** (*Map 6, ☎ 229 9932, 44 Gilmore Place*) has comfortable if small rooms from £20 per person. Named after a former gold-mining town in Australia, **Ballarat Guest House** (*Map 6, ☎ 229 7024, 14 Gilmore Place*) provides clean, non-smoking rooms for £23 per person.

Down Leamington Terrace at No 33, is **Menzies Guest House** (*Map 3, ☎ 229 4629*). It's well run and has rooms from £20 to £28 per person, though you only have one choice of breakfast cereal. The refurbished *Leamington Guest House* (*Map 3*, ☎ *228 3879*), No 57, has eight rooms, each with a different theme, and good breakfasts for £20/26 without/with bathroom.

There are several quiet guesthouses in Hartington Gardens, off Viewforth, itself off Bruntsfield Place. *Aaron Guest House* (*Map 3*, ☎ *229 6459*), at the end of the street, is handy for drivers since it has a private car park. Beds go for £20 to £35 per person in comfortable *en suite* rooms. The comfortable, friendly *Robertson Guest House* (*Map 3*, ☎ *229 2652*), No 5, offers a good range of food at breakfast including yoghurt and fruit, and has rooms from £20 per person.

HOTELS

Not surprisingly, the international hotels in the centre are extremely expensive, although there can be good deals outside summer, especially at weekends. Unless otherwise stated, rates include breakfast.

Old Town

The *Thistle Inn Hotel* (*Map 6*, ☎ *220 2299, 94 Grassmarket*) is in the heart of the Old Town in one of the city's nightlife centres. Singles/doubles with private bath and TV cost from £33/56. The entrance is next to Biddy Mulligan's pub, and every floor is accessible by lift. (Don't confuse it with the bigger, more expensive King James Thistle Hotel beside the shopping centre, off Leith St.) Nearby, *Apex International Hotel* (*Map 6*, ☎ *300 3456, 31-35 Grassmarket*) has 99 *en suite* rooms, a rooftop restaurant and off-street parking. B&B costs from £60/80.

The new, spruce *Ibis Hotel* (*Map 5*, ☎ *240 7000, 6 Hunter Square*), just off the Royal Mile, offers a flat rate of £55 per room per night, but breakfast is an extra £5.25. The stylish *Bank Hotel* (*Map 5*, ☎ *556 9043, 1 South Bridge*), on the corner of the Royal Mile, has a good bar downstairs and singles/doubles for £70/100 including breakfast.

The *Holiday Inn Crowne Plaza* (*Map 5*, ☎ *557 9797, 80 High St*) is a purpose-built hotel whose exterior mimics the Royal Mile's 16th century architecture. The interior is, nonetheless, as modern as you could hope for. Rates are from £125/145 a single/double.

New Town

The three-star *Royal British Hotel* (*Map 4*, ☎ *556 4901, 20 Princes St*) is in a good location opposite the TIC. B&B costs from £70/82 a single/double. The *Old Waverley Hotel* (*Map 4*, ☎ *556 4648, 43 Princes St*) has a prime site opposite the Sir Walter Scott Monument, and many rooms have castle views. Rooms with private bath cost from £90/144. The luxurious *Balmoral Hotel* (*Map 5*, ☎ *556 2414, 1 Princes St*), next to Waverley station and the TIC, is one of Edinburgh's top hotels with rooms for £137. Facilities include a gym, pool and sauna.

Carlton Highland Hotel (*Map 5*, ☎ *472 3000, North Bridge*), south of Princes St, is an imposing Victorian building with a leisure centre, nightclub and *en suite* rooms from £85/120. The elegant *Caledonian Hotel* (*Map 4*, ☎ *459 9988*), at the west end of Princes St on the corner of Lothian Rd, is in a huge, red sandstone building below the castle. Singles/doubles cost £147/220 and hotel facilities include three restaurants.

Royal Terrace has a great position on the north side of Calton Hill, with views over Royal Terrace Gardens to Leith. *Ailsa Craig Hotel* (*Map 5*, ☎ *556 1022, 24 Royal Terrace*) is a refurbished Georgian building where rooms, most with bath, cost from £30/55 a single/double. The *Claymore Hotel* (*Map 5*, ☎ *556 2693, 7 Royal Terrace*), the *Halcyon* (*Map 5*, ☎ *556 1032, 8 Royal Terrace*), and the *Adria Hotel* (*Map 5*, ☎ *556 7875, 11 Royal Terrace*) are similar.

At the *Greenside Hotel* (*Map 5*, ☎ *557 0022, 9 Royal Terrace*) the 15 huge rooms are each furnished differently, are all *en suite* and cost from £25 to £55 per person; snacks are available throughout the day.

The swishest hotel and one of the best in Edinburgh is the *Royal Terrace Hotel* (*Map 5*, ☎ *557 3222*), No 18. It's full of fine furnishings and most rooms include a spa bath; it costs from £120/160 a single/double.

More personal than most hotels is the tastefully decorated *Sibbet House* (*Map 4*, ☎ *556 1078, 26 Northumberland St*), where prices of £80 to £90 per person might include an impromptu bagpipe recital by your host.

The grand, old-world *Roxburghe Hotel* (*Map 4*, ☎ *225 3921, 38 Charlotte Square*) is in one of Edinburgh's most prestigious locations. Rooms with bathroom cost from £100/135 a single/double. The very traditional, elegant *George Inter-Continental Hotel* (*Map 4*, ☎ *225 1251, 19-21 George St*), in the heart of Edinburgh's financial district, has over 500 rooms costing from £95 to £165.

North of the New Town
The *Lovat Hotel* (*Map 2*, ☎ *556 2745, 5 Inverleith Terrace*), near the Royal Botanic Garden, is a small terrace hotel with off-street parking. Rooms cost £30/50. *Christopher North House Hotel* (*Map 4*, ☎ *225 2720, 6 Gloucester Place*), Stockbridge, is a small, genteel Georgian hotel in a quiet area. Rooms cost from £40/60 a single/double, £60/100 with bathroom.

In Leith, Edinburgh's main port, the *Malmaison Hotel* (*Leith Map*, ☎ *555 6868, 1 Tower Place*), in a 19th century sailor's home, is a wonderfully stylish hotel, with rooms from £95.

West End & Haymarket
Good value given the location, the *West End Hotel* (*Map 3*, ☎ *225 3656, 35 Palmerston Place*) has *en suite* rooms from £25 per person, and a bar with a wide selection of whiskies. *Rothesay Hotel* (*Map 2*, ☎ *225 4125, 8 Rothesay Place*), in a quiet, central street, has pleasantly spacious rooms, mostly with bathroom, from £30 to £80 per person.

There's a handy batch of mid-range places on Coates Gardens, off Haymarket Terrace near Haymarket train station. Comfortable *Boisdale Hotel* (*Map 3*, ☎ *337 1134, 9 Coates Gardens*) has rooms with private bath from £25 to £45 per person.

At the top of Coates Gardens in Eglinton Crescent, *Greens Hotel* (*Map 3*, ☎ *337 1565*), at No 24, occupies four terrace houses and caters mostly to business people, but is reasonably priced from £35 per person.

Lothian Rd & Around
The *Sheraton Grand Hotel* (*Map 3*, ☎ *229 9131, 1 Festival Square*), is opposite the Royal Lyceum Theatre, off Lothian Rd, east of the castle. You pay for, and get, luxury. Rooms cost from £155/195. Further south, the *Point Hotel* (*Map 6*, ☎ *221 5555, 34 Bread St*), off Lothian Rd, has a strikingly modern, stark, Art Deco interior, and a trendy café-bar called Monboddo (see Places to Eat). Rates are from £70/90.

Newington
In a quiet residential area south of Holyrood Park, *Marchhall Hotel* (*Map 3*, ☎ *667 2743, 14-16 Marchhall Crescent*), a three-storey Victorian terrace, offers B&B from £23 per person. *Thrums Hotel* (*Map 3*, ☎ *667 5545, 14 Minto St*) is a small but popular place with off-street parking. B&B costs from £30 per person and it's advisable to book in advance. *Arthur's View Hotel* (*Map 3*, ☎ *667 3468*) is on the corner of Mayfield Gardens and Bright's Crescent. Although its name is stretching credibility a bit, it's a friendly place with a private car park and evening meals. B&B costs from £40/70 a single/double.

Bruntsfield
Hotels here have the advantage of being close to Bruntsfield Links and Meadow Park and to some good eateries.

Next to the SYHA hostel, the *Nova Hotel* (*Map 3*, ☎ *447-6437, 5 Bruntsfield Crescent*) is in a quiet, three-storey Victorian terrace, with views across the links. Its 12 *en suite* rooms cost from £35. *Bruntsfield Hotel* (*Map 3*, ☎ *229 1393*) is well positioned on the corner of Bruntsfield Place and Leamington Terrace facing Bruntsfield Links. It charges £89/125 a single/double, but has a standby rate of £50 per person for the first night and other specials.

SELF-CATERING

There's plenty of self-catering accommodation in Edinburgh and staying in a flat or house in the city gives you an opportunity to get a feel for a community. The minimum stay is usually one week in the summer peak season, three nights or less at other times.

The *Edinburgh Holiday Guide*, free from the TIC, contains a list of these (with contact addresses) in Edinburgh and the Lothians. Depending on facilities, location and time of year, prices range from £150 to £750 per week.

Dundas (*Leith Map*, ☎ 554 6480, 8 *Claremont Gardens*) provides a comfortable two-bedroom flat in Leith near the golf course. It's open from July to September, has a minimum period of four days and charges from £150.

Less personal but more central is ***Glen House Apartments*** (*Map 6*, ☎ 228 4043, fax 229 8873, 22 Glen St), off Lauriston Place south of the Old Town. It has a range of units with one to four bedrooms and charges from £160 to £750 a week. The minimum stay is three nights.

Open year round, ***Jane Armstrong*** (*Map 2*, ☎/fax 558 9868, 13 Inverleith Row), close to the Royal Botanic Garden north of the centre, has two units that can sleep up to five people. The weekly rate is from £250 and there's a minimum stay of three nights.

LONG TERM RENTALS

In general, prices for rented accommodation are high and standards low, but many are furnished so you won't have to buy much. At the lower end of the market, bedsits are single furnished rooms, usually with a shared bathroom and kitchen, although some have basic cooking facilities. The next step up is a studio, which normally has its own bathroom and kitchen. Shared houses and flats are probably the best value. Rates start from around £170 per calendar month. Many landlords demand a security deposit (normally one month's rent) plus a month's rent in advance; some also request some sort of reference.

When you inspect a flat it's wise to take someone else with you, both for safety reasons and for help in spotting any shortcomings. A few things to check before signing a tenancy agreement are:

- the cost of gas, electricity, the phone, the TV and how they're to be paid for
- whether there's street parking and/or how close it is to public transport
- the arrangements for cleaning the house or flat
- whether you can have friends to stay

To find a place, look in the classified ads in the local newspapers and in the Flatshare section of *The List* magazine. Hostel noticeboards are also a good source. For agents check the Yellow Pages. One agent is DRM Residential (☎ 466 4661, fax 466 4662, www.drm-residential.co.uk), 3 Comiston Place in Morningside. It has holiday apartments and properties to let and doesn't charge the tenant for finding accommodation.

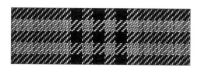

Places to Eat

FOOD

Scotland's chefs have an enviable range of fresh meat, seafood and vegetables at their disposal. And the country has gone a long way to shake off its once dismal culinary reputation. Most Edinburgh restaurants are good while some are internationally renowned.

Most pubs do food, with either a cheap bar menu or a more formal restaurant or both. Supermarkets and department stores have reasonable (and reasonably priced) cafés.

Lunch is served from 12.30 to 2 pm, dinner from 7 to around 9 pm. An alternative to dinner is high tea (from about 4.30 to 6.30 pm), when a main dish is served with tea and cakes.

Some of the best places to eat are members of the Taste of Scotland scheme. The STB's annual *Taste of Scotland Guide* (£7.99) is worth buying to track down these restaurants and hotels. The excellent, annual *Edinburgh & Glasgow Eating & Drinking Guide* contains reviews of cafés, restaurants and bars and is published by *The List* magazine.

Vegetarianism has a long tradition in Edinburgh, and vegetarians can get a reasonable meal pretty well anywhere, especially if they like pizza, pasta or curry. Vegans will find the going tougher, but many places with vegetarian menus often include vegan dishes. The *Cruelty Free Guide to Edinburgh* has a list of these.

The cheapest way to eat is to cook for yourself. Even if you lack great culinary skills, you can buy good quality pre-cooked meals from supermarkets.

Scottish Breakfast

Surprisingly few Scots eat porridge and even fewer eat it in the traditional way as a savoury dish not a sweet one – that is with salt to taste, then eaten with milk, but no sugar. You'll rarely be offered porridge in a B&B. Generally, a glass of fruit juice accompanies a bowl of cereal or muesli, followed by a cooked breakfast which may include: bacon, sausage, black pudding (a type of sausage made from dried blood), grilled tomato, grilled mushrooms, fried bread or tattie (potato) scones (if you're lucky), and an egg or two. More upmarket hotels may offer porridge followed by kippers (smoked herrings). As well as toast, there may be oatcakes (oatmeal biscuits) to spread your marmalade upon.

Snacks

As well as ordinary scones (similar to American biscuits), Scottish bakeries often offer milk scones, tattie scones and girdle scones. Bannocks are a cross between scones and pancakes. Savoury pies include the *bridie* (a pie filled with meat, potatoes and sometimes other vegetables) and the Scotch pie (minced meat in a plain round pastry casing – best eaten hot). A *toastie* is a toasted sandwich.

Dundee cake, a rich fruit cake topped with almonds, is highly recommended. Black bun is another type of fruit cake, eaten over Hogmanay (New Year's Eve).

Soups

Scotch broth, made with barley, lentils and mutton stock, is highly nutritious and very good. Cock-a-leekie is a substantial soup made from a cock, or chicken, and leeks.

You may not be drawn to *powsowdie* (sheep's-head broth) but it's very tasty. More popular is *cullen skink*, a fish soup containing smoked haddock.

Meat & Game

Steak eaters will enjoy a thick fillet of world-famous Aberdeen Angus beef, while beef from Highland cattle is much sought after. Venison, from the red deer, is leaner and appears on many menus. Both may be served with a wine-based or creamy whisky sauce.

Gamebirds like pheasant and the more expensive grouse, traditionally roasted and served with game chips and fried breadcrumbs, are also available. They're definitely worth trying, but watch your teeth on the shot, which is not always removed before cooking.

Then there's haggis, Scotland's much-maligned national dish ...

Fish & Seafood

Scotland offers a wide variety of fish and seafood. Scottish salmon is well known but there's a big difference between farmed salmon and the leaner, more expensive, wild version. Both are available either smoked (served with brown bread and butter) or poached. Wild brown trout is cheaper than salmon and almost as good; there's also a farmed variety and it's often served fried in oatmeal.

As an alternative to kippers (smoked herrings) you may be offered Arbroath smokies (lightly smoked fresh haddock), traditionally eaten cold. Herrings in oatmeal are good if you don't mind the bones. *Krappin heit* is cod's head stuffed with fish livers and oatmeal. Mackerel paté and smoked or peppered mackerel (both served cold) are also popular.

Prawns, crab, lobster, oysters, mussels and scallops are available in coastal towns and around lochs, although much is exported.

Cheeses

Cheddar is the Scottish cheese industry's main output, but there are speciality cheese-makers whose products are definitely worth sampling. Many are based on the islands, particularly Arran, Bute, Gigha, Islay, Mull and Orkney. Brodick Blue is a ewes' milk blue cheese made on Arran. Lanark Blue is rather

---

Haggis – Scotland's National Dish

A popular rhyme, penned by an English poet, goes:

For the land of Burns
The only snag is
The haggis

Scotland's national dish is frequently ridiculed by foreigners because of its ingredients which don't sound too mouthwatering. However, once you get over any delicate sensibilities towards tucking in to chopped lungs, heart and liver mixed with oatmeal and boiled in a sheep's stomach, with the accompanying glass of whisky it can taste surprisingly good.

Haggis should be served with tatties and neeps (mashed potatoes and turnips, with a generous dollop of butter and a good sprinkling of black pepper).

Although it's eaten year-round, haggis is central to the celebrations of 25 January in honour of Scotland's national poet, Robert Burns. Scots worldwide unite on Burns Night to revel in their Scottishness. A piper announces the arrival of the haggis and Burns' poem *Address to a Haggis* (otherwise known as the *Selkirk Grace*) is recited to this 'Great chieftan o' the puddin'-race'. The bulging stomach is then lanced with a dirk (dagger) to reveal the steaming offal within.

Vegetarians (and quite a few carnivores, no doubt) will be relieved to know that veggie haggis is available in some restaurants in Edinburgh.

PLACES TO EAT

like Roquefort. There are several varieties of cream cheese (Caboc, St Finan, Howgate) which are usually rolled in oatmeal.

Scottish oatcakes make the perfect accompaniment for cheese.

Puddings

Traditional Scottish puddings are irresistibly creamy, calorie-enriched concoctions. *Cranachan* is made with toasted oatmeal, raspberries, or some other fresh fruit, and whisky, all mixed into thick cream. *Atholl brose* is similar but without the fruit – rather like English syllabub. *Clootie dumpling* is delicious, a rich steamed pudding filled with currants and raisins.

DRINKS
Nonalcoholic Drinks

On quantity drunk, tea probably qualifies as Scotland's national drink, but coffee is widely available and it's easy to get a cappuccino or espresso in large towns. Definitely an acquired taste is the virulent orange-coloured fizzy drink, Irn-Bru; it's 100% sugar plus some pretty weird flavouring.

Alcoholic Drinks

Takeaway alcoholic drinks are sold from neighbourhood off-licences (liquor stores) rather than pubs. Opening hours vary, but although some stay open daily to 9 or 10 pm, many keep ordinary shop hours. Alcohol can also be bought at supermarkets and corner shops.

Most restaurants are licensed to sell alcoholic drinks which are always expensive. There are a few BYO (Bring Your Own booze) restaurants. Most charge an extortionate sum for 'corkage' – opening your bottle for you. See Pubs under Entertainment.

Whisky Whisky (always spelt without an 'e' if it's Scottish) is Scotland's best-known product and biggest export. The spirit was first distilled in Scotland in the 15th century; over 2000 brands are now produced.

There are two kinds of whisky: single malt, made from malted barley, and blended whisky, which is distilled from unmalted grain (maize) and blended with selected

Making Malt Whisky

The process of making malt whisky begins with malting. Barley is soaked in water and allowed to germinate so that enzymes are produced to convert the starch in the barley to fermentable sugar. The barley is then dried in a malt kiln over the peat fire that gives malt whisky its distinctive taste. Since most distilleries now buy in their malted barley, tourists rarely see this part of the process.

The malt is milled, mixed with hot water and left in a large tank, the mash tun. The starch is converted into sugar and this liquid, or 'wort', is drawn off into another large tank, the washback, for fermentation.

This weak alcoholic solution, or wash, is distilled twice in large copper-pot stills. The process is controlled by the stillman, who collects only the middle portion of the second distillation to mature in oak barrels. The spirit remains in the barrels for at least three years, often much longer. During bottling, water is added to reduce its strength.

malts. Single malts are rarer (there are only about 100 brands) and more expensive than blended whiskies. Although there are distilleries all over the country, there are concentrations around Speyside and on the Isle of Islay.

As well as blends and single malts, there are also several whisky-based liqueurs like Drambuie. If you must mix your whisky with anything other than water try a whisky-mac (whisky with ginger wine). After a long walk in the rain there's nothing better to warm you up.

When out drinking, Scots may order a 'half' or 'nip' of whisky as a chaser to a pint of beer. Only tourists say 'Scotch' – what else would you be served in Scotland? The standard measure is 50mL.

Beer There's a wonderfully wide range of beers, ranging from light (almost like lager) to extremely strong and treacly. What New Worlders call beer is actually lager; to the distress of local connoisseurs, lagers constitute a huge chunk of the market. Fortunately, thanks to the Campaign for Real Ale (CAMRA) organisation, the once threatened traditional beers are thriving.

The best ales are hand-pumped from the cask, not carbonated and drawn under pressure. They're usually served at room temperature, which may come as a shock to lager drinkers, and have subtle flavours that a cold, chemical lager can't match. Most popular is what the Scots call 'heavy', a dark beer similar to English bitter. Most Scottish brews are graded in shillings so you can tell their strength, the usual range being 60 to 80 shillings (written 80/-). The greater the number of shillings, the stronger the beer.

The market is dominated by the big brewers: Younger, McEwan, Scottish & Newcastle and Tennent. Look out for beer from local breweries, some of it strong – the aptly-named Skullsplitter from Orkney is a good example. Caledonian 80/-, Maclay 80/- Belhaven 80/- and Traquair House Ale are others worth trying.

Long before hops arrived in Scotland, beer was brewed from heather. Reintroduced, heather ale is surprisingly good and available in some pubs.

Stout is a dark, rich, foamy drink; Guinness is the most famous brand.

Beers are usually served in pints (from £1.50 to £2), but you can also ask for a 'half' (a half pint). The stronger brews are usually 'specials' or 'extras'. Potency can vary from around 2 to 8%.

Wine For centuries people made wine from wild flowers, fruits and tree saps. This cottage industry is continued at Moniack Castle, near Beauly in the Highlands, and at Cairn o' Mohr winery in the Carse of Gowrie.

Good international wines are widely available and reasonably priced (except in pubs and restaurants). In supermarkets an ordinary but drinkable bottle can be found for around £4.

PLACES TO EAT

There are good-value restaurants and cafés scattered all round the city. For cheap eats, the best areas are Union Place, near the Playhouse Theatre; around Grassmarket, just south of the castle; near the university around Nicolson St, the extension of North/South Bridge, and in Bruntsfield. Most restaurants offer cheap set menus at lunchtime. Many close on Sunday evening, so ring ahead to make sure.

Royal Mile & Around

Despite being a tourist Mecca, the Royal Mile has lots of good-value, enjoyable eating oases.

Restaurants The excellent, small *Polo Fusion* (Map 6, ☎ 622 7722, 503 Lawnmarket) is reasonably priced by Edinburgh standards, and specialises in Asian dishes. Noodle dishes are good value at £5.50 to £6.50.

Viva Mexico (*Map 5, ☎ 226 5145, Cockburn St*) is a very cheerful, atmospheric restaurant. Some tables have views across to the New Town, and the food is good quality. Nachos cost from £2.50, burritos from £8.95.

Those who like a good wine with their meal should try the congenial *Doric Wine Bar & Bistro* (*Map 5, ☎ 225 1084, 15 Market St*). It has a good-value bar menu (meals from £2.50 to £3.50) noon to 6.30 pm and the small upstairs bistro offers classic Scottish dishes like haggis, neeps and tatties for £8.95.

Pleasant *Black Bo's* (*Map 7, ☎ 557 6136, 57 Blackfriars St*) offers an imaginative vegetarian menu. Mains like mushrooms and olives in filo pastry cost around £8.95.

You can sample traditional Scottish cooking at *The Grange* (*Map 5, ☎ 558 9992, 267 Canongate*) where three course lunches are £9.95; in the evening venison in a prune and wine glaze costs £15.35. *Dubh Prais* (*Map 5, ☎ 557 5732, 123 High St*), considered one of the best places to try Scottish cuisine, is popular with locals and tourists. As well as traditional meals the menu features interesting dishes like asparagus and parmesan risotto for £4.90 and aubergine with goat's cheese for £9.90.

Cafés Secluded *Deacon's House Café* (Map 6), down Brodie's Close, serves traditional Scottish food like Dundee cake or Scottish salmon sandwiches for £3.95.

Patisserie Florentin (Map 4), St Giles St, with its eye-catching frontage, attracts a rather self-consciously Bohemian crowd, but has excellent light meals and pastries; filled baguettes are £3 and good coffee £1. It stays open till the early hours during the festival period.

The enormously popular *Elephant House* (Map 6, ☎ 220 5355, 21 George IV Bridge) is a café with delicious pastries, newspapers, some of the best variety of coffee and tea (£1.70) in Edinburgh ... and lots of elephants.

Lower Aisle Restaurant (Map 6), beneath St Giles' Cathedral in Parliament Square, is peaceful outside peak lunchtimes. Soup and a roll costs £1.50. *Elephant's Sufficiency* (Map 5, ☎ 220 0666, 170 High St) is a bustling lunch spot. Try the Orkney burger for £3.75.

Open daily *Bann's Vegetarian Café* (Map 5, ☎ 226 1112, 5 Hunter Square), behind the Tron Kirk, is a relaxed Art Deco place with newspapers to read and music playing in the background. Most mains are under £7; vegetarian haggis with creamed turnip tartlets is £6.50.

Bright *Gustos Café* (Map 5, ☎ 558 3083, 105 High St) does delicious gourmet sandwiches from £1.95. *Netherbow Theatre Café* (Map 5, ☎ 556 9579, 43 High St), beside John Knox's House, serves cheap breakfasts in an outdoor courtyard up to noon, then lunches (big portions), salads and quiche for £3.15.

Charming *Clarinda's Tea Room* (Map 5, ☎ 557 1888, 69 Canongate) lurks at the quieter Holyrood end of the Mile. There are a variety of teas from 50p and delicious cakes from 93p. *Brambles Tearoom* (Map 5, ☎ 556 3503, 158 Canongate), close to Huntly

House, is similar; it does soup and a roll for £1.50 and has a good selection of cakes.

Grassmarket

The lively pubs and restaurants on the north side of Grassmarket cater to a young crowd and is a good starting point for a night out.

Ristorante Gennaro (Map 6, ☎ 226 3706), No 64, serves standard but good

Edinburgh Oyster Bars

Dotted around Edinburgh are a number of oyster bars, part of a chain operated by Oyster Bar Enterprises (☎ 554 6200, 1 Quayside St), Leith. The bars are all casual places where you can eat or drink daily from noon till late, and the menu includes beef and chicken dishes as well. Half a dozen Loch Fyne oysters cost £4.60, snacks like nachos £4.20.

The largest of the chain is *St James Oyster Bar* (Map 5, ☎ 557 2925, 2 Calton Rd), down some steps below the Black Bull pub, opposite the St James shopping centre. The *Queen St Oyster Bar* (☎ 226 2530, 16A Queen St), on the corner of Hanover St, is more intimate. In the West End the *West End Oyster Bar* (Map 3, ☎ 225 2530) can be found at 28 West Maitland St near Haymarket train station. *The Bare Story* (Map 7, ☎ 556 3953, 253-55 Cowgate), an anagram of the name, is a popular student hangout. Finally, the large *Leith Oyster Bar* (☎ 554 6294, 12 Burgess St) is near the Malt & Hops pub in Leith.

All of them serve real ale, while the Bare Story has DJs on Sunday, the St James has a juke box and the Queen St and West End bars have live music on weekends.

Of course, these aren't the only oyster bars in town and one of the best of the rest is at the *Café Royal Bar* (Map 4, ☎ 556 4124, 17 West Register St), in magnificent, wood-panelled Victorian surroundings.

PLACES TO EAT

Italian fare, with minestrone at £2.20, cannelloni at £6.20 and pizzas from £4.70 to £7. Popular *Mamma's Pizzas* (*Map 6, ☎ 225 6464*), No 28, does excellent pizzas with imaginative toppings (from £3.95).

Pierre Victoire (*Map 6, ☎ 226 2442, 38 Grassmarket*) is part of the chain that serves good-value French food. There's also a branch at 10 Victoria St, which curves up to George IV Bridge from the north-east corner of Grassmarket. Also part of Pierre's empire, *Beppe Vittorio* (*Map 6, ☎ 226 7267, 7 Victoria St*), follows the same formula – authentic, good-value food – although in this case it's Italian. You can mix and match sauces and pastas from £5. At the time of writing the Pierre Victoire chain was in financial difficulties but was continuing to operate.

New Town

The New Town is neither particularly well endowed with eating places nor a particularly interesting part of town at night, but there are a few reasonable options, especially in Hanover and Frederick Sts.

Restaurants The self-serve *Henderson's* (*Map 4, ☎ 225 2131, 94 Hanover St*) is an Edinburgh institution which has been churning out vegetarian food for more than 30 years. Hot dishes start at £3.50, but it's worth checking if there's a lunch or dinner special.

Gringo Bill's (*Map 4, ☎ 220 1205, 110 Hanover St*) is a good Mexican restaurant which serves food with an off-beat sense of humour. It does a huge meal and a drink at lunchtime for £5. *Bar Napoli* (*Map 4, ☎ 225 2600, 75 Hanover St*) is a cheerful Italian restaurant, open until 3 am, with pasta and pizza for £4 to £6. Another reliable Italian option, the traditional *Alfredo's* (*Map 4, ☎ 226 6090, 109 Hanover St*) is good value for money; it offers a three-course lunch for £4.95, and lets you BYO beer.

Chez Jules (*Map 4, ☎ 225 7893, 61 Frederick St*) is a Pierre Victoire spin-off offering similar simple, cheap, but good-quality French food in relaxed surroundings. A three-course lunch is £5.90. In the same French vein there's a branch nearby of the popular *Café Rouge* (*Map 4, ☎ 225 4515, 43 Frederick St*); lamb casserole here is £7.95. Below street level, *Vito's Ristorante* (*Map 4, ☎ 225 5052, 55 Frederick St*) is a very busy Italian restaurant specialising in seafood served in large proportions. King prawns in garlic cost £5.95.

The long-standing *Singapura Restaurant* (*Map 4, ☎ 538 7878, 69 North Castle St*) serves an array of excellent Malaysian-Singaporian food and offers a five-course banquet for £17.90. It's closed Sunday.

Cafés Midway along Princes St are two pleasant cafés. On the 2nd floor of Waterstone's bookshop, near the corner of South Charlotte St, is a branch of the *Starbucks* (Map 4), on the 1st floor overlooking Princes St from its bay window. Nearby is *Bewley's Café* (*Map 4, ☎ 220 1969, 4 South Charlotte St*), a branch of the Irish chain of traditional cafés. Sandwiches are £1.95 to £2.50, pastries £1.20; it also serves lunch and breakfast.

At the western end of Princes St on the corner of Lothian Rd, below St John's Church, *Cornerstone Coffee House* (*Map 4, ☎ 229 0212*) has good views of the castle and St Cuthbert's Church.

At the east end of Princes St at 1 Waterloo Place the French-style *Delifrance* (*Map 5, ☎ 557 4171*) does reasonably priced, good food; baguettes are £3.25 to £4.20. More upmarket French food is provided by *Café 1812* (*Map 5, ☎ 556 5766, 29 Waterloo Place*), with great views of Calton Hill and good-value two-course lunches for £5.40.

While you're in the Scottish National Portrait Gallery, Queen St, check out the delicious home-baked cooking at its *Queen Street Café* (Map 4), open from 10 am to 4.30 pm.

The popular *Hard Rock Café* (*Map 4, ☎ 260 3000, 20 George St*) has huge, tasty burger meals for around £9, plus all the usual merchandising and intriguing rock music memorabilia.

The Forth Road Bridge, South Queensferry

Monument to Greyfriars Bobby, Greyfriars Kirkyard

Everyone loves a parade - Hearts' fans celebrate their team's 1998 victory in the Scottish FA Cup

Pub sign, Grassmarket

Pub sign, Grassmarket

A quiet afternoon with Edinburgh's most famous son, washed down with whisky and shortbread

Fast Food Princes St is the main area in Edinburgh for fast food. There are the usual international chains like *Burger King* plus food courts in Waverley train station, at the bottom level of Waverley Market shopping centre and in St James shopping centre.

Leith Walk & Broughton St

Restaurants A number of places on Leith Walk pitch for Playhouse Theatre-goers, including several Italian options. Pick of the bunch is friendly, informal *Giuliano's* (*Map 5*, ☎ 556 6590, 18 Union Place) opposite the theatre. It's open to 2 am, and serves pastas and pizzas for under £6. *Ferri's Italiano Pizzeria* (*Map 5*, ☎ 556 5592, 1 Antigua St*) does pasta and pizza at similar prices, and has a good vegetarian selection.

Pierre Victoire (*Map 5*, ☎ 557 8451, 8 Union St*) offers a relaxed style and main courses for around £8.

Cafés & Bars The informal, downstairs *Café Libra* (*Map 2*, ☎ 556 9602, 5A Union St*) has all-day breakfasts for £4 and walls covered in posters advertising the latest events.

Nearby, alternative, Bohemian Broughton St has a couple of organic food shops and a few interesting low-cost café-bars that are good for a drink as well as a meal, and are especially busy on weekends.

The busy *Basement Bar* (*Map 5*, ☎ 557 0097, 10A Broughton St*) has reasonable prices and opens from noon to 1 am. Most dishes are under £4.50 and its weekend Mexican menu is especially popular. *Blue Moon Café* (*Map 5*, ☎ 557 0476, 36A Broughton St*) is a gay café but straights are welcome. It has a wide selection of dishes including vegetarian. Boldly painted in orange and purple *Baroque* (*Map 5*, ☎ 557 0627, 39-41 Broughton St*) is hard to miss. In fine weather it has tables outside and serves fare like toasted baguettes (£3.95) and salads (£2.95).

West End

Restaurants A few places on Dalry Rd are convenient for those staying in or near the West End. Offering a good mix of French-Scottish cuisine, *Howie's Restaurant* (*Map 3*, ☎ 313 3334, 63 Dalry Rd*) is so popular that advance booking is wise. The two-course lunch is a bargain at £6.95. House specialities include banoffi pie. At the northern end of Dalry Rd, the *Verandah Restaurant* (*Map 3*, ☎ 337 5828*), No 17, is an excellent tandoori restaurant with tasty food and three-course lunches for £5.95.

Raffaelli's (*Map 4*, ☎ 225 6060, 10 Randolph Place*) is one of Edinburgh's top Italian restaurants; main dishes are expensive but its pastas are reasonably priced at £4.50 to £7.50.

Cafés & Bars *Ryan's Café-Bar* (*Map 4*, ☎ 226 7005*), on the corner of Hope and Queensferry Sts, has an Irish name but is very much in the style of a Parisian street café. The food is a mix of traditional and French. Mussels in garlic cost £4.95. The *Granary* (*Map 4*, ☎ 220 0550*), next door on Queensferry St, is rather like a downmarket Hard Rock Café, but is noted for its burger meals (£5.95) and the portions are generous.

Stockbridge & Around

Village-like, sleepy Stockbridge is popular with the young and affluent and has some interesting eateries.

Restaurants Upmarket *Lancers* (*Map 2*, ☎ 332 3444, 5 Hamilton Place*) is reputed to be one of Edinburgh's best Indian restaurants; the food is mostly North Indian and mains like tandoori murgh (roasted chicken) cost £6.95 to £12.95.

Pizza Express (*Map 2*, ☎ 332 7229, 1 Deanhaugh St*) overlooking the Water of Leith, offers above average pizzas from £3.85. Small *Passepartout* (*Map 4*, ☎ 332 4476, 24 Deanhaugh St*) takes its name from Jules Verne's *Around the World in 80 Days* and reflects its international menu. A three-course dinner costs £6.

The Watershed (*Map 2*, ☎ 557 0627, 44 St Stephen St*) is popular and serves good inexpensive food, some of it traditional like sausage and mash (£5.50), some of it more Mediterranean like seafood pasta (£4.85).

Near Stockbridge, **Ducks at Le Marché Noir** (*Map 2, ☎ 558 1608, 2-4 Eyre Place*) is a gourmet French-Scottish restaurant with mains like *confit* of duck for £12.25 to £17. Next door, the Spanish **Tapas Olé** (*Map 2, ☎ 556 2754, 10 Eyre Place*) mostly serves the dishes for which it is named; seafood tapas are £3 to £5, vegetarian ones £2 to £4.

Cafés & Bars *Caffe Italia* (*Map 2, ☎ 332 3864, 1 Raeburn Place*), on the corner of Dean St, is a popular trattoria where pastas cost a modest £4 to £6. It's closed Sunday. **Patisserie Florentin** (*Map 4, ☎ 220 0225, 5 North West Circus Place*) has excellent quiche, pastries and coffee like its sister shop off the Royal Mile.

River Café (*Map 2, ☎ 332 3322, 36 Deanhaugh St*) offers ample all-day breakfasts for £2.75, but also includes a small range of Persian specialities.

The **Bailie Bar** (*Map 4, ☎ 225 4673, 2 St Stephen St*) has an excellent moderately priced, varied menu; stuffed baked aubergine is £4.85.

Lothian Rd & Around

Restaurants A few places around the southern end of Lothian Rd cater for the Royal Lyceum Theatre's clientele. Big, jolly **Dario's Pizzeria Ristorante** (*Map 6, ☎ 229 9625, 85 Lothian Rd*) opens until 5 am daily. Set lunches cost £4 and its wide range of pastas and pizzas start from around £5.

Opposite the theatre, **Jasmine** (*Map 6, ☎ 229 5757, 32 Grindlay St*) has excellent Chinese cooking, especially seafood. You can eat well for under £15. A weekday three-course lunch costs £6.

Lazio (*Map 6, ☎ 229 7788, 95 Lothian Rd*) has won awards for its pizzas and pastas (£4.80 to £6.20); it opens from noon onwards.

Cafés & Bars *Starbucks* (Map 6), on the corner of Lothian Rd and Bread St, has a simple décor, a relaxed atmosphere and a variety of coffees and teas. Savouries and pastries cost from £1.20.

Open till late, **Uluru** (*Map 6, ☎ 228 5407, 133 Lothian Rd*) is a café-bar whose name and décor are Australian inspired. Pizzas cost from £3.20 and sandwiches £2.95; there's also a good selection of teas and coffees.

The **Monboddo** café-bar in the Point Hotel (*Map 6, ☎ 221 5555, 34 Bread St*), off Lothian Rd, is stylish but reasonably priced. Main dishes from the extensive menu cost £5.50.

Bruntsfield

There's a batch of moderately-priced eateries on Home and Leven Sts (which lead to Bruntsfield Place), but some of the more interesting places are further south around the junction of Bruntsfield Place, Montpelier Park and Murchison Place.

Restaurants *Efes* (*Map 6, ☎ 229 7833, 42 Leven St*) sells various Turkish kebabs and pizzas. They're cheaper to take away, but if you eat in a doner kebab costs £6.50. **Caley's Bistro** (*Map 6, ☎ 622 7170, 32 Leven St*) provides contemporary Scottish cuisine, with its three-course lunch great value at £6.75. You can bring your own alcohol.

Jacques' Bistro (*Map 3, ☎ 229 6080, 8 Gillespie Place*) is a cosy French restaurant catering to the King's Theatre crowd. It offers a pre/post-theatre, two-course meal and coffee for £8.90.

Parrots (*Map 3, ☎ 229 3252, 3 Viewforth*), off Bruntsfield Place, is a deservedly popular non-smoking restaurant that sells excellent-value evening meals in pleasant parrot-themed surroundings. The extensive menu offers everything from baltis for £5.95, to mushroom and nut fettuccine for £3.75. It's even possible to eat alone here without feeling like a leper. It's closed Sunday and Monday.

Montpelier's (*Map 3, ☎ 229 3115, 159 Bruntsfield Place*) serves cappuccinos and cakes all day, and excellent Scottish breakfasts. The interesting dinner menu includes swordfish in mango sauce for £8.95. **La Grande Cafetière** (*Map 3, ☎ 228 1188, 184*

Bruntsfield Place), opposite, is similar; it serves delicious meals for around £5.25 and agreeably wicked desserts.

At 208 Bruntsfield Place there's a branch of **Howie's Restaurant** (*Map 3*, ☎ *221 1777*) in an old bank (see West End earlier).

Cafés *Ramsden's Luncherie* (Map 3), Bruntsfield Place, is a basic, friendly café with breakfasts for £2.30. The large *Estate Coffee Lounge* (Map 6), on Leven St opposite the King's Theatre, has posters advertising the latest happenings. Sandwiches are £2 and the coffee is good.

On Home St, colourful *Filfila* (Map 6) serves mostly Middle Eastern food. Meals are filling but perhaps not as flavoursome as you'd expect. Beef with couscous is £3.60 and there is a good vegetarian selection. Opposite, young people are continually dropping into *Ndebele* (*Map 6*, ☎ *221 1141, 57 Home St*), which serves healthy, good-value, tasty South African style food; sugar bean stroganoff is £3.50.

University

There are lots of places near the university. Many student favourites are between Nicolson St and Bristo Place at the end of George IV Bridge.

Restaurants *Kebab Mahal* (*Map 7*, ☎ *667 5214, Nicolson Square*) is a legendary source of cheap sustenance with excellent kebabs from £2.25, and curries from £3.25. You sit at a counter bathed in fluorescent light.

Vegetarian *Susie's Diner* (*Map 7*, ☎ *667 8729, West Nicolson St*), west off Nicolson St, has good, inexpensive food – mains costs £3.45 to £4.75 – and a belly dancer for entertainment in the evenings. Pigs feature in the décor at *Pigs Bistro* (*Map 7*, ☎ *667 6676, 41 West Nicolson St*), but not on the diverse menu. Lunchtime mains are good value – chicken enchilada costs £3.95.

Spartan, atmospheric *Khushi's* (*Map 7*, ☎ *556 8996, 16 Drummond St*) is the original Edinburgh curry house and little has changed since it opened in 1947. You can bring your pint in from the pub next door.

Lamb bhuna at £4.60 is said to be the local favourite.

Kalpna (*Map 7*, ☎ *667 9890, 2 St Patrick's Square*) is a highly acclaimed, reasonably priced Gujarati (Indian) vegetarian restaurant. Each week on Wednesday night it lays on a gourmet buffet (£8.95) of 20 dishes from a different region of India.

Cafés & Bars *Nile Valley Café* (*Map 7*, ☎ *667-8200, Potterow*) serves an interesting mix of Mediterranean and Sudanese food; you can bring your own beer. Mains cost £6 to £8. *Negociant's* (*Map 7*, ☎ *225 6313, 45 Lothian St*) is a very hip café and music venue with good-value food – main courses cost from £5.95 for cajun salmon to £6.50 for beef chilli. The basement bar opens until 3 am.

Newington & Around

If you're staying in Minto St or Mayfield Gardens, you need to head back towards the centre to find several good choices on either side of the main road.

Restaurants *Chinese Home Cooking* (*Map 3*, ☎ *668 4946, 34 West Preston St*) is a real bargain BYO restaurant with spartan décor but filling, tasty food. Its three-course lunch is great value at £4.

There's another branch of *Howie's Restaurant* (*Map 7*, ☎ *668 2917, 75 St Leonard's St*) near the corner of Montague St.

La Bonne Vie (*Map 7*, ☎ *622 9111, 113 Buccleuch St*) is a highly regarded French restaurant specialising in vegetarian and seafood. Vegetarian strudel is £5.75 and smoked haddock £6. Nearby at No 79 is *King's Balti* (*Map 7*, ☎ *622 9212*), a large BYO balti restaurant with a wide selection of dishes including vegetarian ones. Three-course lunch specials cost £6.95.

Cafés *The Metropole* (*Map 3*, ☎ *668 4999, 33 Newington Rd*), a good place to relax with a newspaper, magazine or book, serves a wide choice of coffees and teas from 85p, plus delicious pies and pastries. *Isabel's Café* (*Map 7*, ☎ *662 4014, 83 South Clerk*

St) sells tasty, inexpensive vegetarian/vegan snacks and meals. Pasta and green vegetable bake is £3.50.

Leith

North of the centre picturesque Leith, Edinburgh's main port, has some good cafés and bars plus some more upmarket restaurants. See the Leith map for references.

Restaurants On the corner of Commercial St and Dock Place, there are some good mid-range restaurants in converted warehouses with views across to the huge Scottish Office.

Daruma-ya (☎ 554 7660) is a Japanese restaurant that has modern decor but has kept the original brick ceiling. You could eat well for under £20 from its extensive menu. (A daruma is a little potbellied figure of luck; the Japanese paint one of its eyes at the beginning of a project, the other at its successful conclusion.)

Daniel's Bistro (☎ 553 5933) is a mainly French-style restaurant with a strong Alsatian bias. Mains like *confit de canard* are under £10 and its three course lunches for £5.95 are excellent value. It also operates a delicatessen selling meats and cheeses.

Saray (☎ 553 7887) is a spacious Turkish restaurant with delicious starters including

mussels fried in batter for £4.30. Mains are £11 to £15.

The Ship (☎ 555 0409, 24-26 The Shore) is a relaxed, intimate restaurant specialising in fish that is beautifully prepared. Baked haddock in cheese sauce costs £9.95 and the two-course lunch is good value at £6.50.

Cafés & Bars *Malmaison Hotel* (☎ 555 6868, 1 Tower Place) has a chic café-bar and a brasserie where mains, including plenty of vegetarian options, cost £8.50 to £16.50.

There are other eateries nearby along The Shore, including *The Shore* (☎ 553 5080), an informal place with three-course lunches for £7.95 and live traditional music Wednesday and Saturday at 9 pm. At upmarket *Fishers Bistro* (☎ 554 5666), in a 17th century signal tower, seafood mains (£12 to £16) include marinated swordfish. You can eat on the cruise ship *The Edinburgh*, moored in the dock, on weekends; a full breakfast including haggis is £5.75.

Filling bar meals and real ales are available in two historic pubs, the *Malt & Hops* (☎ 555 0083), the oldest in Leith, and *King's Wark* (☎ 554 9260).

PLACES TO EAT

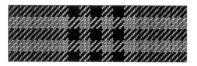

Entertainment

To some, Edinburgh may have an image of staid, middle-class respectability, but this is belied by its vibrant nightlife. There's a lively club scene, and many pubs offer entertainment ranging from live traditional Scottish folk music, to pop, rock and jazz to disco and quiz nights. Some places stage a ceilidh or Highland show featuring Scottish song and dance. The city also has a number of fine theatres and concert halls and there are independent arthouse cinemas as well as cinemas showing commercial films.

For full coverage buy *The List* (£1.90) Edinburgh's (and Glasgow's) fortnightly events guide. The Saturday edition of *The Scotsman* also has a good section on entertainment.

PUBS

The local pub is the place to go for a drink and often live music; you'll get a warm reception at most. Edinburgh has over 700 pubs and bars which are as varied as the population ... everything from Victorian palaces to rough and ready drinking holes. Given how much Scotland and Edinburgh are epitomised by the pub, it's odd how unenthusiastic the big breweries seem to be in hanging on to them. Many traditional brewery-owned pubs are being converted to café-bars or brasseries, or being reinvented as Irish or Australian theme bars. Ask at your hostel, B&B or hotel for recommendations.

Pubs generally open Monday to Saturday from 11 am to 11 pm, Sunday from 12.30 pm. Some have a late licence at weekends. The bell for last orders rings about 15 minutes before closing time.

Royal Mile & Around

The pubs on the Royal Mile aren't very inspiring, although there are some classics along the side streets. The *Jolly Judge* (*Map 6*, ☎ *225 2669, 7A James Court*) retains its distinctive 17th century character, has live music and a cheering fire in cold weather.

Malt Shovel Inn (*Map 4*, ☎ *225 6843, 11-15 Cockburn St*) has a good range of beers and whiskies and jazz on Tuesday night.

One of Edinburgh's most entertaining pubs is *The Ceilidh House* (*Map 7*, ☎ *220 1500*), below the Tron Tavern, Hunter Square. It's the atmospheric home to the Edinburgh Folk Club. Most nights there are informal, but high-quality, jam sessions.

'Give me a Firkin Pint'

To supplement the many traditional Scottish pubs and the growing number of trendy café-bars, Edinburgh has a number of theme pubs.

There are Irish pubs, like *O'Neill's* (*Map 4*, ☎ *225 0911, 99 Hanover St*), where they pull a good, slow pint of Guinness or Caffrey's and put on folk music. There are Australian theme pubs like *Bar Oz* (*Map 6*), on Forrest Rd, a big barn of a place, with clocks showing current times in Australia and New Zealand, and mileposts with distances to towns and suburbs in those countries. And of course, they sell antipodean as well as local beers.

You'll also see a number of pubs with 'Firkin' in the name; these are all part of a chain. The *Physician & Firkin* (*Map 3*, ☎ *662 4746, 58 Dalkeith Rd*), on the corner of Salisbury Rd in Newington, is the main one. It houses the brewery which supplies the Firkin beer for the other Firkin pubs – these are the *Fiscal & Firkin* (*Map 5*), 7 Hunter Square off the Royal Mile, *Fling & Firkin* (*Map 4*), 49 Rose St in New Town, and *Footlights & Firkin* (*Map 6*), 7 Spittal St, just south of the castle.

For those who don't know, a firkin is a small wooden barrel.

Entry to the more formal sessions is £7. The *Hebrides Bar* (*Map 4*, ☎ *220 4213, 17 Market St*) provides a mix of Scottish and Irish folk music on Friday and Saturday nights; on Sunday afternoon anyone is invited to play.

Instead of watching TV you can sit and see the comings and goings along the Mile from the trendy *Logie Baird's Bar* (☎ *556 9043, 1 South Bridge*), on the corner of High St.

The Tass (*Map 5*, ☎ *556 6338*), on the corner of High and St Mary's Sts, has guest ales each week and traditional Scottish music on Thursday and Saturday nights and Sunday afternoon. Opposite is the *World's End* (*Map 5*, ☎ *556 3628*) where part of the Flodden Wall can still be seen in the basement.

Grassmarket & Around

Traditional *Bow Bar* (*Map 6*, ☎ *226 7667, 80 West Bow*) is a popular pub serving real ales and a huge selection of malt whiskies. Despite its picturesque name, *The Last Drop* (*Map 6*, ☎ *225 4851, 74 Grassmarket*) actually commemorates the executions that used to take place nearby.

The White Hart (*Map 6*, ☎ *226 2688, 34 Grassmarket*) is another traditional pub once visited by Robbie Burns. The *Fiddlers Arms* (*Map 6*, ☎ *229 2665, 9-11 Grassmarket*) is an unpretentious pub with old fiddles lining the walls and live music during the week.

There are a couple of cheerful, friendly places on Cowgate. The *Green Tree* (*Map 7*, ☎ *225 1294, 182 Cowgate*) is a student hang-out and one of Edinburgh's few pubs with a beer garden. *Bannerman's* (*Map 7*, ☎ *556 3254, 212 Cowgate*) attracts students, locals and backpackers, and there's often live music or disco.

Greyfriars Bobby's Bar (*Map 6*, ☎ *225 8328, 34 Candlemaker Row*) is popular with students and tourists, and serves inexpensive meals. *Peartree House* (*Map 7*, ☎ *667 7533, 38 West Nicolson St*) is another student favourite partly because of the reasonably priced food, but also for the large outdoor courtyard which fills up in fine weather.

New Town & Around

Rose St may have lots of pubs, but they're not all worth frequenting. One exception is the *Abbotsford* (*Map 4*, ☎ *225 5276, 3 Rose St*), which has Victorian décor and a restaurant. Another is the *Rose St Brewery* (*Map 4*, ☎ *220 1227, 55 Rose St*), which has a good range of beers, most brewed on the premises.

At the western end in Hope St between Princes St and Charlotte Square, *Whigham's Wine Cellars* (*Map 4*, ☎ *225 9717*) is an old (and pricey) wine bar in atmospheric cellars.

It's worth sticking your nose through the door of the *Café Royal Bar* (*Map 4*, ☎ *556 1884, 17 West Register St*) to see its amazing stained-glass windows, Victorian interior and period portraits of famous people. *Tiles Bar-Bistro* (*Map 4*, ☎ *558 1507, 1 St Andrew Square*) is similarly lavish.

In stylish Broughton St, the friendly *Basement Bar* (☎ *557 0097, 10A Broughton St*) is one of Edinburgh's busiest bars and the music (jazz funk, hip hop etc) is loud. By contrast, *Mathers* (*Map 5*, ☎ *556 6754, 25 Broughton St*) is good for a quiet drink, and has inexpensive real ales and a huge selection of malts. Not far from Broughton St, *Route 66* (*Map 5*, ☎ *524 0061, 6 Baxter's Place*) is a gay pub with real ales, cheap food and a pool table.

The small *Wally Dug* (*Map 4*, ☎ *556 3271, 32 Northumberland St*) serves cask conditioned ales and is where weary workers wind down at the end of the day. Its name translates as 'woolly dog'.

At the sophisticated, basement level *Harry's Bar* (*Map 4*, ☎ *539 8100, 7B Randolph Place*), in the West End, you can drink (and eat) in the evenings until late.

Stockbridge

Trendy *Maison Hector* (*Map 2*, ☎ *332 5328, 47 Deanhaugh St*) is a café-bar with live music on Thursday night from 10 pm to 1 am, and jazz on Sunday from 4.30 pm. The long-established *Antiquary* (*Map 2*, ☎ *225 2858, 72-78 St Stephen St*), popular with students and locals, offers folk music on Thursday night, when all comers are welcome to perform. The relaxed *Bailie Bar* (☎ *225 4673, 2 St Stephen St*) attracts a mixed clientele and serves good pub grub.

Bruntsfield

Bennet's Bar (*Map 6, ☎ 229 5143, 8 Leven St*), beside the King's Theatre, is a smokey Victorian pub whose chief feature is the beautiful, large curved mirrors with tiled surrounds. Decorated with golfing memorabilia, *Ye Olde Golf Tavern* (*Map 3, ☎ 229 5040, 30 Wright's Houses*) dates from 1486 and overlooks Bruntsfield Links. The popular *Auld Toll* (*Map 6, ☎ 229 1010, 39 Leven St*) is an old, delightfully unpretentious place serving real ales.

Leith

The down-to-earth *Port o'Leith* (☎ *554 3568, 58 Constitution St*) is a traditional, relaxed pub that's bucking Leith's upmarket trend. The refurbished *Burns Alehouse* (☎ *554 7515, 7 Bernard St*) is a friendly, family run place with a range of beers and other drinks. Two historic pubs serving real ales are the *Malt & Hops* (☎ *555 0083*), the

Beer drinkers will love the great selection of ales available in the Edinburgh pubs

oldest in Leith, and *King's Wark* (☎ *554 9260*); both are on The Shore near the bridge. See the Leith map for references.

CLUBS

Entry to Edinburgh's clubs costs from around £3 to £10 with most charging £5 or £6.

Old Town

The Old Town has Edinburgh's largest concentration of nightclubs. There are some interesting music/club venues in old vaults under the George IV and South Bridges. *The Vaults* (*Map 7, ☎ 558 9052, 15 Niddry St*), under South Bridge, has a variety of reliable club nights offering reggae, rap and R&B. On the same street, *Whistle Binkie's* (*Map 5, ☎ 557 5114*) has been around a long time and provides live music nightly till 3 am.

The *Venue Night Club* (*Map 5, ☎ 557 3073, 15 Calton Rd*) has live music and is well worth checking out. Its fortnightly *Disco Inferno* is a favourite session with dance music on three floors. It's open from 10 pm to 3 am and entry is £6.

It's a bit hard to know where to slot the *City Café* (*Map 7, ☎ 220 0125, 19 Blair St*). It's a seriously cool bar, but there are also meals and downstairs there's a dance floor, *City 2*, with different music depending on the night.

There are several clubs around the junction of Blair St and Cowgate where you can drink and dance to the wee small hours. *The Honeycomb* (*Map 7, ☎ 220 4381, 36-38A Blair St*) provides a varied range of music nights including house, garage, groove, disco and soul. Further west, *Subway* (*Map 6, ☎ 225 6766, Cowgate*) has different music themes each night. Next door, *Legends* (*Map 6, ☎ 225 8382*) has good live bands most nights; entry is £3 to £5. Offering a bit more variety, *The Kitchen* (*Map 7, ☎ 226 6550, 233 Cowgate*) puts on comedy shows as well as live bands and other performances.

New Town & West End

Below Chez Jules' restaurant in Frederick St, *Fingers Piano Bar* (☎ *225 3026*) dishes up a

ENTERTAINMENT

mix of rock and blues nightly untill 3 am. Every night at *Po Na Na* (☎ *226 2224, 43B Frederick St*), with its Arab bazaar décor, DJs play their music from funk to hip hop; there's a small dance floor and the club gets busy on weekends. Also in Frederick St, *Club 30* (☎ *220 1226*), for the over 25s, plays disco music from the 1970s, 80s and 90s.

Thursday night to Monday night from 9 pm to 1 am the *Catwalk* (☎ *225 5583, Broughton St*) puts on a musical blend of funk, garage and house.

In the West End, *CC Blooms* (☎ *556 9331, 23-24 Greenside Place*) is a gay and lesbian pub with a free club downstairs open from 11 pm to 3 am offering dance and house music. For those who like to start partying early, *Walkers* (☎ *476 7613, 12 Shandwick Place*) has a happy hour from 4 to 8 pm, free entry till 10.30 pm and DJs till 3 am.

THEATRE & MUSIC

Probably because of the frantic festival activity, Edinburgh has more than its fair share of theatres in relation to the size of its population.

The *Edinburgh Festival Theatre* (*Map 7*, ☎ *529 6000, 13-29 Nicolson St*) stages everything from ballet to the Chippendales. The *Royal Lyceum Theatre* (*Map 6*, ☎ *229 9697*), opposite Festival Square, hosts concerts, children's shows and ballet. Nearby, the architecturally impressive *Usher Hall* (*Map 6*, ☎ *228 1155*) puts on classical and popular concerts. Beside Usher Hall, *Traverse Theatre* (*Map 6*, ☎ *228 1404, Cambridge St*) is noted for its production of experimental drama.

The small *Netherbow Theatre* (*Map 5*, ☎ *556 9579, 43-45 High St*), on the Royal Mile, features modern drama, cabaret and children's story-telling. The program at slightly run-down *King's Theatre* (*Map 6*, ☎ *220 4349, 2 Leven St*), Bruntsfield, often features revivals. The restored *Playhouse Theatre* (*Map 5*, ☎ *557 2590, 18-22 Greenside Place*) in Leith Walk, stages musicals, dance shows and Christmas pantomimes.

Bedlam Theatre (*Map 6*, ☎ *225 9893, 2 Forrest Rd*) is at the southern end of George IV Bridge in a converted church. It's the home of the University Theatre Company made up of students from Edinburgh University.

Tickets can be purchased from Ticketline (☎ *220 4349*).

SCOTTISH EVENINGS

Several hotels offer an evening of eating, singing and dancing with a Scottish theme. The *Carlton Highland Hotel* (*Map 5*, ☎ *472 3000, North Bridge*) has a Hail Caledonia night for £35.50 which includes five courses, entertainment and a nip of whisky. The action kicks off at 7.30 pm and ends around 10.20 pm, depending on how much the audience gets into the swing of things.

Other hotels that have Scottish evenings are the *George Inter-Continental Hotel* (*Map 4*, ☎ *225 1251, 19-21 George St*) and *The King James* (☎ *556 0111, 107 Leith St*).

COMEDY

If you're in need of a laugh, *The Stand Comedy Club* (*Map 4*, ☎ *558 7272, 5 York Place*), around the corner from St Andrew Square, is one of the main venues for Edinburgh stand-up comedy. It often has well-known names and opens Wednesday to Sunday from 8 pm to 11 pm.

The *Gilded Balloon Studio* (*Map 7*, ☎ *226 6550, 233 Cowgate*) has international and emerging comedians performing from Friday night to Sunday night with doors opening at 8 pm.

CINEMA

Filmhouse (*Map 6*, ☎ *228 2688, 88 Lothian Rd*) is an excellent arthouse cinema which shows foreign, offbeat and current but less commercial films. Near Tollcross, the *Cameo Cinema* (*Map 6*, ☎ *228 4141, 38 Home St*) has late-night cult screenings as well as showing independent and arthouse films. Entry is £4.

For mainstream films there's the three-screen *ABC Cinema* (*Map 6*, ☎ *228 1638, 120 Lothian Rd*), or the *Dominion* (*Map 3*, ☎ *447 4771, 18 Newbattle Terrace*) south of Bruntsfield. In Newington, the *Odeon* (*Map 7*, ☎ *668 2101, 7 Clerk St*) has five screens and a bar.

SPECTATOR SPORTS

The Scots love their games, watch them with fierce, competitive dedication and identify closely with teams and individuals that compete both locally and internationally.

Football, also known as soccer to distinguish it from rugby football, is Scotland's largest spectator sport. The Scottish Football League is the main national competition and has a number of divisions. The best clubs form the Scottish Premier League. Edinburgh has two rival football teams playing in the Scottish Premier League: Heart of Midlothian (Hearts) and Hibernian (Hibs). Hearts' home ground is **Tynecastle Park** (*Map 3*, ☎ *337 6132*), south-west of the centre on Gorgie Rd. Hibs plays at **Easter Rd Park** (*Map 2*, ☎ *652 0630*), about 1¼ miles east of the centre, north of London Rd.

The domestic football season lasts from August to May and most matches are played at 3 pm on Saturday or 7.30 pm on Tuesday or Wednesday.

Rugby union football is administered by the Scottish Rugby Union based at **Murrayfield Stadium** (☎ *346 5000*), about 1½ miles west of the centre and south of Corstorphine Rd. International games are played here. Each year, starting in January, Scotland takes part in the Six Nations Rugby Union Championship. The most important fixture is the clash against England for the Calcutta Cup. At the club level, the season runs from September to May.

For golfing enthusiasts, the **Old Course** at St Andrews is 55 miles north of Edinburgh across the Firth of Forth (see the Excursions chapter). The Alfred Dunhill Cup, the world's most renowned international team tournament, takes place here in mid-October. The British Open Championship is also held here regularly.

Most other spectator sports, including athletics and cycling, are played at **Meadowbank Sports Centre** (☎ *661 5351, 139 London Rd*), Scotland's main sports arena, east of the centre.

Horse-racing enthusiasts need to head 6 miles east to **Musselburgh Racecourse** (☎ *665 2859*), Scotland's oldest racecourse, where meetings occur throughout the year. The dates of meetings are published in the STB's free twice-yearly brochure, *Events in Scotland*.

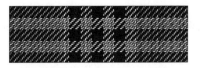

Shopping

WHAT TO BUY

Making things to sell to tourists is big business in Scotland, and almost every visitor attraction seems to have been redesigned to funnel you through the gift shop. Among the tourist kitsch are some good-value, high-quality goods.

Tartan, Tweed & Other Fabrics

Scottish textiles, particularly tartans, are popular and tartan travelling rugs or scarves are often worth buying. There are said to be over 2000 designs, some officially recognised as clan tartans. Many shops have a list and can tell you if your family belongs to a clan, but these days if you can pay for the cloth you can wear the tartan. There are some universal tartans, like the Flower of Scotland, that aren't connected with a clan.

For about £350 to £400, you can have a kilt made in your clan tartan, but this shouldn't be worn without a *sporran* (purse), which can cost from £40 for a plain version up to £1000 for an ornate silver dress sporran. Full kilts are traditionally worn only by men, while women wear kilted or tartan skirts.

There are mill shops in many parts of Scotland, but the best known textile manufacturing areas are the Borders and Central regions, particularly around Stirling and Perth. Scotland is also renowned for a rough woollen cloth known as tweed – Harris tweed is world famous. There are various places on this Hebridean island where you can watch your cloth being woven.

Sheepskin rugs and jackets are also popular.

Knitwear

Scottish knitwear can be great value and is sold throughout Scotland. Shetland is most closely associated with high-quality wool, and at knitwear factory shops you can buy genuine Shetland sweaters for as little as £11. The most sought-after sweaters bear the intricate Fair Isle pattern – the genuine article from this remote island costs at least £25.

Jewellery & Glassware

Silver brooches set with cairngorms (yellow or wine-coloured gems from the mountains of the same name) are popular. Jewellery decorated with Celtic designs featuring mythical creatures and intricate patterns is particularly attractive, although some pieces are actually made in Cornwall. Glassware, particularly Edinburgh crystal and Caithness glass, is another good souvenir.

Food & Drink

Sweet, butter-rich Scottish shortbread makes a good gift. The biggest manufacturer, Walkers, bakes such prodigious quantities of the stuff that the Speyside town of Aberlour smells of nothing else. Dark, fruity Dundee cake lasts well and is available in a tin, but is heavy to take by air. Heather honey can give you a reminder of Scotland when your visit is over.

If you haven't far to go, smoked salmon or

Tartan is everywhere!

any other smoked product (venison, mussels etc) are worth buying, but some countries don't allow you to import meat and fish.

You're better off buying duty-free souvenir bottles of Scotch at the airport rather than in high street shops, unless it's a rare brand. If you go on a distillery tour, you may be given £1 or so discount to buy a bottle there. Miniature bottles make good presents.

Books

Edinburgh has an interesting array of bookshops scattered around. A good local general bookshop with several locations is James Thin. Its main outlet (Map 7, ☎ 556 6743) is at 53-59 South Bridge St on the corner of Infirmary St, while the branch (Map 4, ☎ 225 4495) at 57 George St has a small café.

The national chain, Waterstone's (not to be confused with George Waterston shops which sell stationery and office supplies), has two well-stocked, well organised branches at either end of Princes St. One is at No 13 (☎ 556 3034) near the Royal British Hotel and the other is at No 128 (Map 4, ☎ 226 2666) and has a Starbucks café on the 1st floor.

There are quite a few second-hand bookshops. One of the biggest is McNaughtan's Bookshop (Map 2, ☎ 556 5897), downstairs at 3A Haddington Place on Leith Walk near the corner of Annandale St. It houses a huge range of second-hand and antiquarian books with many Scottish titles. It's closed on weekends. Alternatively, there's Second Edition (☎ 556 9403), 9 Howard Place on Inverleith Row near the Royal Botanic Garden; it's home to thousands of pre-loved books on just about every subject.

The government run Stationery Office Bookshop (Map 4, ☎ 228 4181), 71 Lothian Rd, as well as carrying some dry academic publications, contains an excellent selection of books and maps on Scotland.

If you're looking for something less mainstream, try Word Power (Map 7, ☎ 662 9112), 43 West Nicolson St, in Lauriston south of the Old Town. It's an alternative bookshop covering such issues as the environment, feminism, homosexuality and radical politics. West & Wilde (Map 4, ☎ 556 0079), 25A Dundas St (the northern extension of Hanover St) in the New Town, is Edinburgh's only gay and lesbian bookshop.

Bauermeister Booksellers (Map 6, ☎ 226 5561), 19 George IV Bridge, is a cavernous shop with a large, wide-ranging collection of titles.

WHERE TO SHOP
Old Town & Around

Royal Mile In the Old Town, the Royal Mile is the most tourist oriented shopping area, but, the kitsch notwithstanding, it does offer a good selection of tartans, tweeds, whiskies and crafts.

Hector Russell (☎ 558 1254), 137 High St, is a specialist kiltmaker; if you want one made, it'll cost from £345 and take up to six weeks. It also sells sporrans from £40 and a selection of Scottish gifts. John Morrison (☎ 225 8149), 461 Lawnmarket, supplies Scottish tweeds and tartans, and can give you an off the peg kilt for £190. The Woollen Mill (☎ 225 8023), 179 High St on the corner of Cockburn St, can sell you full evening wear for £599.

The Edinburgh Woollen Mill (☎ 225 1525), 453 Lawnmarket, sells reasonably priced woollen clothing, while Old Town Knitwear (☎ 556 2186), 125 Canongate, will handknit clothes to your design. For Fair Isle sweaters head to Canongate Jerseys (☎ 557 2976), 166 Canongate.

Two shops specialising in quality Scottish cashmere are The Cashmere Store (☎ 225 5178), 379 High St, which probably has the largest selection in Scotland; and Designs on Cashmere (☎ 556 6394), 53 High St, which has both traditional and modern styles.

Clan Bagpipes (☎ 225 2415), 13A James Court, Lawnmarket, makes bagpipes according to your clan name. Scottish Gems (☎ 557 5731), 24 High St, has one of Scotland's best selections of traditional gold and silver jewellery with Celtic and Pictish designs.

Royal Mile Whiskies (☎ 225 3383), 379 High St, and Cadenheads Whisky Shop (☎ 556 5864), 172 Canongate, offer a wide range of malt whiskies and miniatures. You can also purchase whiskies from the shop at the Scotch Whisky Heritage Centre (☎ 220 0441), Castle Hill.

Geoffrey (Tailor) Highland Crafts (☎ 557 0256), 57-59 High St near John Knox House, is a one-stop emporium selling tartan textiles, kilts, jewellery, crystal, whisky and gifts.

West Bow/Victoria St Steep, curving West Bow/Victoria St, between the George IV Bridge and Grassmarket, has lots of interesting specialist shops. Bacchus (☎ 225 6183), 95 West Bow, and Bow-Well (☎ 225 3335), 103 West Bow, are worth exploring for their antiques. Kinnells (☎ 220 1150), 36 Victoria St, lets you taste before you purchase any of its enormous variety of teas and coffees. Byzantium (Map 6, ☎ 225 1768), 9A Victoria St, a flea market, is a great place to buy all manner of merchandise, though the food buffet in the café upstairs is best avoided.

Elsewhere Along Bank St off Lawnmarket, Coda Music (Map 4, ☎ 622 7246) has a wide selection of CDs and tapes including a good selection of Scottish folk and traditional music. (It has another branch in the Waverley Market shopping centre.)

South-east of the Old Town in St Leonard's, Scayles Music (Map 7, ☎ 667 8341), 40-42 West Crosscauseway, sells, hires out and repairs musical instruments.

New Town & Around

Princes St, George St and the streets around them form Edinburgh's main shopping precinct.

Princes St Princes St has many of the standard British high street stores. It also has two large shopping centres: the sprawling, St James, just off its eastern end in Leith St, and the more upmarket Waverley Market, next to the train station. In Waver-

ley Market, you can buy hand-painted miniatures of famous Scottish locations at Scotland in Miniature (☎ 557 8291) or purchase a bottle or three of fine whisky at The Whisky Shop (☎ 556 5688).

On the corner of David St, holding its own against the chainstore onslaught is the elegant, baroque-style Jenners (Map 4, ☎ 225 2442), the world's oldest independent department store. Jenners opened for business in 1838 (though the current building dates from 1895) and sells a wide range of quality goods.

The Scotch House (Map 4, ☎ 556 1252), 39-41 Princes St, sells Scottish knitwear, tartans and gifts and upstairs on the 3rd floor it houses the Scottish Tartans Museum. At No 95 is a branch of Hector Russell (☎ 225 3315), the specialist kiltmaker. There are also two branches of the Edinburgh Woollen Mill; one at No 62 (☎ 225 466) the other at No 139 (☎ 226 3840).

Rose St Behind Princes St, narrow and partly pedestrianised Rose St is home to lots of small, speciality craft shops. Les Cadeaux (☎ 225 9120), 121 Rose St, is one of Edinburgh's leading stores selling china and crystal. Tiso's (☎ 225 9486), 115 Rose St, is an excellent, well-stocked outdoor equipment shop.

George St George St is the place to go to for high-quality, upmarket stores. A clothing outfitter specialising in Scottish tweeds is Aitken & Niven (☎ 225 1461), 79 George St. The long-established Hamilton & Inches (☎ 225 4898), at No 87, and Mappin & Webb (☎ 225 5502), at No 88, both stock expensive antique and modern silver and gold jewellery. James Allan (☎ 225 2261), at No 32, is a high-class shoe shop.

The venerable Justerini & Brooks (☎ 226 4202), 45 George St, has been purveying fine malts and wines since the mid-18th century.

Thistle & Queen Sts These streets are north of and parallel to George St. On Thistle St you will find Aldric Young

(☎ 226 4101), at No 49, a long running retailer of antiques and paintings. Stewart Christie & Co (☎ 225 6639), 69 Queen St, is a traditional Scottish tailor that has been operating here for more than 200 years.

Stockbridge North-west of the New Town, Stockbridge is worth strolling around for its charming boutiques and antique shops. Mon Trésor (☎ 220 6877), 35 St Stephen St, is full of antique treasures, and amongst the bric-a-brac at Reid & Reid (☎ 225 9660), at No 134, there are old prints, silverware and antiquarian books. More antiques can be found nearby at the chock-a-block Quadrant Antiques (☎ 226 7282), 39 Circus Lane, and at Dunedin Antiques (☎ 220 1574), 4 North-West Circus Place.

Leith Kinloch Anderson (☎ 555 1390), at the corner of Commercial and Dock Sts, has been kiltmaker to the royal family since 1868; it sells Highland dress and other traditional Scottish clothing.

Bruntsfield
In Bruntsfield, Kilberry Bagpipes (Map 6, ☎ 221 9925), 38 Lochrin Buildings, Gilmore Place, manufactures and sells bagpipes and their accessories. The best example of that other symbol of Scotland, the haggis, can be purchased from Macsween of Edinburgh (Map 3, ☎ 229 9141), 118 Bruntsfield Place.

Penicuik
In this town 10 miles south of the city, you can buy Edinburgh crystal directly from the manufacturer in its showroom at the Edinburgh Crystal Visitor Centre (☎ 01968-675128). See the Excursions chapter.

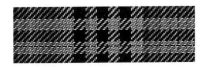

Excursions

HIGHLIGHTS

- St Andrews
- Jedburgh
- Melrose and the Eildon Hills
- Dryburgh Abbey
- Traquair House
- Pentland Hills for walking
- Linlithgow Palace
- Thirlestane Castle
- The east coast near Eyemouth for diving

When you need a break from the city, the beautiful countryside surrounding Edinburgh is nearby. And Scotland is small enough that few places are too far away for a day or weekend trip, much of it accessible by public transport. This chapter concentrates on sights closer to the city. For details of places farther afield, see Lonely Planet's *Scotland* guide.

The Lothians

This is the collective name given to the three counties surrounding Edinburgh.

EAST LOTHIAN & MIDLOTHIAN

East of Edinburgh, East Lothian stretches from Musselburgh along the coast to North Berwick and Dunbar. In the centre, attractive Haddington is worth visiting both in its own right and as a site from which to explore the hinterland; nearby Gifford is the gateway to the northern slopes of the Lammermuir Hills.

Midlothian, directly south of Edinburgh, is bordered in the south by the Moorfoot Hills and in the west by the Pentland Hills, both of which afford excellent walks and great views.

Trains from Edinburgh stop in Musselburgh, Prestonpans, North Berwick and Dunbar and there are regular buses to these and other towns and villages. For information on public transport call the East and Midlothian Traveline (☎ 0800-232323).

Musselburgh to North Berwick

The small town of **Musselburgh** sits on the River Esk about 6 miles east of Edinburgh. There's not much here except for the small but pretty, terraced **Inveresk Lodge Garden** (☎ 01721-722502; NTS) open April to September, Monday to Friday from 10 am to 4.30 pm, weekends from 2 to 5 pm; admission is £1. There's also a riverside path and good views from the harbour.

In **Prestonpans**, 3 miles north-east of Musselburgh, coal was mined for centuries and at the former colliery you can visit the somewhat bleak **Prestongrange Industrial Heritage Museum** (☎ 0131-653 2904), open daily April to October from 11 am to 4 pm; admission is free.

Past Port Seton the countryside opens up. At the mouth of the River Peffer 17 miles from Edinburgh, Georgian cottages stretch along the main street of the village of **Aberlady**. The mud flats and salt marshes here are the site of the **Aberlady Bay Nature Reserve**, where numerous seabirds nest and feed.

Next along the road, the fashionable resort town of **Gullane** is home to a number of golf courses including the prestigious Muirfield.

Two miles east lies **Dirleton Castle** (☎ 01620-850330; HS) surrounded by well-tended walled gardens. Originally built in the 13th century it was altered and added to over the next 300 years until destroyed by General Monck in 1650. Nevertheless, the ruins are still massive enough to dwarf Dirleton village. The castle opens April to September, daily from 9.30 to 6.30 pm; October to March, Monday to Saturday from 9.30 am to 4.30 pm, Sunday from 2 to 4.30 pm. Entry is £2.30/1.

North Berwick & Around
• **pop 4860 ☎ 01620**

An easy day trip from Edinburgh, North Berwick is an attractive Victorian seaside resort with long sandy beaches, three golf courses and a small harbour. The TIC (☎ 892197), on Quality St, opens Monday to Saturday from 9 am to 6 pm. The public toilets are very clean and even have flowers in vases beside the washbasins!

Things to See Off High St a short steep path climbs up **North Berwick Law** (184m,

613 feet), a ... nates the to... there are gre...

By the harb... **Kirk**, the 12th ... the first parish ...

Several sm... **Rock**, 3 miles ... prison for Cov... thousands of ga... ....er seabirds. To visit, you need to be a dedicated birdwatcher and not mind the smell of guano. Puffins nest in burrows on nearby **Craig Rock** and

112 Excursions – The L...

Fidra Island. Fr... runs trips out ... the rest of ... and Fid... abou... o...

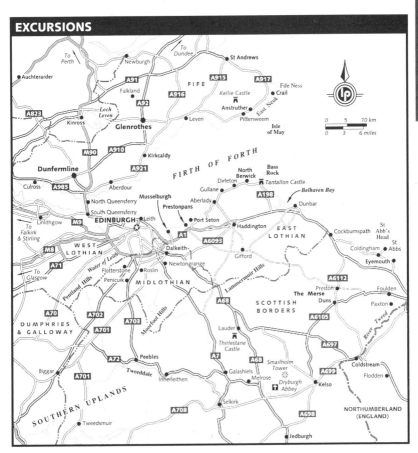

EXCURSIONS

To Perth • Auchterarder • Newburgh • St Andrews To Dundee

A91 FIFE A915 A917 Fife Ness
Falkland Kellie Castle • Crail
A92 A916 Anstruther East Neuk
A823 Loch Leven Pittenweem • Leven
Kinross **Glenrothes** Isle of May

0 5 10 km
0 3 6 miles

M90 A910 • Kirkcaldy FIRTH OF FORTH
Dunfermline A921 North Berwick Bass Rock
Culross A985 Aberdour Dirleton • ⚔ Tantallon Castle
North Queensferry Musselburgh Gullane • Belhaven Bay
South Queensferry Prestonpans Aberlady • A198 • Dunbar
To Falkirk & Stirling M9 **EDINBURGH** Leith • Port Seton
M8 WEST LOTHIAN A1 A6093 Haddington EAST LOTHIAN Cockburnspath St Abb's Head
To Glasgow A71 Water of Leith Dalkeith Coldingham • Abbs St Abbs
Flotterstone • Roslin Newtongrange Gifford Eyemouth •
Pentland Hills Penicuik **MIDLOTHIAN** Lammermuir Hills A6112
A68 The Merse Preston Foulden
A70 A702 A703 SCOTTISH BORDERS Duns Paxton •
DUMPRIES & GALLOWAY A701 Moorfoot Hills Lauder A6105 River Tweed
A72 Peebles A7 Thirlestane Castle A697
Biggar A701 Tweeddale Innerleithen Galashiels A68 Smailholm Tower Coldstream
SOUTHERN UPLANDS A708 Melrose Dryburgh Abbey Kelso A699 Flodden •
• Tweedsmuir Selkirk NORTHUMBERLAND (ENGLAND)
A698
• Jedburgh

Marr (☎ 01620-892838)
daily in summer, on weekends
the year. Trips around Bass Rock
a Island cost £4.60/2.60 and take
70 minutes. Fred will also drop you
on Bass Rock for two to three hours
then return and pick you up (£10).

Places to Stay North Berwick has lots of places to stay, though they can fill quickly on weekends when golfers are in town. *Palmerston* (☎ *892884, 115 High St*) is a central B&B with spacious *en suite* rooms from £18 and private parking. Popular *Craigview* (☎ *892529, 5 Beach Rd*) overlooks the harbour and Bass Rock and offers B&B from £16 per person.

Getting There & Away The bus stop outside the TIC is for Haddington (bus No 121) and Dunbar (bus No 120). The one at the other end of High St is for Edinburgh (bus Nos 124, 125 and X5). There are frequent ScotRail trains to Edinburgh (33 minutes).

The Witches of North Berwick

In 1590, the Church of St Andrews was the scene of a gathering of witches of both sexes, under the leadership of 'the Devel', who was in reality Francis Stuart, Earl of Bothwell. He tried by means of witchcraft to cause a storm in the Forth which was to drown James VI as he returned by sea from Denmark, accompanied by Princess Anne of Denmark, his wife.

The attempt failed and several witches were subsequently tortured, tried and executed. Bothwell was imprisoned but later escaped. The North Berwick events became widely known. James VI took a great interest in the trial and even wrote a book about witchcraft.

Nearly 200 years later, it's believed that Robbie Burns drew on stories about the witches when writing *Tam O'Shanter* and the *Old Kirk of Alloway*.

Tantallon Castle

Built around 1350, Tantallon Castle (☎ 01620 892727; HS), 3 miles east of North Berwick, was a fortress residence of the Douglas Earls of Angus (the 'Red Douglases'). On one side it's an almost sheer drop to the sea below, and fulmars nest in the cliffs. It opens April to September daily from 9.30 am to 6.30 pm; October to March, Monday to Saturday from 9.30 am to 4.30 pm, Sunday from 2 to 4.30 pm; admission is £2.30/1.

Dunbar
• pop 5800 ☎ 01368

Attractive Dunbar is a holiday resort and small fishing port on the east coast, 30 miles from Edinburgh. It was the site of two important battles, both resulting in Scottish losses. Edward I invaded in 1296 and General Monck defeated a larger Scots army in 1650, facilitating Cromwell's entry into Edinburgh. John Muir (1838-1914), pioneer conservationist and 'father' of the US national park system, was born here.

The TIC (☎ 863353), 143 High St, opens October to March, weekdays from 9 am to 5 pm, and from April to September it's open daily (extended hours in July and August).

Things to See & Do In the Middle Ages, Dunbar was an important Scottish fortress town, but little remains of **Dunbar Castle** except for some small ruins, inhabited by seabirds, by the harbour. From the castle a 2-mile cliff-top trail follows the coastline west to the sands of Belhaven Bay and **John Muir Country Park** (☎ 863886), where there's sea fishing and horse riding.

John Muir House (☎ 862595), 128 High St, the man's childhood home, has a small exhibition and audio-visual display on his life. It opens June to September, Monday to Saturday from 11 am to 1 pm, and 2 to 5 pm, Sunday from 2 to 5 pm; admission is free. The **Dunbar Town House Museum** (☎ 863734), also on High St, gives an introduction to local history and archaeology. It opens April to October, daily from 2 to 4.30 pm; admission is free.

Royal Mile Whisky shop, Royal Mile

How much is that whisky in the window?

Sporrans – a uniquely Scottish product

Beppe Caffe & Ristorante, Old Town

GLENN BEANLAND

Crail, one of East Neuk's prettiest villages

TOM SMALLMAN

Looking past Tantallon Castle to Bass Rock, East Lothian

GLENN BEANLAND

Crail's harbour is a good place to buy fresh lobster and shellfish

Turning right here leads you to the tall Gothic **Sir Walter Scott Monument** (15), then to Waverley Bridge from where sightseeing and other buses depart. Continuing east a little farther brings you back to the piazza above **Waverley Market** shopping centre and the TIC.

EDINBURGH CASTLE

Edinburgh Castle dominates the city centre, sitting astride the core of an extinct volcano, its three sides scoured almost vertical by glacial action. The castle is overrun with tourists, and although the views are great, you may decide it's more impressive from the outside looking in.

The castle (☎ 225 9846, HS) opens April to September, daily from 9.30 am to 6 pm (5 pm in winter). The admission price of £6/1.50 includes provision of an audio tape commentary.

History

There was a settlement here as early as 850 BC, although the first historical references date from the 6th century when the Northumbrian king, Edwin, rebuilt a fortress here as a defence against the Picts.

A favoured royal residence from the 11th to the 16th centuries, Edinburgh only became Scotland's capital at the end of the Middle Ages. The oldest surviving part of the castle is St Margaret's Chapel.

Although it looks impregnable, the castle often changed hands between the Scots and English. It last saw action in 1745, when Bonnie Prince Charlie's army tried but failed to breach its walls.

During the Wars of Independence (1174 to 1356), the English captured it several times. In 1313 it was demolished by the Scots as part of Robert the Bruce's scorched earth policies and wasn't rebuilt until 1371

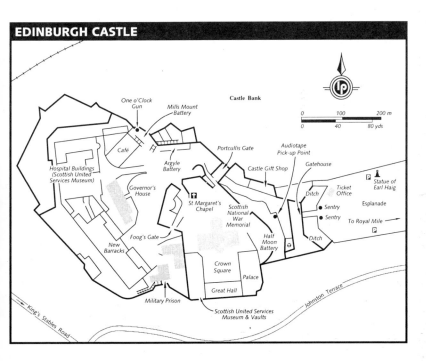

EDINBURGH CASTLE

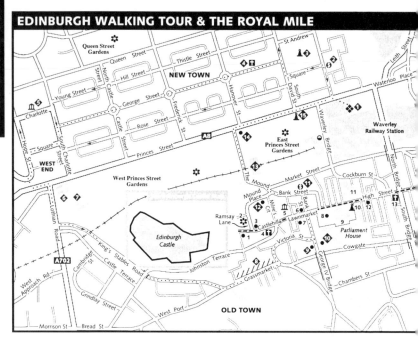

EDINBURGH WALKING TOUR & THE ROYAL MILE

by David II. Little of this work survives, however, because the castle was strengthened and renovated in the 16th, 17th and 18th centuries.

From the 16th century the royal family built more comfortable domestic accommodation at places like Holyrood, and the castle developed as a seat of government and military power. However, in 1566 Mary Queen of Scots underlined its continuing symbolic importance when she chose to give birth to her son in the castle. In 1573 much of it was destroyed when loyalists attempted to hold it for Mary; the oldest substantial work – including the Half Moon Battery and Portcullis Gate – survives from the subsequent rebuilding.

The castle was then taken in turn by the Covenanters (in 1640), Cromwell (in 1650) and King William and Queen Mary (the last true siege, in 1689). In 1715 and 1745 the

Stuarts tried unsuccessfully to recapture it. In the gaps between sieges more defences were added, and (apart from some 19th and 20th century additions) by the mid-18th century the castle looked much as it does today.

Partly thanks to Sir Walter Scott, in the 19th century the castle began to recover its importance as a Scottish symbol. Efforts were made to improve its appearance and to restore important buildings.

The Castle

Visitors enter from the **Esplanade**, a parade ground where the Military Tattoo takes place each August. The changing of the guard occurs on the hour, and on summer evenings a piper plays here. On the right as you enter the Esplanade is a statue of Field Marshall Earl Haig on horseback. Haig was commander-in-chief of British forces during WWI and was responsible for the

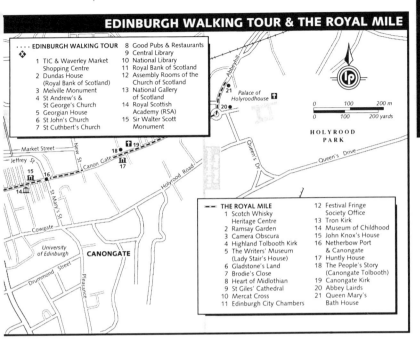

EDINBURGH WALKING TOUR & THE ROYAL MILE

···· **EDINBURGH WALKING TOUR**
1 TIC & Waverley Market Shopping Centre
2 Dundas House (Royal Bank of Scotland)
3 Melville Monument
4 St Andrew's & St George's Church
5 Georgian House
6 St John's Church
7 St Cuthbert's Church
8 Good Pubs & Restaurants
9 Central Library
10 National Library
11 Royal Bank of Scotland
12 Assembly Rooms of the Church of Scotland
13 National Gallery of Scotland
14 Royal Scottish Academy (RSA)
15 Sir Walter Scott Monument

–– **THE ROYAL MILE**
1 Scotch Whisky Heritage Centre
2 Ramsay Garden
3 Camera Obscura
4 Highland Tolbooth Kirk
5 The Writers' Museum (Lady Stair's House)
6 Gladstone's Land
7 Brodie's Close
8 Heart of Midlothian
9 St Giles' Cathedral
10 Mercat Cross
11 Edinburgh City Chambers
12 Festival Fringe Society Office
13 Tron Kirk
14 Museum of Childhood
15 John Knox's House
16 Netherbow Port & Canongate
17 Huntly House
18 The People's Story (Canongate Tolbooth)
19 Canongate Kirk
20 Abbey Lairds
21 Queen Mary's Bath House

policy of attrition in the trench warfare that killed thousands of troops. He later founded the Royal British Legion.

After entering the castle proper through the **Gatehouse** (added in the late 19th century) with its drawbridge, the pathway curves round to the right. It passes through the 16th century **Portcullis Gate**, whose upper section was added in 1886-87, before coming to **Argyle Battery** then **Mills Mount Battery**. There are good views to the north from both batteries and at Mills Mount the weekday 1 pm gun salute takes place.

Continuing round, you pass the **Governor's House** and the **New Barracks**, both dating from the 18th century, but which aren't open to the public. Behind the Governor's House, in the old hospital buildings, is an annexe of the Scottish United Services Museum. In the **Military Prison** (1842) you

can view the cells where recalcitrant soldiers were held in solitary confinement.

You enter the central defensive area through **Foog's Gate**. Here you'll find the small Norman **St Margaret's Chapel**, the oldest building in Edinburgh. It's a simple stone edifice that was probably built by David I or Alexander I in memory of their mother sometime around 1130. Following Cromwell's capture of the castle in 1650 it was used to store ammunition until Queen Victoria had it restored; it was rededicated in 1934.

On the eastern end of Crown Square is the **Palace** built between the 15th and 16th centuries. Among the royal apartments is the bedchamber where Mary Queen of Scots gave birth to her son James, who was to unite the crowns of Scotland and England. Another room is used to house the Scottish crown jewels, made up of sceptre,

The Stone of Destiny

Alleged to have accompanied the Scots in all their mythical journeyings, the original Stone of Destiny (the Fatal Stone) was a carved block of sandstone on which the Scottish monarchs placed their feet during the coronation.

Stolen by Edward I in 1296, this venerable talisman was incorporated into the Coronation Chair, used by English (and later British) monarchs, in London's Westminster Abbey. Apart from being taken to Gloucester during air raids in WWII, the Stone lay undisturbed for centuries.

On Christmas Eve 1950, however, a plucky band of Scottish students drove down from Glasgow, jemmied the door of Westminster Abbey and made off with the Stone. English officialdom was outraged. The border roads had roadblocks on them for the first time in 400 years, but while Scots living in London jeered the English police as they searched the Serpentine Lake and the River Thames, the Stone was smuggled back to Scotland.

King George VI was 'sorely troubled about the loss', but the students issued a petition affirming their loyalty to him, stating that they would give back the Stone as long as it could remain on Scottish soil. The authorities refused to negotiate and, three months after it was stolen, the Stone turned up on the altar of the ruined Abbey of Arbroath. It was here, in 1320, that the Arbroath Declaration had been signed, reaffirming the right of Scots to self-rule and independence from England. Before the public were aware that the Stone had even been found, it was back in London. No charges were brought and Ian Hamilton, the student who led this jolly caper, published his story in *The Taking of the Stone of Destiny*.

Many Scots, however, hold that the original Stone is safely hidden somewhere in Scotland, and that Edward I was fobbed off with a shoddy imitation. This is possibly true, for descriptions of the original state that it was decorated with carvings, not that it was a plain block of sandstone. Given that Scottish nationalism is running high, this powerful symbol of Scotland would surely have been brought out by now if it hadn't been quite so safely hidden.

Imitation or not, the Scottish Secretary and Conservative MP, Michael Forsyth, arranged for the return of the sandstone block to Edinburgh Castle, with much pomp and circumstance, in 1996. If it was an attempt to boost his flagging political standing, it failed dismally: Forsyth lost his seat in the House of Commons in the May 1997 general election.

---

sword and crown; with them now lies the Stone of Destiny (see boxed text).

Adjacent to the Palace is the **Great Hall**, built for James IV as a ceremonial hall and used as a meeting place for the Scottish Parliament until 1639. In former barracks opposite, the massive, sombre **Scottish National War Memorial** was added to the castle complex in the 1920s and is a memorial to the Scots dead of WWI.

At the western end of the square in the Queen Anne Building, the **Scottish United Services Museum** houses displays on the history of Scottish regiments as well as the air force and navy. From this end of the square you can descend into the dark, dank **Vaults**, a former prison for foreigners. One of its rooms contains **Mons Meg**, a huge 15th century siege cannon.

ROYAL MILE

Following a ridge that runs from Edinburgh Castle to the Palace of Holyroodhouse, the Royal Mile is one of the world's most fascinating streets. From the west end you can see beyond craggy Arthur's Seat and over the waters of the Firth of Forth, with tantalising glimpses of the Old and New Towns through the *closes* (entrances) and *wynds* (alleyways) on either side. Although there are tourists and shops stuffed with tacky Scottish souvenirs aplenty, the street still feels a real part of a thriving city. It's lined with extraordinary buildings, including multistoreyed *lands* (tenements) dating from the 15th century.

To see the numerous sites would take several days, but even with limited time, it's worth ducking through a *pend* (arched gateway) or close to explore the narrow wynds and courts beyond.

The map reference in brackets beside each item corresponds to the map on which the item is found, while the number beside it corresponds to the number in the key of the Edinburgh Walking Tour & The Royal Mile map.

Scotch Whisky Heritage Centre (Maps 1 & 6)

If you'd like to know how whisky is manufactured the Scotch Whisky Heritage Centre (☎ 220 0441), Castle Hill, offers a tour with several audiovisual presentations followed by a ride in a car past a tableau explaining the history of the 'water of life'. You can take the ride only (15 minutes) for £3.80/2, but it's not really worth it. It's better value to do the full tour or put the money toward the purchase of one (or more) of the hundreds of different brands of whisky sold in the shop. The centre opens daily from 10 am to 5.30 pm; the full experience including a tasting costs £4.95/2.50.

Ramsay Garden (Maps 2 & 6)

Constructed around the mid-18th century home of the poet Alan Ramsay, the attractive apartments here overlook The Esplanade and the small garden from which they get their name. They were designed in the 1890s by an early town planner, Patrick Geddes, in an attempt to revitalise the Old Town. They're now very expensive, very wonderful private apartments.

Camera Obscura (Maps 3 & 6)

Just beyond Ramsay Lane, the Camera Obscura (☎ 226 3709) offers great views over the city. The 'camera' itself is a curious device (originally dating from the 1850s, although improved in 1945) a bit like a periscope, which uses lenses and mirrors to throw a 'live' image onto a large interior bowl. The accompanying 'guided tour' is entertaining, and the whole exercise has a quirky charm. It's open Monday to Friday from 9.30 am to 6 pm, weekends from 10 am; admission is £3.85/1.95, family £11.50.

Highland Tolbooth Kirk (Maps 4 & 6)

With the tallest spire (71.7m, 239 feet) on one of Edinburgh's highest points, the Highland Tolbooth Kirk is an important feature of the skyline. It was built in the 1840s by James Graham and Augustus Pugin (architect of the London Houses of Parliament).

It gets its name from the Gaelic services that were held here for Edinburgh's Highland congregations (which now occur at Greyfriars Kirk). It's being refurbished and will eventually be the home of the Edinburgh Festival office.

Opposite the kirk are the **Assembly Rooms** of the Church of Scotland, which are the temporary home of the new Scottish Parliament.

The Writers' Museum (Maps 4 & 5)

The Writers' Museum (☎ 529 4901) is in Lady Stair's House, built in 1622, and contains manuscripts and memorabilia belonging to Robert Burns, Sir Walter Scott and Robert Louis Stevenson.

The static displays will only entertain enthusiasts of these writers but it's open Monday to Saturday from 10 am to 5 pm and, during the Edinburgh Festival, on Sunday from 2 to 5 pm; admission is free.

Gladstone's Land (Map 6)

Gladstone's Land (☎ 226 5856; NTS), 477 Lawnmarket, gives a fascinating glimpse of the Old Town's past. The house was built in about the mid-16th century and extended around 1617 by wealthy merchant Thomas

Gledstanes. Its comfortable interior contains fine painted ceilings, walls and beams and some splendid furniture from the 17th and 18th centuries. It's open April to October, Monday to Saturday from 10 am to 5 pm, Sunday from 2 to 5 pm; admission is £2.80/1.90.

Brodie's Close (Maps 6 & 7)

Brodie's Close is named after the father of the notorious William Brodie, a deacon and respected citizen by day, a burglar by night. William Brodie was the inspiration for Robert Louis Stevenson's *Dr Jekyll and Mr Hyde* and, some would say, a dramatic reflection of Edinburgh's darker undercurrents. He met his end on the gallows in 1788.

Parliament Square (Map 6)

Lawnmarket ends at the crossroads of Bank St and George IV Bridge; at the south-east corner, brass strips set in the road mark the site of the scaffold where public hangings took place until 1864. From there the Royal Mile continues as High St.

Parliament Square, largely filled by St Giles' Cathedral (see below), the High Kirk of St Giles, is on the north side. This was the heart of Edinburgh until the 18th century, and a cobblestone **Heart of Midlothian** (8) is set in the paving. Passers-by traditionally spit on it for luck. This was the site of the entrance to the Tolbooth, originally built to collect tolls, but subsequently a meeting place for parliament, the town council and the General Assembly of the Reformed Kirk, then law courts and, finally, a prison and place of execution.

The 19th century **Mercat Cross** (10) replaced the original 1365 cross and marks the spot where merchants and traders met to transact business and Royal Proclamations were read.

The square's southern side is flanked by **Parliament House**, the meeting place of the Scottish Parliament from 1639; its neoclassical façade was added in the early 19th century. After the Act of Union in 1707 the building became the centre for the Scottish legal system – the Court of Session and High Court – which retained their independence. The most interesting feature is **Parliament Hall**, where the parliament actually met, which is now used by lawyers and their clients as a meeting place.

St Giles' Cathedral (Maps 6 & 9)

There has been a church on this site since the 9th century. A Norman-style church was built in 1126, but this was burnt by the English in 1385; the only substantial remains are the central piers that support the tower. The present church was then built in stages, with the crown spire completed in 1495.

Inside, near the entrance is a life-size statue of John Knox, minister from 1559 to 1572; from here he preached his uncompromising Calvinist message and launched the Scottish Reformation. The new austerity this ushered in led to changes in the building's interior – decorations, stained glass, altars and the relics of St Giles were thrown into the Nor Loch.

The High Kirk of St Giles was at the heart of Edinburgh's struggle against episcopacy (the rule of the church by bishops). In 1637 when Charles I attempted to re-establish episcopacy and made the kirk a cathedral, he provoked a possibly apocryphal outburst by Jenny Geddes which, according to popular belief, led to the signing of the National Covenant at Greyfriars the following year. Jenny hurled a stool at the dean who was using the English prayer book (a symbol of episcopacy); a tablet marks the spot and a copy of the National Covenant is displayed on the wall.

One of the most interesting corners of the kirk is the Thistle Chapel built 1909-11 for the Knights of the Most Ancient & Most Noble Order of the Thistle. The carved Gothic-style stalls have canopies topped with the helms and arms of the 16 knights.

Entry to the kirk is free, but a £1 donation is requested.

Edinburgh City Chambers (Maps 5 & 11)

The City Chambers were originally built by John Adam (brother of Robert) in 1761 to replace the Mercat Cross and serve as a Royal Exchange. However, the merchants continued to prefer the street, and the building was taken over by the town council which has been using it since 1811.

Tron Kirk (Maps 5 & 13)

At the south-western corner of the intersection with South Bridge, Tron Kirk owes its name to a salt *tron* or public weighbridge that stood on the site. It was built in 1637 on top of Marlin's Wynd which has been excavated to reveal a cobbled street with cellars and shops on either side. Run by the Edinburgh Old Town Renewal Trust (☎ 225 8818), the church acts as a visitor centre for the Old Town. It's open early April to mid June, Thursday to Monday from 10 am to 5 pm, and mid June to early September daily from 10 am to 7 pm.

Museum of Childhood (Maps 5 & 14)

This museum (☎ 529 4142), 42 High St, attempts to cover the serious issues related to childhood – health, education, upbringing and so on – but more enjoyable is the enormous collection of toys, dolls, games and books which fascinate children and, for adults, brings childhood memories back. It includes a video history of the various Gerry Anderson puppet TV series, like *Thunderbirds*, made in the 1960s. The museum opens Monday to Saturday from 10 am to 5 pm, and, during the Edinburgh Festival only, Sunday from 2 to 5 pm; admission is free.

John Knox's House (Maps 5 & 15)

Perhaps the most extraordinary building on the Royal Mile, John Knox's House (☎ 556 9579), 43-45 High St, dates from around 1490. The outside staircase, overhanging upper floors and crow-stepped gables are all typical of a 15th century town house. John Knox is thought to have occupied the 2nd floor from 1561 to 1572. The labyrinthine interior has an interesting display on his life including a recording of his interview with Mary Queen of Scots, whose mother was a target of his diatribe *First Blast of the Trumpet Against the Monstrous Regiment of Women*. It's open Monday to Saturday, from 10 am to 4.30 pm; admission is £1.95/75p.

Netherbow Port & Canongate (Maps 5 & 16)

High St ends at the intersection with St Mary's and Jeffrey Sts, where the city's eastern gate, Netherbow Port, part of the Flodden Wall, once stood. Though it no longer exists, it's commemorated by brass strips set in the road.

The next stretch of the Mile, Canongate, takes its name from the canons (priests) of Holyrood Abbey. From the 16th century, it was home to aristocrats attracted to the Palace of Holyroodhouse. Originally governed by the canons, it remained an independent burgh until 1856.

Huntly House (Maps 5 & 17)

Huntly House, built in 1570, is a good example of the luxurious accommodation that aristocrats built for themselves along Canongate; the projecting upper floors of plastered timber are typical of the time. It now contains a local history museum (☎ 529 4143) with some interesting displays, including a copy of the National Covenant of 1638 signed in protest against Charles I's attempt to re-establish episcopacy and the English prayer book. It opens Monday to Saturday, from 10 am to 5 pm, and, during the Edinburgh Festival only, Sunday from 2 to 5 pm; admission is free.

The People's Story (Maps 5 & 18)

Canongate Tolbooth, with its picturesque turrets and projecting clock, is an interesting example of 16th century architecture. Built in 1591, it served successively as a collection point for tolls (taxes), a council house, a courtroom and a jail. It now houses a fascinating museum (☎ 331 5545) telling the story of the life, work and pastimes of ordinary Edinburgh folk from the 18th century to the present day. It opens Monday to Saturday, from 10 am to 5 pm, and, during the Edinburgh Festival only, Sunday from 2 to 5 pm; admission is free.

Canongate Kirk (Maps 5 & 19)

Attractive Canongate Kirk was built in 1688. In 1745 Prince Charles Stuart (Bonnie Prince Charlie, the Young Pretender) used it to hold prisoners taken at the Battle of Prestonpans. The churchyard has good views and several famous people are buried there. These include the economist Adam Smith, author of *The Wealth of Nations*, who lived nearby in Panmure Close, and the 18th century poet Robert Fergusson.

Abbey Lairds (Maps 5 & 20)

On the north side of Abbey Strand, flanking the entrance to the Palace of Holyroodhouse, the Abbey Lairds provided sanctuary for aristocratic debtors from 1128 to 1880. It was one of a number of hovels, most of which were pulled down when Queen Victoria occupied the palace. The debtors or 'lairds' could avoid prison as long as they remained within the palace and Holyrood Park, although they were allowed out on Sunday.

Queen Mary's Bath House (Maps 5 & 21)

According to legend, Mary Queen of Scots used to bathe in white wine and goat's milk in this small, 16th century turreted lodge – but only twice a year! More likely, it was a dovecote or summer house.

PALACE OF HOLYROODHOUSE & HOLYROOD ABBEY (MAP 5)

The Palace of Holyroodhouse developed from a guesthouse attached to medieval Holyrood Abbey. It was a royal residence at various times from the 16th century, and is still the Queen's official residence in Scotland, so access is very restricted. You're only allowed to view a few apartments, walk around part of the grounds and visit the abbey ruins.

The abbey was founded by David I in 1128, and was probably named after a fragment of the Cross (*rood* is an old word for cross) said to have belonged to his mother St Margaret. As it lay outside the city walls it was particularly vulnerable to English attacks, but the church was always rebuilt and survived as Canongate parish church until it collapsed in 1768. Most of the surviving ruins date from the 12th and 13th centuries, although a doorway in the far south-eastern corner has survived from the original Norman church.

King James IV extended the abbey guesthouse in 1501 to create more comfortable living quarters than were possible in bleak and windy Edinburgh Castle; the oldest surviving section of the building, the north-west tower, was built in 1529 as a royal apartment. Mary Queen of Scots spent 16 eventful years living in the tower. During this time she married Darnley (in the abbey) and Bothwell (in what is now the Picture Gallery), and this is where she debated with John Knox and witnessed the murder of her secretary Rizzio.

Although Holyrood was never again a permanent royal residence after Mary's son James VI departed for London, it was further extended during Charles II's reign.

Although you're carefully shepherded through a limited part of the palace, there's a certain fascination to following in Mary's footsteps and seeing the room where Rizzio was cut down.

Opening hours are normally April to October, daily from 9.30 am to 5.15 pm; November to March, daily from 9.30 am to 3.45 pm. Entry is £5.30/2.60. However, the complex is sometimes closed for state functions or when the Queen is in residence, usually in mid-May, and mid-June to around early July; phone ☎ 556 7371 to check.

Close to Holyroodhouse construction is under way for the new purpose-built **Scottish Parliament** and the **Dynamic Earth** exhibition presenting the geological story of the planet.

HOLYROOD PARK & ARTHUR'S SEAT

In Holyrood Park, Edinburgh is blessed in having a real wilderness on its doorstep. The former hunting grounds of Scottish monarchs, it covers 650 acres of varied landscape, including hills, moorland, lochs and fields. The highest point is the 251m (823 feet) extinct volcano, Arthur's Seat.

The park can be circumnavigated along Queen's Drive by car or bike, but it's closed to motorised traffic on Sunday. There are several excellent walks. Opposite the palace's southern gate, a footpath named Radical Road runs up immediately along the base of the Salisbury Craigs, but is partly blocked off because of danger from falling rocks. A fairly easy half-hour walk leads from Dunsapie Loch to the summit of Arthur's Seat. There are magnificent views of the city to the Pentland Hills and across the Firth of Forth.

To the south, **Duddingston Loch** is a natural lake and a bird sanctuary.

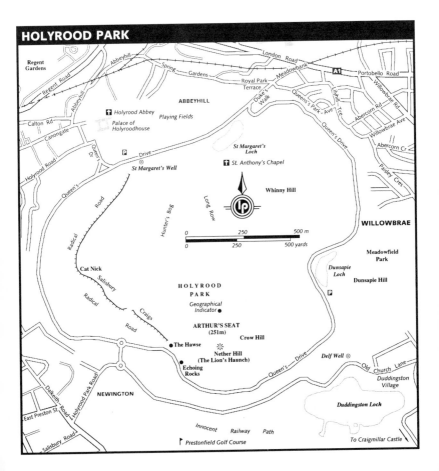

Arthur's Seat

Arthur's Seat, the eroded stump of a lava flow that erupted around 325 million years ago, sits in Holyrood Park, the ancient hunting ground of Scottish kings. It forms part of a volcano that includes Calton Hill and Castle Rock.

It's not certain where the name derives from. There's no evidence to connect it with the King Arthur of Camelot and round table fame. It may have been named after the 6th century Arthur of Strathclyde. Alternatively, it may come from the Gaelic *Ard-na-Saighead*, which means 'Height of Arrows'.

SOUTH OF THE ROYAL MILE

The area south of the Royal Mile includes some of the oldest, most crowded and atmospheric parts of the Old Town at the foot of Castle Rock and the Mile. Around the university and the beautiful Meadow Park it opens up to run into sturdy Victorian suburbs like Bruntsfield, Marchmont and Grange.

One of the city's main traffic arteries (carrying traffic to/from the A68 and A7), with many shops, restaurants and guesthouses, runs down the eastern side – beginning as North Bridge and becoming successively South Bridge, Nicolson St, Clerk St, Newington Rd, Minto St, Mayfield Gardens and Craigmillar Park.

Grassmarket

Grassmarket is one of Edinburgh's nightlife centres, with numerous restaurants and pubs, including the White Hart Inn which was patronised by Robert Burns. An open area hedged by tall tenements and dominated by the looming castle, it can be approached from George IV Bridge, via Victoria St, an unusual two-tiered street clinging to the ridge below the Royal Mile, with some excellent shops.

The site of a market from at least 1477 to the start of the 20th century, Grassmarket was always a focal point for the Old Town. This was the main place for executions and over 100 hanged Covenanters are commemorated with a cross at the east end. The notorious murderers Burke and Hare operated from a now vanished close off the west end. In around 1827 they enticed at least 18 victims here, suffocated them and sold the bodies to Edinburgh's medical schools.

Leading off from the south-east corner, Candlemaker Row climbs back up to the George IV Bridge and Chambers St with the Royal Museum of Scotland and the University of Edinburgh's Old College.

Cowgate

Cowgate, which runs off the eastern end of Grassmarket parallel to the Royal Mile, is less a canyon than a bleak tunnel, thanks to the bridges that were built above it. Once a fashionable place to live, it now has a couple of Fringe Festival venues and one or two good pubs.

Royal Museum of Scotland

The Royal Museum of Scotland (☎ 225 7534), Chambers St, is a Victorian building whose grey, solid exterior contrasts with its large, bright, galleried entrance hall of slim wrought-iron columns and glass roof. The museum houses an eclectic, comprehensive series of exhibitions. These range from the natural world (evolution, mammals, geology, fossils etc) to scientific and industrial technological development, with one section featuring the world's oldest steam locomotive, *Wylam Dilly* (1813) and to the decorative arts of ancient Egypt, Islam, China, Japan, Korea and the west.

The adjacent **Museum of Scotland**, opened in 1998, houses archaeological artefacts from the old Museum of Antiquities. It shows the history of Scotland in chronological order starting with the country's earliest history in the basement.

The museums open Monday to Saturday from 10 am to 5 pm (to 8 pm Tuesday), and

Sunday from noon to 5 pm. Entry is £3 (free on Tuesday from 5 to 8 pm), children free.

University of Edinburgh

The University of Edinburgh is one of Britain's oldest, biggest and best universities: founded in 1583, it now has around 17,000 undergraduates. The students make a major contribution to the lively atmosphere of Grassmarket, Cowgate, and the nearby restaurants and pubs. The university sprawls for some distance, but the centre is the **Old College** (also called Old Quad), at the junction of South Bridge and Chambers St, a Robert Adam masterpiece designed in 1789, but not completed till 1834.

Inside the Old College is the **Talbot Rice Art Gallery** (Map 7, ☎ 650 2210) which houses a permanent, small collection of old masters, plus regular exhibitions of new work.

Greyfriars Kirk & Kirkyard (Map 6)

At the bottom of a stone canyon made up of tenements, churches, volcanic cliffs and the castle, Greyfriars Kirkyard is one of Edinburgh's most evocative spots – a peaceful oasis dotted with memorials and surrounded by Edinburgh's dramatic skyline.

The kirk was built on the site of a Franciscan friary and opened for worship on Christmas Day 1620. In 1638, the National Covenant was signed inside near the pulpit. The covenant rejected Charles I's attempts to reintroduce episcopacy and a new English prayer book, and affirmed the independence of the Scottish church. Many who signed were later executed in Grassmarket and, in 1679, 1200 Covenanters were held prisoner in terrible conditions in an enclosure in the yard. There's a small exhibition inside.

Tour groups, however, come to pay homage to a tiny statue of Greyfriars Bobby (Map 6) in front of the nearby pub. Bobby was a Skye terrier who maintained a vigil over the grave of his master, an Edinburgh police officer, from 1858 to 1872. The story was immortalised (and distorted) in a novel by Eleanor Atkinson in 1912 and later

turned into a film. In the kirk you can buy *Greyfriars Bobby – The Real Story at Last* (£3.50), Forbes Macgregor's debunking of some of the myths. Bobby's grave is just inside the entrance to the kirkyard.

CALTON HILL (MAP 5)

Calton Hill, at the east end of Princes St, is another distinctive component of Edinburgh's skyline, 100m (333 feet) high and scattered with grandiose memorials mostly dating from the first half of the 19th century. Here you get one of the best views of Edinburgh, taking in the entire panorama – the castle, Holyrood, Arthur's Seat, the Firth of Forth, the New Town and Princes St.

Approaching from Waterloo Place, you pass the imposing **Royal High School**, Regent Rd, dating from 1829 and modelled on the Temple of Theseus in Athens. Former pupils include Robert Adam, Alexander Graham Bell and Sir Walter Scott. Now called St Andrew's House, it was at one time cited as a potential home for the new Scottish parliament, and houses part of the Scottish Office. To the east, on the other side of Regent Rd, is the **Burns Monument** (1830), a Greek-style memorial to Robert Burns. It was designed by Thomas Hamilton, another former pupil of the school.

The largest structure is the **National Monument**, an over-ambitious attempt to replicate the Parthenon, in honour of Scotland's dead in the Napoleonic Wars. Construction began in 1822, but funds ran dry when only 12 columns were complete.

The design of the **City Observatory** (1818) was based on the Greek Temple of the Winds. Here you'll find the **Edinburgh Experience** (☎ 556 4365), a 20 minute, 3-D audio-visual portrayal of Edinburgh's history. It's open April to October, daily from 10 am to 5 pm; admission is £2/1.20.

Looking a bit like an upturned telescope, the **Nelson Monument** was built to commemorate Nelson's victory at Trafalgar. It's open (for great views) April to September, Monday from 1 to 6 pm, Tuesday to Saturday from 10 am to 6 pm; October to March,

Monday to Saturday from 10 am to 3 pm; admission is £2.

There's also the small, circular **Monument to Dugald Stewart** (1753-1828), an obscure professor of philosophy.

NEW TOWN

The New Town, dating from the 18th century, lies north of the Old Town, separated from it by Princes St Gardens and occupying a ridge that runs below, but parallel to, the Royal Mile. It's in complete contrast to the chaotic tangle of streets and buildings that evolved in the Old Town, and typifies the values of the Scottish Enlightenment.

Despite being confined behind city walls, the Old Town was periodically sacked by the English or torn by civil wars and disputes. The overcrowding and numerous domestic chimneys gave it its nickname, Auld Reekie (Old Smokey). So when the Act of Union in 1707 brought the prospect of long-term stability, aristocrats were keen to find healthier, more spacious surroundings. Cowgate was bridged to open up the south, Nor Loch at the northern foot of Castle Rock was drained and the North Bridge constructed.

In 1767, 23-year-old James Craig won a competition to design a New Town. His plan was brilliant in its simplicity. George St followed the line of the ridge between Charlotte and St Andrew Squares. Building was restricted to one side of Princes St and Queen St only, so the town opened onto the Firth of Forth to the north, and to the castle and Old Town to the south.

The New Town continued to sprout squares, circuses, parks and terraces, and some of its finest neoclassical architecture was designed by Robert Adam. Today, the New Town is the world's most complete and unspoilt example of Georgian town planning and architecture.

Princes St

Princes St was originally envisaged as the back of the New Town, as it was literally and figuratively turning away from its Jacobite past. However, the transport links and stunning outlook soon led to its development as Edinburgh's principal thoroughfare.

The main train station at the east end is now overshadowed by the uninspiring **Waverley Market** (Map 5) shopping centre. The entrance to the TIC is via the street level piazza which is frequently used by buskers and other street performers.

The street's north side is lined with standard High St shops, and few 18th century buildings survive. One exception is the beautiful **Register House** (1788) (Map 5), designed by Robert Adam, at the eastern end of Princes St, with the statue of the Duke of Wellington on horseback in front. It's home to the Scottish Record Office.

Back on the south side, about halfway along, the massive Gothic spire of the **Sir Walter Scott Monument** (Map 4), built by public subscription after his death in 1832, testifies to a popularity largely inspired by his role in rebuilding pride in Scottish identity. At the time of research it was closed for refurbishment (costing about £2 million), but when it reopens you'll be able to climb the 287 steps to the top.

Behind the monument are the **Princes St Gardens** (Map 4) a public park which stretch east west from Waverley Bridge to Lothian Rd, and up the hillside to the castle. The Princes St Gardens are cut by **The Mound** (Map 4), a pile of earth dumped during the construction of the New Town to provide it with a road link to Old Town. It was completed in 1830. The Royal Scottish Academy and the National Gallery of Scotland are also here (see later).

St John's Church (Map 4), at the west end of Princes St on the corner of Lothian Rd, stands above some interesting shops and is worth visiting for its fine Gothic Revival interior. It overlooks **St Cuthbert's Church** (Map 4) below, off Lothian Rd, which has a watch tower in the graveyard – a reminder of the Burke and Hare days when graves had to be guarded against robbers. Inside are ornate furnishings and many murals.

Royal Scottish Academy (RSA) (Map 4)

The RSA (☎ 225 6671), fronting Princes St, was designed by William Playfair and built in Grecian style in 1826, with its fluted Doric columns added later. It contains artwork by academy members and hosts temporary exhibitions throughout the year. It's open Monday to Saturday from 10 am to 5 pm, Sunday from 2 to 5 pm; admission is free (although there are charges for some exhibitions).

National Gallery of Scotland (Map 4)

Also designed by William Playfair, the National Gallery (☎ 556 8921) behind the RSA at the foot of The Mound, is an imposing classical building dating from the 1850s. It houses an important collection of European art from the 15th century Renaissance to 19th century postimpressionism. There are paintings by Verrocchio (Leonardo da Vinci's teacher), Tintoretto, Titian, Holbein, Rubens, van Dyck, Vermeer, El Greco, Poussin, Rembrandt, Gainsborough, Turner, Constable, Monet, Pissaro, Gauguin and Cezanne.

The USA is also represented by the works of Frederick Church, John Singer Sargent and Benjamin West. The section specifically on Scottish art, in the basement, includes portraits by Allan Ramsay and Sir Henry Raeburn, rural scenes by Sir David Wilkie and impressionistic landscapes by William MacTaggart.

Antonio Canova's statue of the Three Graces (room X) is owned jointly with London's Victoria & Albert Museum. In Greek mythology the Three Graces – Aglaia, Euphrosyne and Thalia – daughters of Zeus and Euryonome, embodied beauty, gracefulness and youth.

The gallery opens Monday to Saturday from 10 am to 5 pm, Sunday from 2 to 5 pm; admission is free.

St Andrew Square & George St (Map 4)

Dominated by the fluted Doric column of the Melville Monument, St Andrew Square isn't particularly architecturally distinguished (partly thanks to the bus station at the northeast corner). On the eastern side, however, is the impressive Palladian-style **Dundas House** which has a spectacular dome, best seen from the interior banking hall, and frieze. It's the head office of the Royal Bank of Scotland, which has been there since 1825.

George St, parallel to Princes St and connecting St Andrew Square with Charlotte Square, was originally envisaged as the main thoroughfare of the residential New Town. It's now Scotland's Wall St, home to highly successful Scottish financial institutions which control billions of pounds. **St Andrew & St George Church**, built in 1784, boasts a wonderful oval plaster ceiling, and was where the Church of Scotland split in two in 1843.

Charlotte Square (Map 4)

At the western end of George St, Charlotte Square, designed in 1791 by Robert Adam shortly before his death, is regarded as the architectural jewel of the New Town. On Hope St, the west side of Charlotte Square, St George's Church (1811) is now **West Register House**, an annexe to Register House in Princes St. It houses part of Scotland's official records which appear in occasional exhibitions in the entrance hall.

The north side of Charlotte Square is a Robert Adam's masterpiece, and one of the finest examples of Georgian architecture anywhere. **Bute House**, at No 6, is the office of the Secretary of State for Scotland. Next door at No 7, the **Georgian House** (☎ 225 2160; NTS), has been beautifully restored and refurnished to show (albeit in idealised form) how Edinburgh's wealthy elite lived at the end of the 18th century. The walls are decorated with paintings by Allan Ramsay, Henry Raeburn and Sir Joshua Reynolds. A 35 minute video brings it all to life rather well. It's open April to October, Monday to Saturday from 10 am to 5 pm, Sunday from 2 to 5 pm; admission is £4.20/2.80, family £11.20.

Scottish National Portrait Gallery (Map 4)

The gallery (☎ 556 8921), at the junction of St Andrew and Queen Sts, is in a large, red sandstone, Italian-Gothic building dating from 1882. It records Scottish history through portraits and sculptures. Although the subjects are probably the main source of interest, some portraits are also fine paintings.

The entrance hall is decorated with a frieze showing the chief protagonists in Scottish history and the balcony with frescoes of important moments in Scottish history painted by William Hole in 1897. The collection's subjects range from the kings, queens and nobles of earlier times to modern-day Scots from various walks of life.

There's a good café (see the Places to Eat chapter). The gallery opens Monday to Saturday, from 10 am to 5 pm, Sunday from 2 to 5 pm; admission is free.

WEST END

The last part to be built, the West End is an extension of the New Town. Huge **St Mary's Episcopal Cathedral** (Map 3), Palmerston Place, built in the 1870s, was Sir George Gilbert Scott's last major work.

If you follow Palmerston Place north over the Water of Leith, you come to **Dean Village** ('dean' means deep valley), an odd corner of Edinburgh. Once a milling community, it has been restored and taken over by yuppies. A pleasant walk begins by the Water of Leith at Belford Bridge. The footpath takes you up onto Dean Path, then onto Dean Bridge, from where you can look down on the village. You can continue on the south bank of the Leith, north-east through Stockbridge, then detour to the Royal Botanic Garden.

Scottish National Gallery of Modern Art (Map 2)

West of Dean Village, the Scottish National Gallery of Modern Art (☎ 556 8921), off Belford Rd, repays the effort of getting there (walk from Belford Bridge or take bus No 13 from George St). It's in an impressive classical Greek-style building that's surrounded by a sculpture park, which features work by Henry Moore and Barbara Hepworth among others.

Inside, the collection concentrates on 20th century art, with various European art movements represented by the likes of Matisse, Picasso, Kirchner, Magritte, Miro, Mondrian and Giacometti. American and English artists are also represented, but most space is given to Scottish painters – from the Scottish colourists early in the 20th century to contemporary artists. The gallery is small enough not to overwhelm and opens Monday to Saturday from 10 am to 5 pm, Sunday from 2 to 5 pm; admission is free.

NORTH OF THE NEW TOWN

The New Town's Georgian architecture extends north to Stockbridge and the Water of Leith, a rewarding area to explore since it's well off the tourist trail. **Stockbridge** is a trendy area with its own distinct identity, some interesting shops, and a good choice of pubs and restaurants. The painter, Sir Henry Raeburn, was born in Stockbridge, and he helped develop part of the area, most notably **Ann St**, one of the most exclusive addresses in Edinburgh.

Just north of Stockbridge is the lovely **Royal Botanic Garden** (Map 2, ☎ 552 7171) on Inverleith Row. It's worth visiting for the different perspective you get on the Edinburgh skyline from the Terrace Café. The garden opens daily November to January from 10 am to 4 pm; February and October to 5 pm; March and September to 6 pm; April to August to 7 pm; admission is free. Bus Nos 8, 19, 23, 27 and 37 will get you there.

GREATER EDINBURGH

Outside the centre there are some worthwhile attractions in the suburbs and beyond.

Craigmillar Castle

Edinburgh's suburbs are beginning to surround the castle, and the approach road, Craigmillar Castle Rd, is strewn with litter. Nevertheless, massive Craigmillar Castle (☎ 244 3101; HS), about 2½ miles south of the city centre off the A68 to Dalkeith, is still impressive.

Dating from the 15th century, the tower house rises above two sets of walls that enclose an area of 1½ acres. Mary Queen of Scots took refuge here after the murder of Rizzio; it was here too that plans to murder her husband Darnley were laid. Look for

Art Galleries

You shouldn't miss the National Gallery of Scotland, the Royal Scottish Academy (RSA), the Scottish National Portrait Gallery or the Scottish National Gallery of Modern Art. But there are also many other smaller galleries.

The Edinburgh Gallery Guide is a free monthly booklet available around town containing an index of current exhibitions and venues. *The List* magazine and *The Scotsman* also provide a list of what's on. You can find out more at the web site www.scottish-gallery.co.uk.

Some of the galleries are:

Calton Gallery (Map 5)
(☎ 556 1010), 10 Royal Terrace, displays paintings, watercolours and sculpture by British and European artists from 1750 to 1940; open Monday to Friday from 10 am to 6 pm, Saturday from 10 am to 1 pm.
City Art Centre (Map 5)
(☎ 529 3993), 2 Market St, the largest of the smaller galleries, it comprises six floors of exhibitions with a variety of themes, including an extensive collection of Scottish art; open Monday to Saturday from 10 am to 5.30 pm, Sunday from noon to 5 pm.
Collective Gallery (Map 4)
(☎ 220 1260), 22-24 Cockburn St, an artist-run gallery with exhibitions by contemporary, innovative Scottish and other artists; open Tuesday to Saturday from 11 am to 5.30 pm.
Edinburgh Printmakers' Workshop & Gallery (Map 5)
(☎ 557 2479), 23 Union St off Leith Walk; workshops and courses on the ground floor, exhibitions of lithographs, screenprints etc by local artists on the 1st floor; open Tuesday to Saturday from 10 am to 6 pm.
Fruitmarket Gallery (Map 5)
(☎ 225 2383), 29 Market St, showcases contemporary Scottish and international artists; open Tuesday to Saturday from 10.30 am to 5.30 pm, Sunday from noon to 5 pm.
The Leith Gallery
(☎ 553 5255), 65 The Shore, has exhibitions on young Scottish artists; open Tuesday to Friday from 11 am to 6 pm, Saturday from 11 am to 4 pm.
Portfolio Gallery (Map 6)
(☎ 220 1911), 43 Candlemaker Row, a photographic gallery with the emphasis on local and Scottish themes; open Tuesday to Saturday from noon to 5.30 pm.
The Scottish Gallery (Map 4)
(☎ 558 1200), 16 Dundas St (the northern extension of Hanover St), has exhibitions on both contemporary artists and past masters, including crafts as well as paintings; open Monday to Friday from 10 am to 6 pm, Saturday from 10 am to 4 pm.
Stills Gallery (Map 4)
(☎ 225 9876), 23 Cockburn St, refurbished photographic gallery; open Tuesday to Saturday from 11 am to 5 pm.

the prison cell complete with built-in sanitation, something some 'modern' British prisons only finally managed in 1996.

It's open daily April to September from 9.30 am to 6.30 pm; October to March, Monday to Saturday from 9.30 am to 4.30 pm, and Sunday from 2 to 4.30 pm; admission is £1.80/75p. Bus Nos 14, 21, C3 and C33 pass by.

Royal Observatory (Map 3)

Directly south of the centre on Blackford Hill, the observatory (☎ 668 8100) was moved here from Calton Hill in 1896. In the visitor centre there's a multimedia gallery with computers and CD ROMS on astronomy and there are terrific views of Edinburgh from the rooftop. It's open Monday to Saturday from 10 am to 5 pm, Sunday from noon to 5 pm. Entry costs £2.50/1.50. Take bus No 40 or 41 from the Mound to Blackford Ave.

Leith

Leith is and was Edinburgh's main port, although it remained an independent burgh until the 1920s. It's still among Britain's busiest ports, but in the 1960s and 70s it fell into decay. Since the 1980s a revival has been taking place and the area is now noted for its interesting eateries and pubs. It's a popular stopping-off point for cruise ships, and the former royal yacht *Britannia* is permanently docked here.

Parts are still rough, but it's a distinctive corner of Edinburgh and the prettiest area is around The Shore. From here a footpath follows the Water of Leith south-west through Edinburgh to Balerno, a distance of about 10 miles.

Take bus No 87, 88 or 88A from St Andrew Square. See the Leith map for references.

Britannia (Map 2) You'll find the former royal yacht *Britannia* (☎ 555 5566 for ticket reservation) moored in Leith harbour, just off Ocean Drive (the ship will be relocated at the new Ocean Terminal, also in Leith, in 2001). She's well worth visiting and you'll

learn some surprising things in the visitors centre and on board. Allow at least 1½ hours to look around, and note that the use of cameras on board is prohibited.

After a four minute introductory video, you enter the visitors centre. Take care to have a good look around – you can't get back in once you've boarded the ship. Among other things, you'll discover that the Queen travelled with five tonnes of luggage when making state visits, shouting by officers and crew was forbidden, and a three month deployment required 2200 toilet rolls.

The ship was launched by the Queen at John Brown's shipyard, Clydebank, on 16 April 1953, then sailed 1.1 million miles over the next 44 years, calling at nearly every Commonwealth country and making 25 state visits. After decommissioning at Portsmouth on 11 December 1997 the final voyage took *Britannia* to Leith.

On leaving the visitors centre, you'll embark on a self-guided 23-stop audio tour of the ship (also available in French, German, Italian and Spanish). You'll see that the ship does not have her name on the hull, and the well-appointed but certainly not lavish royal apartments for the Queen and the Duke of Edinburgh are equipped with single beds. The silver pantry has an impressive array of Edwardian silver. The grand royal dining room, which can accommodate 52 guests, has a mahogany dining table, and the drawing room (with its anteroom) can hold up to 250 guests. Visitors have included Nelson Mandela, Bill Clinton and Indira Gandhi.

Britannia is open daily, except Christmas Day, from 10.30 am to 6 pm (last admission at 4.30 pm). Entry to the visitors centre and the ship costs £7.50/5.75/3.75 for adults/seniors/children and there's an £18 family ticket for two adults and two children. Tickets should be reserved in advance by telephone or purchased from the Tattoo Office, 32 Market St.

Portobello

About 2¼ miles south-east of Leith along the coast, the suburb of Portobello has been

Edinburgh's seaside resort since the late 19th century. Although its heyday has long passed, its promenade and beach still attract crowds on warm summer days. Famous music-hall entertainer, Sir Harry Lauder (1870-1950) was born on Bridge St.

Take bus No 15, 20, 26, 42 or 46 from the centre.

Newhaven

Immediately west of Leith is Newhaven, once a small, distinctive fishing community, now absorbed into the Edinburgh conurbation. The old fish-market building has a **Heritage Centre** which is worth a visit. A 15 minute video reveals the astonishingly tribal lifestyle that survived here until the 1950s when overfishing put paid to the traditional source of income. In a matriarchal society, women in distinctive dress dominated the fish market and life in the home. The centre opens daily from noon to 5 pm; admission free.

Most people come here, however, to taste the delights of the enormously popular Harry Ramsden's (☎ 551 5566), purveyor of fish and chips, next to the centre.

Take bus No 7 or 11 from Princes St.

Edinburgh Zoo

Parents of young children will be relieved to know there's a zoo (☎ 334 9171), 3 miles west of the centre on the A8, offering an alternative to the museums. What will delight kids most are the zoo's penguins, especially when they (the penguins) are allowed out of their enclosure to go walkabout. The zoo also takes care of some rare and endangered animals such as the snow leopard, pygmy hippo and red panda.

It's open April to September, Monday to Saturday from 9 am to 6 pm, October and March to 5 pm, November to February to 4.30 pm (it opens Sunday at 9.30 am). Admission costs £6/3.20. Bus Nos 2, 26, 31, 69, 85 and 86 pass by.

Lauriston Castle

Three miles north-west of the centre, Lauriston Castle (☎ 336 2060), Cramond Rd South,

Sir Harry Lauder

These days not everyone will have heard of the Scottish music hall entertainer Sir Harry Lauder (1870-1950), but they almost certainly have heard one or more of his songs.

Born in Portobello, he worked as a flax spinner in Arbroath while still at school, then in his teens as a pitboy in a Lanarkshire coal mine. He travelled around entering and winning talent competitions before achieving professional success in Glasgow. When he moved to London he was an immediate hit, and he then went on to wow them in the USA and around the world.

Two of his most famous songs are 'Roamin' in the Gloamin'' and 'I Love a Lassie', both written for his wife. Another, 'Keep Right on to the End of the Road' was written after their only son was killed in battle in WWI. Although he continued to perform he never fully recovered from this tragedy.

Sometimes derided for his stage persona of a stereotypical bekilted Scot, he was enormously talented and his musical legacy endures.

started life in the 16th century as a tower house. It was built by Archibald Napier, whose son, John, invented logarithms. The castle was extended and 'modernised' in 19th century baronial style and now contains a collection of fine art and furniture. It's set in peaceful grounds and allows great views north across the Firth of Forth to Fife.

There are 40-minute guided tours of the castle April to October, Saturday to Thursday, from 11 am to 5 pm; November to March, weekends only, 2 to 4 pm; £4/3. Bus Nos 40 and 41 from Hanover St pass by.

South Queensferry & the Forth Bridges

South Queensferry lies on the south bank of the Firth of Forth, at its narrowest point. From early times it was a ferry port, but ferries no longer operate and it's now overshadowed by two bridges.

The magnificent Forth Rail Bridge is one of the finest Victorian engineering achievements. Completed in 1890 after seven years work and the deaths of 58 men, it's over a mile long and the 50,000 tons of girders take three years to paint. The Forth Road Bridge wasn't completed until 1964 and is a graceful suspension bridge.

In the pretty High St there are several places to eat and the small **South Queensferry Museum** (☎ 331 5545) contains some interesting background information on the bridges. The prize exhibit is a model of the Furry Man; on the first Friday of August, some hapless male still has to spend nine hours roaming the streets covered from head to toe in burrs and clutching two floral staves in memory of a medieval tradition. It's open Thursday to Saturday from 10 am to 1 pm and from 2.15 to 5 pm, Sunday from noon to 5 pm; admission is free.

The *Maid of the Forth* (☎ 331 4857) leaves from Hawes Pier and cruises under the bridges to Inchcolm Island (see following section) and Deep Sea World (☎ 01383-411411), the huge aquarium in North Queensferry. There are daily sailings mid-July to early September (weekends

only April to June and October). In summer, evening cruises with jazz or folk music cost £9.50 a head.

Inchcolm Island & Abbey Inchcolm Island has one of Scotland's best preserved medieval abbeys which was founded for Augustinian priors in 1123. In well-tended grounds stand remains of a 13th century church and a remarkably well-preserved octagonal chapter house with stone roof.

It's half an hour to Inchcolm, and you're allowed 1½ hours ashore. Admission to the abbey is £2.30/1, included in the £7.50/3.60 ferry cost (HS members should show their cards for reduction); non-landing tickets cost £5.20/2.60 and allow you to see the island's grey seals, puffins and other seabirds.

Getting There & Away From St Andrew Square numerous buses (Nos 43, X43, 47, 47A) run to South Queensferry. From Edinburgh there are frequent trains to Dalmeny station (15 minutes).

Hopetoun House

Two miles west of South Queensferry, Hopetoun House (☎ 331 2451), one of Scotland's finest stately homes, has a superb location in lovely grounds beside the Firth of Forth. There are two parts, the older built to Sir William Bruce's plans between 1699 and 1702 and dominated by a splendid stairwell, the newer designed between 1720 and 1750 by three members of the Adam family, William and sons Robert and John.

The rooms have splendid furnishings and staff are on hand to make sure you don't miss details like the revolving oyster stand for two people to share. The Hope family supplied a Viceroy of India and a Governor-General of Australia so the upstairs museum displays interesting reminders of the colonial life of the ruling class. Even further up there's a viewing point on the roof, ideal for photos.

It's open April to September daily from

10 am to 5.30 pm; admission is £4.70/2.60 (for the grounds only it's £2.60/1.60).

Hopetoun House can be approached from South Queensferry, or from Edinburgh turn off the A90 onto the A904 just before the Forth Bridge Toll and follow the signs.

Edinburgh Canal Centre

The Edinburgh Canal Centre (☎ 333 1320) is beside the Union Canal in **Ratho**, 8 miles south-west of Edinburgh. The centre offers 1½-hour sightseeing barge trips on the canal for £4.50/2.50 April to October. Take bus No 37 from St Andrew Square. By car, follow the Calder Rd (A71), then turn right (north) onto Dalmeny Rd.

ACTIVITIES

Edinburgh offers numerous opportunities for recreational activities and the TIC can provide particular details. Favourite outdoor venues are Holyrood Park, Meadow Park and Bruntsfield Links.

There are plenty of good walks. Following the Water of Leith offers a relaxed stroll through the city, while more strenuous climbs to Arthur's Seat or along the Radical Rd in Holyrood Park are rewarded with great views. For longer hill-walking head for the Pentland Hills in the south.

Edinburgh has a network of signposted cycle paths that can get you around the city and out into the surrounding countryside.

Tracing Your Ancestors

For visitors with Scottish ancestors a trip here is a good chance to find out more about them and their lives; you may even discover relatives you never knew about.

You should first go to the General Register Office (GRO, Map 5, ☎ 334 0380), New Register House, 3 West Register St, Edinburgh EH1 3YT. This office holds birth, marriage and death records since 1855, the census records and old parochial registers. Contact the GRO for leaflets giving details of its records and fees. The office opens weekdays from 9 am to 4.30 pm. Before you go, contact the office to reserve a search-room seat, particularly if you have limited time.

Next door is part of the Scottish Record Office (☎ 535 1314), HM General Register House, 2 Princes St, Edinburgh EH1 3YY. There are two search rooms: the historical search room, where you should go to research ancestors (no charge); and the legal search room, where you can see records for legal purposes (a fee is payable). Staff answer simple inquiries, by correspondence, if you give precise details. If you want more research done for you (perhaps before you come), the office will send a list of professional searchers. All correspondence should be addressed to The Keeper of the Records of Scotland, Scottish Record Office, and sent to the above address.

The other place to try is the Scottish Genealogy Society (☎ 220 3677), 15 Victoria Terrace (above Victoria St), Edinburgh EH1, which has a library, microfiche, books for sale and helpful staff.

Visiting graveyards may seem morbid but it's something many tourists do as part of tracing their ancestors (and paying their respects). This address is useful: Anne King, Scottish Ancestral Research (email aking53104@aol.com), Tigh Righ, 4 Esplanade Terrace, Joppa, Edinburgh EH15 2ES.

If you're serious about ancestry research, it may be worth buying one or more of the following: *Tracing Your Scottish Ancestors* (Stationery Office) by Cecil Sinclair; *Tracing Your Scottish Ancestry* (Polygon, Edinburgh) by Kathleen B Cory; *My Ain Folk – an easy guide to Scottish family history*, by Graham S Holton & Jack Wind; and *Surnames of Scotland* by George F Black and published by the New York Library.

Queen's Drive, that circles Holyrood Park, is popular especially on Sunday when it's closed to motorised traffic. The Innocent Railway Path from Holyrood Park takes you through Duddingston village to Craigmillar and Musselburgh.

Not surprisingly, golf is a favourite pastime and there are lots of courses around Edinburgh. Many people practise their golf stroke on Bruntsfield Links; others head for Braid Hills public course (Map 3) or the nearby floodlit driving range at Braid Hills Golf Centre (☎ 658 1755), 91 Liberton Drive. Some private courses also welcome visitors including Craigmillar Park Golf Club (☎ 667 0047), Observatory Rd, near the Royal Observatory.

Alien Rock (Map 2, ☎ 552 7211), Old St Andrew's Church, 8 Pier Place, Newhaven, is an indoor climbing centre open daily. Training courses are available. It costs £5 per session plus £3 for boots and harness hire.

On the southern boundary of the city off the A702 the Midlothian Ski Centre (☎ 445 4433), Hill End, is a large artificial ski area, open daily year round. Take bus No 4 from the city centre. The Edinburgh Ski Club (☎ 220 3121), 2 Howe St, Edinburgh EH3 6TD offers lessons, day trips, discounts to ski areas and equipment hire. For cross-country skiing contact the Edinburgh Nordic Ski Club (☎ 220 4371), c/o 60A Palmerston Place, Edinburgh, EH12 5AY.

Canoeing and sailing in the Firth of Forth are available from Port Edgar Marina & Sailing School (☎ 331 3330), in South Queensferry west of Edinburgh.

Good indoor sports centres providing swimming, squash, badminton etc include Meadowbank Sports Centre (☎ 661 5351), 139 London Rd, off Leith Walk, and the Royal Commonwealth Pool (Map 3, ☎ 667 7211), 21 Dalkeith Rd, Newington.

LANGUAGE COURSES

Given Edinburgh's high standard in education and Scotland's significant contribution to English literature, it's not surprising that the city is a good place to learn English (as well as other languages). Schools usually offer a range of programs including intensive courses, summer schools, weekend workshops and specialised-English courses (eg for business or tourism). Below are some of the schools where you could start making inquiries; also check the Yellow Pages under 'Language Courses & Schools'.

Edinburgh Language Centre
(☎/fax 343 6596), 10B Oxford Terrace, Edinburgh EH4

Edinburgh School of English
(☎ 557 9200, fax 557 9192), 271 Canongate, Edinburgh EH8 8BQ

English Language Institute
(☎ 447 2398, fax 447 7131), 69 Nile Grove, Edinburgh EH10

International Language Academy
(☎ 220 4278, fax 220 1107), 11 Great Stuart St, Edinburgh EH3 7T8

Institute for Applied Language Studies
(☎ 650 6200), University of Edinburgh, 21 Hill Place, Edinburgh EH8 9DP

Those interested in learning about French language and culture should contact the Institut Français d'Écosse (Map 6, ☎ 225 5366, fax 220 0648), 13 Randolph Crescent, just west of the centre.

If you're interested in learning more about Gaelic contact the Celtic department (Map 7, ☎ 650 1000) of the University of Edinburgh, David Hume Tower, George Square, Edinburgh EH8 9JX.

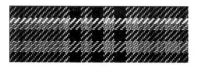

Places to Stay

Edinburgh has masses of accommodation, but the city can still fill up quickly over the New Year, at Easter and between mid-May and mid-September, especially while the festivals are in full swing. Book in advance if at all possible, or use an accommodation booking service.

The TIC's accommodation reservation service (☎ 473 3855) charges a steep £4 fee for booking accommodation. If you have the time, get its free accommodation brochure, the *Edinburgh Holiday Guide*, and ring round yourself.

For £5, three branches of Thomas Cook also make hotel reservations: the Edinburgh airport office (☎ 333 5119); the office (☎ 557 0905) in Waverley Steps near the TIC; and the office (☎ 557 0034) on Platform One of Waverley train station.

CAMPING

Edinburgh has two well-equipped campsites reasonably close to the centre. *Edinburgh Caravan Club Site* (☎ 312 6874, Marine Drive) overlooks the Firth of Forth, 3 miles north-west of the centre, and has full facilities and tent sites for £3. From North Bridge take bus No 8A, 9A or 14A. *Mortonhall Caravan Park* (☎ 664 1533, 38 Mortonhall Gate), off Frogston Rd East, Mortonhall, is 5 miles south-east of the centre. Sites are £8 to £12 and it's open March to October. Take bus No 11 from North Bridge.

HOSTELS & COLLEGES

If you're travelling on a budget, the numerous hostels offer cheap accommodation and are great centres for meeting fellow travellers. Hostels have facilities for self-catering and some provide cheap meals. From May to September and on public holidays, hostels can be heavily booked but so are most other places. Advance booking is advisable.

SYHA Hostels

The office of the Scottish Youth Hostels Association (SYHA, Map 3, ☎ 229 8660, fax 229 2456, www.shya.org.uk) is at 161 Warrender Park Rd in Bruntsfield. The SYHA produces a handbook (£1.50) giving details on around 80 hostels in Scotland, including transport links. Below, higher hostel prices for seniors are given first, followed by the reduced price for juniors.

There are four good SYHA hostels. *Eglinton Youth Hostel* (Map 3, ☎ 337 1120, 18 Eglinton Crescent) is about 1 mile west of the city near Haymarket train station; beds cost £12.50/9.95. To get there, walk down Princes St and continue on Shandwick Place which becomes West Maitland St; veer right at the Haymarket along Haymarket Terrace, then turn right into Coates Gardens which runs into Eglinton Crescent.

Bruntsfield Youth Hostel (Map 3, ☎ 447 2994, 7 Bruntsfield Crescent) has an attractive location overlooking Bruntsfield Links about 2½ miles from Waverley train station. Catch bus No 11 or 16 from the garden side of Princes St and alight at Forbes Rd. It's closed in January and rates are £8.60/7.10 (£9.60/8.10 in July and August).

The other two are summer only (late June to early September): *Central Youth Hostel* (Map 7, ☎ 337 1120, Robertson Close/College Wynd, Cowgate); and *Pleasance Youth Hostel* (Map 7, ☎ 337 1120, New Arthur Place).

Independent Hostels

There's a growing number of independent backpackers' hostels, some of them right in the centre. The long-established, well equipped *High St Hostel* (Map 5, ☎ 557 3984, 8 Blackfriars St) is popular although some have found it noisy. Beds cost £9.50 per night in a 10 bed dorm. It's opposite the Haggis Backpackers tour-booking office.

Not far away is *Royal Mile Backpackers* (Map 5, ☎ 557 6120, 105 High St), which charges £9.90 for beds in dorms of up to 10 beds. **Edinburgh Backpackers Hostel** (*Map 5,* ☎ *220 1717, 65 Cockburn St*) is close to the action; dorm beds cost from £10 and doubles are £35; a continental breakfast is available for £1.75.

Princes St Backpackers (*Map 4,* ☎ *556 6894, 5 West Register St*) is well positioned, behind Princes St and close to the bus station. It's a fun place, but you do have to negotiate 77 exhausting steps to reach reception. Dorm beds cost £9.50, doubles £24. A full breakfast costs just £2, and Sunday night dinner is free!

Princes St West Backpackers (*Map 4,* ☎ *226 2939, 3-4 Queensferry St*) is close to the nightlife. Rates are £10 for a dorm bed or £13 per person in a double; the seventh night is free, and there's a free meal on Sunday.

Belford Youth Hostel (*Map 2,* ☎ *225 6209, 6 Douglas Gardens*) is in a converted church and although some people have complained of noise, it's well run and cheerful with good facilities. Dorm beds cost £8.50.

Quiet **Palmerston Lodge** (*Map 3,* ☎ *220 5141, 25 Palmerston Place*), on the corner of Chester St, is in a listed building. There are no bunks, only single beds, and showers and toilets on every floor. The rates, which include a continental breakfast, start at £10 for a dorm bed; singles/doubles with bathroom are £30/40.

Women and married couples are welcome at the **Kinnaird Christian Hostel** (*Map 3,* ☎ *225 3608, 13-14 Coates Crescent*), where beds in a Georgian house cost from £14. Singles/doubles cost £20/34.

Colleges

Edinburgh has a large student population and during vacations colleges and universities offer accommodation on their campuses, though most are a fair way from the centre and cost as much as lower-end, more central B&Bs. Most rooms are comfortable, functional single bedrooms with shared bathroom. Increasingly, however, there are

rooms with private bathroom, twin and family units, self-contained flats and shared houses. Full-board, half-board, B&B and self-catering options are available. Rooms are usually available from late June to late September.

Closest is **Pollock Halls of Residence** (*Map 3,* ☎ *667 0662, 18 Holyrood Park Rd*), which has Arthur's Seat as a backdrop. Modern (often noisy) single rooms cost from £23.90 per person including breakfast. **Napier University** (☎ *455 4291, Colinton Rd off Bruntsfield Place*) in Craiglockhart offers B&B in summer from £18 per person. **Queen Margaret College** (☎ *317 3310, 36 Clerwood Terrace*) is 3 miles west in Corstorphine near Edinburgh Zoo. From June to September, B&B with shared bathroom costs from £17.50.

B&BS & GUESTHOUSES

On a tight budget the best bet is a private house; get the TIC's free accommodation guide and phone around. At the bottom end you get a bedroom in a private house, a shared bathroom and an enormous cooked breakfast (juice, cereal, bacon, eggs, sausage, baked beans and toast). Small B&Bs may only have one room to let. More upmarket B&Bs have private bathrooms and TVs in each room. Guesthouses, often large converted houses with half a dozen rooms, are just an extension of the B&B concept.

Outside festival time you should get something for around £18, although it'll probably be a bus ride away in the suburbs. Places in the centre aren't always good value if you have a car, since parking is restricted; when booking check whether the establishment has off-street parking. Guesthouses are generally two or three pounds more expensive, and to get a private bathroom you'll have to pay around £25.

The main concentrations are around Pilrig St, Pilrig; Minto St (a southern continuation of North Bridge), Newington; and Gilmore Place and Leamington Terrace, Bruntsfield.

North of the New Town

Pilrig St, left off Leith Walk, has lots of guesthouses, all within about a mile of the centre. Take bus No 11 from Princes St or walk north from the east end of the street.

Balmoral Guest House (*Map 2, ☎ 554 1857, 32 Pilrig St*) is a comfortable terraced house with beds from £17 to £20 per person. Similar is the *Barrosa* (*Map 2, ☎ 554 3700, 21 Pilrig St*), where B&B costs from £19.50/23.50 without/with bath. The attractive, detached, two-crown *Balquhidder Guest House* (*Map 2, ☎ 554 3377, 94 Pilrig St*) provides neat rooms with bath from £18 to £30 a head. Next door, the larger *Balfour House* (*Map 2, ☎ 554 2106, 92 Pilrig St*) has 19 mostly *en suite* rooms for £20/23 per person without/with bathroom.

There are several elegant places in Eyre Place, near Stockbridge and the Water of Leith, 1 mile from the centre. *Ardenlee Guest House* (*Map 2, ☎ 556 2838, 9 Eyre Place*) is a terraced Victorian townhouse with beds from £22 to £26 per person (£2 more for a private bath). The friendly, Georgian *Dene Guest House* (*Map 2, ☎ 556 2700, 7 Eyre Place*) has 10 rooms with B&B from £19.50/37 a single/double. If these are full try *Blairhaven Guest House* (*Map 2, ☎ 556 3025, 5 Eyre Place*), which does B&B from £18.

Newington

There are lots of guesthouses on and around Minto St/Mayfield Gardens in Newington. It's south of the city centre and university on either side of the continuation of North/South Bridge, with plenty of buses to the centre. This is the main traffic artery from the south and carries traffic from the A7 and A68 (both routes are signposted). The best places are in the streets on either side of the main road.

Salisbury Guest House (*Map 3, ☎ 667 1264, 45 Salisbury Rd*), just east of Newington Rd and 10 minutes from the centre by bus, is quiet, comfortable and non-smoking. Rooms with private bath cost from £23 to £30 per person.

The welcoming, red sandstone *Avondale*

Guest House (*Map 3, ☎ 667 6779, 10 South Gray St*), just west of Minto St, is a comfortable, traditional B&B with singles/doubles from £19/32.

In a quiet street, *Fairholme Guest House* (*Map 3, ☎ 667 8645, 13 Moston Terrace*), just west of Mayfield Gardens, is a pleasant Victorian villa with free parking. The range of rooms includes a single from £15.

Grange Guest House (*Map 3, ☎ 667 2125, 2 Minto St*), near the corner of Salisbury Rd, is a two storey, terrace house convenient for the centre, but only provides a continental breakfast. Rooms with shared bathroom cost £16/28 a single/double. One of the better guesthouses on Minto St is *Sherwood Guest House* (*Map 3, ☎ 667 1200*), No 42, a refurbished Georgian villa with off-road parking. B&B costs £25/40, or £40/64 with bathroom.

Millfield Guest House (*Map 3, ☎ 667 4428, 12 Marchhall Rd*), east of Dalkeith Rd past Pollock Halls of Residence, is a pleasant, two-storey, Victorian house with singles/doubles from £18/33.

Further south, Kilmaurs Rd also east of Dalkeith Rd, has several B&Bs. The spacious *Casa Buzzo* (*Map 3, ☎ 667 8998*), No 8, has two doubles for £16 per person with shared bathroom. If you prefer private facilities the nearby *Kenvie Guest House* (*Map 3, ☎ 668 1964*), No 16, has a couple of *en suite* rooms for £26/46 a single/double.

Bruntsfield

Bruntsfield is less than a mile south-west of the centre; most places are on Gilmore Place and Leamington Terrace. Bus Nos 10 and 10A run to Gilmore Place from Princes St.

On Gilmore Place, busy *Averon Guest House* (*Map 6, ☎ 229 9932, 44 Gilmore Place*) has comfortable if small rooms from £20 per person. Named after a former gold-mining town in Australia, *Ballarat Guest House* (*Map 6, ☎ 229 7024, 14 Gilmore Place*) provides clean, non-smoking rooms for £23 per person.

Down Leamington Terrace at No 33, is *Menzies Guest House* (*Map 3, ☎ 229 4629*). It's well run and has rooms from £20 to £28 per person, though you only have one choice of breakfast cereal. The refurbished *Leamington Guest House* (*Map 3*, ☎ *228 3879*), No 57, has eight rooms, each with a different theme, and good breakfasts for £20/26 without/with bathroom.

There are several quiet guesthouses in Hartington Gardens, off Viewforth, itself off Bruntsfield Place. *Aaron Guest House* (*Map 3*, ☎ *229 6459*), at the end of the street, is handy for drivers since it has a private car park. Beds go for £20 to £35 per person in comfortable *en suite* rooms. The comfortable, friendly *Robertson Guest House* (*Map 3*, ☎ *229 2652*), No 5, offers a good range of food at breakfast including yoghurt and fruit, and has rooms from £20 per person.

HOTELS

Not surprisingly, the international hotels in the centre are extremely expensive, although there can be good deals outside summer, especially at weekends. Unless otherwise stated, rates include breakfast.

Old Town

The *Thistle Inn Hotel* (*Map 6*, ☎ *220 2299*, *94 Grassmarket*) is in the heart of the Old Town in one of the city's nightlife centres. Singles/doubles with private bath and TV cost from £33/56. The entrance is next to Biddy Mulligan's pub, and every floor is accessible by lift. (Don't confuse it with the bigger, more expensive King James Thistle Hotel beside the shopping centre, off Leith St.) Nearby, *Apex International Hotel* (*Map 6*, ☎ *300 3456*, *31-35 Grassmarket*) has 99 *en suite* rooms, a rooftop restaurant and off-street parking. B&B costs from £60/80.

The new, spruce *Ibis Hotel* (*Map 5*, ☎ *240 7000*, *6 Hunter Square*), just off the Royal Mile, offers a flat rate of £55 per room per night, but breakfast is an extra £5.25. The stylish *Bank Hotel* (*Map 5*, ☎ *556 9043*, *1 South Bridge*), on the corner of the Royal Mile, has a good bar downstairs and singles/doubles for £70/100 including breakfast.

The *Holiday Inn Crowne Plaza* (*Map 5*, ☎ *557 9797*, *80 High St*) is a purpose-built hotel whose exterior mimics the Royal Mile's 16th century architecture. The interior is, nonetheless, as modern as you could hope for. Rates are from £125/145 a single/double.

New Town

The three-star *Royal British Hotel* (*Map 4*, ☎ *556 4901*, *20 Princes St*) is in a good location opposite the TIC. B&B costs from £70/82 a single/double. The *Old Waverley Hotel* (*Map 4*, ☎ *556 4648*, *43 Princes St*) has a prime site opposite the Sir Walter Scott Monument, and many rooms have castle views. Rooms with private bath cost from £90/144. The luxurious *Balmoral Hotel* (*Map 5*, ☎ *556 2414*, *1 Princes St*), next to Waverley station and the TIC, is one of Edinburgh's top hotels with rooms for £137. Facilities include a gym, pool and sauna.

Carlton Highland Hotel (*Map 5*, ☎ *472 3000*, *North Bridge*), south of Princes St, is an imposing Victorian building with a leisure centre, nightclub and *en suite* rooms from £85/120. The elegant *Caledonian Hotel* (*Map 4*, ☎ *459 9988*), at the west end of Princes St on the corner of Lothian Rd, is in a huge, red sandstone building below the castle. Singles/doubles cost £147/220 and hotel facilities include three restaurants.

Royal Terrace has a great position on the north side of Calton Hill, with views over Royal Terrace Gardens to Leith. *Ailsa Craig Hotel* (*Map 5*, ☎ *556 1022*, *24 Royal Terrace*) is a refurbished Georgian building where rooms, most with bath, cost from £30/55 a single/double. The *Claymore Hotel* (*Map 5*, ☎ *556 2693*, *7 Royal Terrace*), the *Halcyon* (*Map 5*, ☎ *556 1032*, *8 Royal Terrace*), and the *Adria Hotel* (*Map 5*, ☎ *556 7875*, *11 Royal Terrace*) are similar.

At the *Greenside Hotel* (*Map 5*, ☎ *557 0022*, *9 Royal Terrace*) the 15 huge rooms are each furnished differently, are all *en suite* and cost from £25 to £55 per person; snacks are available throughout the day.

The swishest hotel and one of the best in Edinburgh is the *Royal Terrace Hotel* (*Map 5*, ☎ *557 3222*), No 18. It's full of fine furnishings and most rooms include a spa bath; it costs from £120/160 a single/double.

More personal than most hotels is the tastefully decorated *Sibbet House* (*Map 4*, ☎ *556 1078, 26 Northumberland St*), where prices of £80 to £90 per person might include an impromptu bagpipe recital by your host.

The grand, old-world *Roxburghe Hotel* (*Map 4*, ☎ *225 3921, 38 Charlotte Square*) is in one of Edinburgh's most prestigious locations. Rooms with bathroom cost from £100/135 a single/double. The very traditional, elegant *George Inter-Continental Hotel* (*Map 4*, ☎ *225 1251, 19-21 George St*), in the heart of Edinburgh's financial district, has over 500 rooms costing from £95 to £165.

North of the New Town

The *Lovat Hotel* (*Map 2*, ☎ *556 2745, 5 Inverleith Terrace*), near the Royal Botanic Garden, is a small terrace hotel with off-street parking. Rooms cost £30/50. *Christopher North House Hotel* (*Map 4*, ☎ *225 2720, 6 Gloucester Place*), Stockbridge, is a small, genteel Georgian hotel in a quiet area. Rooms cost from £40/60 a single/double, £60/100 with bathroom.

In Leith, Edinburgh's main port, the *Malmaison Hotel* (*Leith Map*, ☎ *555 6868, 1 Tower Place*), in a 19th century sailor's home, is a wonderfully stylish hotel, with rooms from £95.

West End & Haymarket

Good value given the location, the *West End Hotel* (*Map 3*, ☎ *225 3656, 35 Palmerston Place*) has *en suite* rooms from £25 per person, and a bar with a wide selection of whiskies. *Rothesay Hotel* (*Map 2*, ☎ *225 4125, 8 Rothesay Place*), in a quiet, central street, has pleasantly spacious rooms, mostly with bathroom, from £30 to £80 per person.

There's a handy batch of mid-range places on Coates Gardens, off Haymarket Terrace near Haymarket train station. Com-

fortable *Boisdale Hotel* (*Map 3*, ☎ *337 1134, 9 Coates Gardens*) has rooms with private bath from £25 to £45 per person.

At the top of Coates Gardens in Eglinton Crescent, *Greens Hotel* (*Map 3*, ☎ *337 1565*), at No 24, occupies four terrace houses and caters mostly to business people, but is reasonably priced from £35 per person.

Lothian Rd & Around

The *Sheraton Grand Hotel* (*Map 3*, ☎ *229 9131, 1 Festival Square*), is opposite the Royal Lyceum Theatre, off Lothian Rd, east of the castle. You pay for, and get, luxury. Rooms cost from £155/195. Further south, the *Point Hotel* (*Map 6*, ☎ *221 5555, 34 Bread St*), off Lothian Rd, has a strikingly modern, stark, Art Deco interior, and a trendy café-bar called Monboddo (see Places to Eat). Rates are from £70/90.

Newington

In a quiet residential area south of Holyrood Park, *Marchhall Hotel* (*Map 3*, ☎ *667 2743, 14-16 Marchhall Crescent*), a three-storey Victorian terrace, offers B&B from £23 per person. *Thrums Hotel* (*Map 3*, ☎ *667 5545, 14 Minto St*) is a small but popular place with off-street parking. B&B costs from £30 per person and it's advisable to book in advance. *Arthur's View Hotel* (*Map 3*, ☎ *667 3468*) is on the corner of Mayfield Gardens and Bright's Crescent. Although its name is stretching credibility a bit, it's a friendly place with a private car park and evening meals. B&B costs from £40/70 a single/double.

Bruntsfield

Hotels here have the advantage of being close to Bruntsfield Links and Meadow Park and to some good eateries.

Next to the SYHA hostel, the *Nova Hotel* (*Map 3*, ☎ *447-6437, 5 Bruntsfield Crescent*) is in a quiet, three-storey Victorian terrace, with views across the links. Its 12 *en suite* rooms cost from £35. *Bruntsfield Hotel* (*Map 3*, ☎ *229 1393*) is well positioned on the corner of Bruntsfield Place and Leamington Terrace facing Bruntsfield Links. It charges £89/125 a single/double, but has a standby rate of £50 per person for the first night and other specials.

SELF-CATERING

There's plenty of self-catering accommodation in Edinburgh and staying in a flat or house in the city gives you an opportunity to get a feel for a community. The minimum stay is usually one week in the summer peak season, three nights or less at other times.

The *Edinburgh Holiday Guide*, free from the TIC, contains a list of these (with contact addresses) in Edinburgh and the Lothians. Depending on facilities, location and time of year, prices range from £150 to £750 per week.

Dundas (*Leith Map*, ☎ *554 6480, 8 Claremont Gardens*) provides a comfortable two-bedroom flat in Leith near the golf course. It's open from July to September, has a minimum period of four days and charges from £150.

Less personal but more central is ***Glen House Apartments*** (*Map 6, ☎ 228 4043, fax 229 8873, 22 Glen St*), off Lauriston Place south of the Old Town. It has a range of units with one to four bedrooms and charges from £160 to £750 a week. The minimum stay is three nights.

Open year round, ***Jane Armstrong*** (*Map 2, ☎/fax 558 9868, 13 Inverleith Row*), close to the Royal Botanic Garden north of the centre, has two units that can sleep up to five people. The weekly rate is from £250 and there's a minimum stay of three nights.

LONG TERM RENTALS

In general, prices for rented accommodation are high and standards low, but many are furnished so you won't have to buy much. At the lower end of the market, bedsits are single furnished rooms, usually with a shared bathroom and kitchen, although some have basic cooking facilities. The next step up is a studio, which normally has its own bathroom and kitchen. Shared houses and flats are probably the best value. Rates start from around £170 per calendar month. Many landlords demand a security deposit (normally one month's rent) plus a month's rent in advance; some also request some sort of reference.

When you inspect a flat it's wise to take someone else with you, both for safety reasons and for help in spotting any shortcomings. A few things to check before signing a tenancy agreement are:

- the cost of gas, electricity, the phone, the TV and how they're to be paid for
- whether there's street parking and/or how close it is to public transport
- the arrangements for cleaning the house or flat
- whether you can have friends to stay

To find a place, look in the classified ads in the local newspapers and in the Flatshare section of *The List* magazine. Hostel noticeboards are also a good source. For agents check the Yellow Pages. One agent is DRM Residential (☎ 466 4661, fax 466 4662, www.drm-residential.co.uk), 3 Comiston Place in Morningside. It has holiday apartments and properties to let and doesn't charge the tenant for finding accommodation.

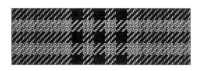

Places to Eat

FOOD

Scotland's chefs have an enviable range of fresh meat, seafood and vegetables at their disposal. And the country has gone a long way to shake off its once dismal culinary reputation. Most Edinburgh restaurants are good while some are internationally renowned.

Most pubs do food, with either a cheap bar menu or a more formal restaurant or both. Supermarkets and department stores have reasonable (and reasonably priced) cafés.

Lunch is served from 12.30 to 2 pm, dinner from 7 to around 9 pm. An alternative to dinner is high tea (from about 4.30 to 6.30 pm), when a main dish is served with tea and cakes.

Some of the best places to eat are members of the Taste of Scotland scheme. The STB's annual *Taste of Scotland Guide* (£7.99) is worth buying to track down these restaurants and hotels. The excellent, annual *Edinburgh & Glasgow Eating & Drinking Guide* contains reviews of cafés, restaurants and bars and is published by *The List* magazine.

Vegetarianism has a long tradition in Edinburgh, and vegetarians can get a reasonable meal pretty well anywhere, especially if they like pizza, pasta or curry. Vegans will find the going tougher, but many places with vegetarian menus often include vegan dishes. The *Cruelty Free Guide to Edinburgh* has a list of these.

The cheapest way to eat is to cook for yourself. Even if you lack great culinary skills, you can buy good quality pre-cooked meals from supermarkets.

Scottish Breakfast

Surprisingly few Scots eat porridge and even fewer eat it in the traditional way as a savoury dish not a sweet one – that is with salt to taste, then eaten with milk, but no sugar. You'll rarely be offered porridge in a B&B. Generally, a glass of fruit juice accompanies a bowl of cereal or muesli, followed by a cooked breakfast which may include: bacon, sausage, black pudding (a type of sausage made from dried blood), grilled tomato, grilled mushrooms, fried bread or tattie (potato) scones (if you're lucky), and an egg or two. More upmarket hotels may offer porridge followed by kippers (smoked herrings). As well as toast, there may be oatcakes (oatmeal biscuits) to spread your marmalade upon.

Snacks

As well as ordinary scones (similar to American biscuits), Scottish bakeries often offer milk scones, tattie scones and girdle scones. Bannocks are a cross between scones and pancakes. Savoury pies include the *bridie* (a pie filled with meat, potatoes and sometimes other vegetables) and the Scotch pie (minced meat in a plain round pastry casing – best eaten hot). A *toastie* is a toasted sandwich.

Dundee cake, a rich fruit cake topped with almonds, is highly recommended. Black bun is another type of fruit cake, eaten over Hogmanay (New Year's Eve).

Soups

Scotch broth, made with barley, lentils and mutton stock, is highly nutritious and very good. Cock-a-leekie is a substantial soup made from a cock, or chicken, and leeks.

You may not be drawn to *powsowdie* (sheep's-head broth) but it's very tasty. More popular is *cullen skink*, a fish soup containing smoked haddock.

Meat & Game

Steak eaters will enjoy a thick fillet of world-famous Aberdeen Angus beef, while beef from Highland cattle is much sought after. Venison, from the red deer, is leaner and appears on many menus. Both may be served with a wine-based or creamy whisky sauce.

Gamebirds like pheasant and the more expensive grouse, traditionally roasted and served with game chips and fried breadcrumbs, are also available. They're definitely worth trying, but watch your teeth on the shot, which is not always removed before cooking.

Then there's haggis, Scotland's much-maligned national dish ...

Fish & Seafood

Scotland offers a wide variety of fish and seafood. Scottish salmon is well known but there's a big difference between farmed salmon and the leaner, more expensive, wild version. Both are available either smoked (served with brown bread and butter) or poached. Wild brown trout is cheaper than salmon and almost as good; there's also a farmed variety and it's often served fried in oatmeal.

As an alternative to kippers (smoked herrings) you may be offered Arbroath smokies (lightly smoked fresh haddock), traditionally eaten cold. Herrings in oatmeal are good if you don't mind the bones. *Krappin heit* is cod's head stuffed with fish livers and oatmeal. Mackerel paté and smoked or peppered mackerel (both served cold) are also popular.

Prawns, crab, lobster, oysters, mussels and scallops are available in coastal towns and around lochs, although much is exported.

Cheeses

Cheddar is the Scottish cheese industry's main output, but there are speciality cheese-makers whose products are definitely worth sampling. Many are based on the islands, particularly Arran, Bute, Gigha, Islay, Mull and Orkney. Brodick Blue is a ewes' milk blue cheese made on Arran. Lanark Blue is rather

Haggis – Scotland's National Dish

A popular rhyme, penned by an English poet, goes:

For the land of Burns
The only snag is
The haggis

Scotland's national dish is frequently ridiculed by foreigners because of its ingredients which don't sound too mouthwatering. However, once you get over any delicate sensibilities towards tucking in to chopped lungs, heart and liver mixed with oatmeal and boiled in a sheep's stomach, with the accompanying glass of whisky it can taste surprisingly good.

Haggis should be served with tatties and neeps (mashed potatoes and turnips, with a generous dollop of butter and a good sprinkling of black pepper).

Although it's eaten year-round, haggis is central to the celebrations of 25 January in honour of Scotland's national poet, Robert Burns. Scots worldwide unite on Burns Night to revel in their Scottishness. A piper announces the arrival of the haggis and Burns' poem *Address to a Haggis* (otherwise known as the *Selkirk Grace*) is recited to this 'Great chieftan o' the puddin'-race'. The bulging stomach is then lanced with a dirk (dagger) to reveal the steaming offal within.

Vegetarians (and quite a few carnivores, no doubt) will be relieved to know that veggie haggis is available in some restaurants in Edinburgh.

like Roquefort. There are several varieties of cream cheese (Caboc, St Finan, Howgate) which are usually rolled in oatmeal.

Scottish oatcakes make the perfect accompaniment for cheese.

Puddings

Traditional Scottish puddings are irresistibly creamy, calorie-enriched concoctions. *Cranachan* is made with toasted oatmeal, raspberries, or some other fresh fruit, and whisky, all mixed into thick cream. *Atholl brose* is similar but without the fruit – rather like English syllabub. *Clootie dumpling* is delicious, a rich steamed pudding filled with currants and raisins.

DRINKS
Nonalcoholic Drinks

On quantity drunk, tea probably qualifies as Scotland's national drink, but coffee is widely available and it's easy to get a cappuccino or espresso in large towns. Definitely an acquired taste is the virulent orange-coloured fizzy drink, Irn-Bru; it's 100% sugar plus some pretty weird flavouring.

Alcoholic Drinks

Takeaway alcoholic drinks are sold from neighbourhood off-licences (liquor stores) rather than pubs. Opening hours vary, but although some stay open daily to 9 or 10 pm, many keep ordinary shop hours. Alcohol can also be bought at supermarkets and corner shops.

Most restaurants are licensed to sell alcoholic drinks which are always expensive. There are a few BYO (Bring Your Own booze) restaurants. Most charge an extortionate sum for 'corkage' – opening your bottle for you. See Pubs under Entertainment.

Whisky Whisky (always spelt without an 'e' if it's Scottish) is Scotland's best-known product and biggest export. The spirit was first distilled in Scotland in the 15th century; over 2000 brands are now produced.

There are two kinds of whisky: single malt, made from malted barley, and blended whisky, which is distilled from unmalted grain (maize) and blended with selected

Making Malt Whisky

The process of making malt whisky begins with malting. Barley is soaked in water and allowed to germinate so that enzymes are produced to convert the starch in the barley to fermentable sugar. The barley is then dried in a malt kiln over the peat fire that gives malt whisky its distinctive taste. Since most distilleries now buy in their malted barley, tourists rarely see this part of the process.

The malt is milled, mixed with hot water and left in a large tank, the mash tun. The starch is converted into sugar and this liquid, or 'wort', is drawn off into another large tank, the washback, for fermentation.

This weak alcoholic solution, or wash, is distilled twice in large copper-pot stills. The process is controlled by the stillman, who collects only the middle portion of the second distillation to mature in oak barrels. The spirit remains in the barrels for at least three years, often much longer. During bottling, water is added to reduce its strength.

malts. Single malts are rarer (there are only about 100 brands) and more expensive than blended whiskies. Although there are distilleries all over the country, there are concentrations around Speyside and on the Isle of Islay.

As well as blends and single malts, there are also several whisky-based liqueurs like Drambuie. If you must mix your whisky with anything other than water try a whisky-mac (whisky with ginger wine). After a long walk in the rain there's nothing better to warm you up.

When out drinking, Scots may order a 'half' or 'nip' of whisky as a chaser to a pint of beer. Only tourists say 'Scotch' – what else would you be served in Scotland? The standard measure is 50mL.

Beer There's a wonderfully wide range of beers, ranging from light (almost like lager) to extremely strong and treacly. What New Worlders call beer is actually lager; to the distress of local connoisseurs, lagers constitute a huge chunk of the market. Fortunately, thanks to the Campaign for Real Ale (CAMRA) organisation, the once threatened traditional beers are thriving.

The best ales are hand-pumped from the cask, not carbonated and drawn under pressure. They're usually served at room temperature, which may come as a shock to lager drinkers, and have subtle flavours that a cold, chemical lager can't match. Most popular is what the Scots call 'heavy', a dark beer similar to English bitter. Most Scottish brews are graded in shillings so you can tell their strength, the usual range being 60 to 80 shillings (written 80/-). The greater the number of shillings, the stronger the beer.

The market is dominated by the big brewers: Younger, McEwan, Scottish & Newcastle and Tennent. Look out for beer from local breweries, some of it strong – the aptly-named Skullsplitter from Orkney is a good example. Caledonian 80/-, Maclay 80/- Belhaven 80/- and Traquair House Ale are others worth trying.

Long before hops arrived in Scotland, beer was brewed from heather. Reintroduced, heather ale is surprisingly good and available in some pubs.

Stout is a dark, rich, foamy drink; Guinness is the most famous brand.

Beers are usually served in pints (from £1.50 to £2), but you can also ask for a 'half' (a half pint). The stronger brews are usually 'specials' or 'extras'. Potency can vary from around 2 to 8%.

Wine For centuries people made wine from wild flowers, fruits and tree saps. This cottage industry is continued at Moniack Castle, near Beauly in the Highlands, and at Cairn o' Mohr winery in the Carse of Gowrie.

Good international wines are widely available and reasonably priced (except in pubs and restaurants). In supermarkets an ordinary but drinkable bottle can be found for around £4.

PLACES TO EAT

There are good-value restaurants and cafés scattered all round the city. For cheap eats, the best areas are Union Place, near the Playhouse Theatre; around Grassmarket, just south of the castle; near the university around Nicolson St, the extension of North/South Bridge, and in Bruntsfield. Most restaurants offer cheap set menus at lunchtime. Many close on Sunday evening, so ring ahead to make sure.

Royal Mile & Around

Despite being a tourist Mecca, the Royal Mile has lots of good-value, enjoyable eating oases.

Restaurants The excellent, small *Polo Fusion* (Map 6, ☎ 622 7722, 503 Lawnmarket) is reasonably priced by Edinburgh standards, and specialises in Asian dishes. Noodle dishes are good value at £5.50 to £6.50.

Viva Mexico (Map 5, ☎ 226 5145, Cockburn St) is a very cheerful, atmospheric restaurant. Some tables have views across to the New Town, and the food is good quality. Nachos cost from £2.50, burritos from £8.95.

Those who like a good wine with their meal should try the congenial *Doric Wine Bar & Bistro* (Map 5, ☎ 225 1084, 15 Market St). It has a good-value bar menu (meals from £2.50 to £3.50) noon to 6.30 pm and the small upstairs bistro offers classic Scottish dishes like haggis, neeps and tatties for £8.95.

Pleasant *Black Bo's* (Map 7, ☎ 557 6136, 57 Blackfriars St) offers an imaginative vegetarian menu. Mains like mushrooms and olives in filo pastry cost around £8.95.

You can sample traditional Scottish cooking at *The Grange* (Map 5, ☎ 558 9992, 267 Canongate) where three course lunches are £9.95; in the evening venison in a prune and wine glaze costs £15.35. *Dubh Prais* (Map 5, ☎ 557 5732, 123 High St), considered one of the best places to try Scottish cuisine, is popular with locals and tourists. As well as traditional meals the menu features interesting dishes like asparagus and parmesan risotto for £4.90 and aubergine with goat's cheese for £9.90.

Cafés Secluded *Deacon's House Café* (Map 6), down Brodie's Close, serves traditional Scottish food like Dundee cake or Scottish salmon sandwiches for £3.95.

Patisserie Florentin (Map 4), St Giles St, with its eye-catching frontage, attracts a rather self-consciously Bohemian crowd, but has excellent light meals and pastries; filled baguettes are £3 and good coffee £1. It stays open till the early hours during the festival period.

The enormously popular *Elephant House* (Map 6, ☎ 220 5355, 21 George IV Bridge) is a café with delicious pastries, newspapers, some of the best variety of coffee and tea (£1.70) in Edinburgh ... and lots of elephants.

Lower Aisle Restaurant (Map 6), beneath St Giles' Cathedral in Parliament Square, is peaceful outside peak lunchtimes. Soup and a roll costs £1.50. *Elephant's Sufficiency* (Map 5, ☎ 220 0666, 170 High St) is a bustling lunch spot. Try the Orkney burger for £3.75.

Open daily *Bann's Vegetarian Café* (Map 5, ☎ 226 1112, 5 Hunter Square), behind the Tron Kirk, is a relaxed Art Deco place with newspapers to read and music playing in the background. Most mains are under £7; vegetarian haggis with creamed turnip tartlets is £6.50.

Bright *Gustos Café* (Map 5, ☎ 558 3083, 105 High St) does delicious gourmet sandwiches from £1.95. *Netherbow Theatre Café* (Map 5, ☎ 556 9579, 43 High St), beside John Knox's House, serves cheap breakfasts in an outdoor courtyard up to noon, then lunches (big portions), salads and quiche for £3.15.

Charming *Clarinda's Tea Room* (Map 5, ☎ 557 1888, 69 Canongate) lurks at the quieter Holyrood end of the Mile. There are a variety of teas from 50p and delicious cakes from 93p. *Brambles Tearoom* (Map 5, ☎ 556 3503, 158 Canongate), close to Huntly

House, is similar; it does soup and a roll for £1.50 and has a good selection of cakes.

Grassmarket

The lively pubs and restaurants on the north side of Grassmarket cater to a young crowd and is a good starting point for a night out.

Ristorante Gennaro (Map 6, ☎ 226 3706), No 64, serves standard but good

Edinburgh Oyster Bars

Dotted around Edinburgh are a number of oyster bars, part of a chain operated by Oyster Bar Enterprises (☎ 554 6200, 1 Quayside St), Leith. The bars are all casual places where you can eat or drink daily from noon till late, and the menu includes beef and chicken dishes as well. Half a dozen Loch Fyne oysters cost £4.60, snacks like nachos £4.20.

The largest of the chain is *St James Oyster Bar* (Map 5, ☎ 557 2925, 2 Calton Rd), down some steps below the Black Bull pub, opposite the St James shopping centre. The *Queen St Oyster Bar* (☎ 226 2530, 16A Queen St), on the corner of Hanover St, is more intimate. In the West End the *West End Oyster Bar* (Map 3, ☎ 225 2530) can be found at 28 West Maitland St near Haymarket train station. *The Bare Story* (Map 7, ☎ 556 3953, 253-55 Cowgate), an anagram of the name, is a popular student hangout. Finally, the large *Leith Oyster Bar* (☎ 554 6294, 12 Burgess St) is near the Malt & Hops pub in Leith.

All of them serve real ale, while the Bare Story has DJs on Sunday, the St James has a juke box and the Queen St and West End bars have live music on weekends.

Of course, these aren't the only oyster bars in town and one of the best of the rest is at the *Café Royal Bar* (Map 4, ☎ 556 4124, 17 West Register St), in magnificent, wood-panelled Victorian surroundings.

Italian fare, with minestrone at £2.20, cannelloni at £6.20 and pizzas from £4.70 to £7. Popular *Mamma's Pizzas* (*Map 6, ☎ 225 6464*), No 28, does excellent pizzas with imaginative toppings (from £3.95).

Pierre Victoire (*Map 6, ☎ 226 2442, 38 Grassmarket*) is part of the chain that serves good-value French food. There's also a branch at 10 Victoria St, which curves up to George IV Bridge from the north-east corner of Grassmarket. Also part of Pierre's empire, *Beppe Vittorio* (*Map 6, ☎ 226 7267, 7 Victoria St*), follows the same formula – authentic, good-value food – although in this case it's Italian. You can mix and match sauces and pastas from £5. At the time of writing the Pierre Victoire chain was in financial difficulties but was continuing to operate.

New Town

The New Town is neither particularly well endowed with eating places nor a particularly interesting part of town at night, but there are a few reasonable options, especially in Hanover and Frederick Sts.

Restaurants The self-serve *Henderson's* (*Map 4, ☎ 225 2131, 94 Hanover St*) is an Edinburgh institution which has been churning out vegetarian food for more than 30 years. Hot dishes start at £3.50, but it's worth checking if there's a lunch or dinner special.

Gringo Bill's (*Map 4, ☎ 220 1205, 110 Hanover St*) is a good Mexican restaurant which serves food with an off-beat sense of humour. It does a huge meal and a drink at lunchtime for £5. *Bar Napoli* (*Map 4, ☎ 225 2600, 75 Hanover St*) is a cheerful Italian restaurant, open until 3 am, with pasta and pizza for £4 to £6. Another reliable Italian option, the traditional *Alfredo's* (*Map 4, ☎ 226 6090, 109 Hanover St*) is good value for money; it offers a three-course lunch for £4.95, and lets you BYO beer.

Chez Jules (*Map 4, ☎ 225 7893, 61 Frederick St*) is a Pierre Victoire spin-off offering similar simple, cheap, but good-quality French food in relaxed surroundings. A three-course lunch is £5.90. In the same French vein there's a branch nearby of the popular *Café Rouge* (*Map 4, ☎ 225 4515, 43 Frederick St*); lamb casserole here is £7.95. Below street level, *Vito's Ristorante* (*Map 4, ☎ 225 5052, 55 Frederick St*) is a very busy Italian restaurant specialising in seafood served in large proportions. King prawns in garlic cost £5.95.

The long-standing *Singapura Restaurant* (*Map 4, ☎ 538 7878, 69 North Castle St*) serves an array of excellent Malaysian-Singaporian food and offers a five-course banquet for £17.90. It's closed Sunday.

Cafés Midway along Princes St are two pleasant cafés. On the 2nd floor of Waterstone's bookshop, near the corner of South Charlotte St, is a branch of the *Starbucks* (Map 4), on the 1st floor overlooking Princes St from its bay window. Nearby is *Bewley's Café* (*Map 4, ☎ 220 1969, 4 South Charlotte St*), a branch of the Irish chain of traditional cafés. Sandwiches are £1.95 to £2.50, pastries £1.20; it also serves lunch and breakfast.

At the western end of Princes St on the corner of Lothian Rd, below St John's Church, *Cornerstone Coffee House* (*Map 4, ☎ 229 0212*) has good views of the castle and St Cuthbert's Church.

At the east end of Princes St at 1 Waterloo Place the French-style *Delifrance* (*Map 5, ☎ 557 4171*) does reasonably priced, good food; baguettes are £3.25 to £4.20. More upmarket French food is provided by *Café 1812* (*Map 5, ☎ 556 5766, 29 Waterloo Place*), with great views of Calton Hill and good-value two-course lunches for £5.40.

While you're in the Scottish National Portrait Gallery, Queen St, check out the delicious home-baked cooking at its *Queen Street Café* (Map 4), open from 10 am to 4.30 pm.

The popular *Hard Rock Café* (*Map 4, ☎ 260 3000, 20 George St*) has huge, tasty burger meals for around £9, plus all the usual merchandising and intriguing rock music memorabilia.

PLACES TO EAT

Forth Rail Bridge at dusk, floodlit – a masterpiece of Victorian engineering, Firth of Forth

NEIL WILSON

St Andrew's ruined cathedral

GLENN BEANLAND

Farmland at harvest-time, near Crail

JOHN DAVIDSON

MAP 2

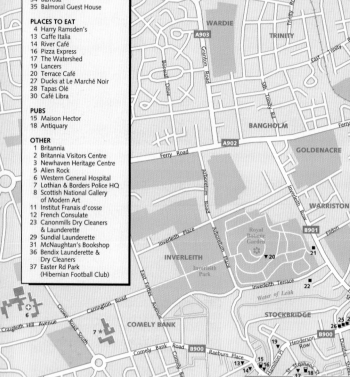

PLACES TO STAY
9 Belford Youth Hostel
10 Rothesay Hotel
21 Jane Armstrong Apartments
22 Lovat Hotel
24 Ardenlee Guest House
25 Dene Guest House
26 Blairhaven Guest House
32 Balquhidder Guest House
33 Balfour House
34 Barrosa
35 Balmoral Guest House

PLACES TO EAT
4 Harry Ramsden's
13 Caffe Italia
14 River Café
16 Pizza Express
17 The Watershed
19 Lancers
20 Terrace Café
27 Ducks at Le Marché Noir
28 Tapas Olé
30 Café Libra

PUBS
15 Maison Hector
18 Antiquary

OTHER
1 Britannia
2 Britannia Visitors Centre
3 Newhaven Heritage Centre
5 Alien Rock
6 Western General Hospital
7 Lothian & Borders Police HQ
8 Scottish National Gallery
  of Modern Art
11 Institut Franais d'cosse
12 French Consulate
23 Canonmills Dry Cleaners
   & Launderette
29 Sundial Launderette
31 McNaughtan's Bookshop
36 Bendix Launderette &
   Dry Cleaners
37 Easter Rd Park
   (Hibernian Football Club)

MAP 2

Western Harbour

FIRTH OF FORTH

LEITH DOCKS

See Leith Map

1

Ocean Drive

Lindsay Road

NORTH LEITH

Commercial Street

Nth Junction Street

Ferry Road

A902

Great Junction Street

Salamander Street

Constitution Street

A901

A199

Duke Street

SOUTH LEITH

LEITH LINKS

Seafield Road

Neuraven Road

Bonnington Road

Pilrig Park

A900

Pilrig Street

32

B900

PILRIG

33

McDonald Road

34

36

35

Leith Walk

Dalmeny Street

Easter Road

Lochend Road

Restalrig Road

RESTALRIG

Albert Street

Arthurdale Street

LOCHEND

Leigh Drive

37

A900

Brunswick Road

BROUGHTON

East London St

29

31

Montgomery Street

30

Lochend Loch

Lochend Park

Lochend Rd Sth

Restalrig Rd Sth

Road

Maryville

Maryville Avenue

MEADOWBANK

B1350 London Road

See Map 5

GREENSIDE

See Edinburgh Walking Tour
& The Royal Mile Map

CALTON

Regent Road

Meadowbank
Sports Centre

See Holyrood Park Map

London Road

A1

Portobello Road

Willowbrae Road

Waterloo Place

A1

ABBEYHILL

Calton Road

North Bridge

Queen's Drive

*HOLYROOD
PARK*

St Margaret's
Loch

Queen's Drive

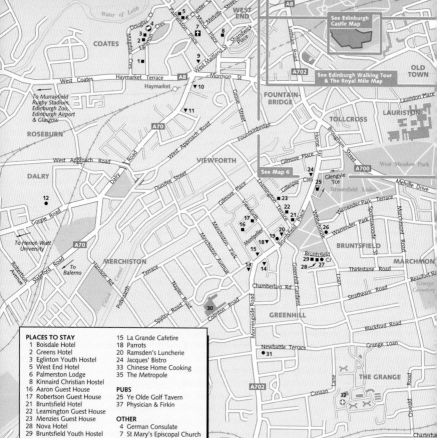

MAP 3

WEST END

OLD TOWN

See Edinburgh Castle Map

See Edinburgh Walking Tour & The Royal Mile Map

COATES

Water of Leith

To Murrayfield Rugby Stadium, Edinburgh Zoo, Edinburgh Airport & Glasgow

ROSEBURN

West Coates

Haymarket Terrace

Haymarket

DALRY

FOUNTAIN-BRIDGE

TOLLCROSS

LAURISTON

Lauriston Place

West Meadow Park

VIEWFORTH

West Approach Road

Gorgie Road

To Heriot-Watt University

MERCHISTON

To Balerno

See Map 6

Glengyle Tce

Bruntsfield Links

BRUNTSFIELD

MARCHMONT

GREENHILL

Grange Cemetery

THE GRANGE

Blackford Hill

To Hill End, Roslin & Penicuik

Braid Burn

Braid Hills Drive

PLACES TO STAY
1 Boisdale Hotel
2 Greens Hotel
3 Eglinton Youth Hostel
5 West End Hotel
7 Palmerston Lodge
8 Kinnaird Christian Hostel
16 Aaron Guest House
17 Robertson Guest House
21 Bruntsfield Hotel
22 Leamington Guest House
23 Menzies Guest House
28 Nova Hotel
29 Bruntsfield Youth Hostel
36 Salisbury Guest House
39 Pollock Halls of Residence
40 Millfield Guest House
41 Marchhall Hotel
42 Casa Buzzo
43 Kenvie Guest House
44 Grange Guest House
46 Sherwood Guest House
47 Thrums Hotel
48 Avondale Guest House
49 Arthur's View Hotel
50 Fairholme Guest House

PLACES TO EAT
9 West End Oyster Bar
10 Verandah Restaurant
11 Howie's Restaurant
13 Howie's Restaurant
14 Montpelier's

15 La Grande Cafetire
18 Parrots
20 Ramsden's Luncherie
24 Jacques' Bistro
33 Chinese Home Cooking
35 The Metropole

PUBS
25 Ye Olde Golf Tavern
37 Physician & Firkin

OTHER
4 German Consulate
7 St Mary's Episcopal Church
12 Tynecastle Park
   (Heart of Midlothian
   Football Club)
19 Macsween of Edinburgh
26 SYHA Office
27 British Council
30 Napier University
31 Dominion Cinema
32 Astley Ainslie Hospital
34 Historic Scotland
38 Royal Commonwealth
   Pool
45 Branch of National Library
51 Cameron Toll Shopping
   Centre
52 Royal Observatory
53 Braid Hills Public
   Golf Course
54 City Hospital

MAP 3

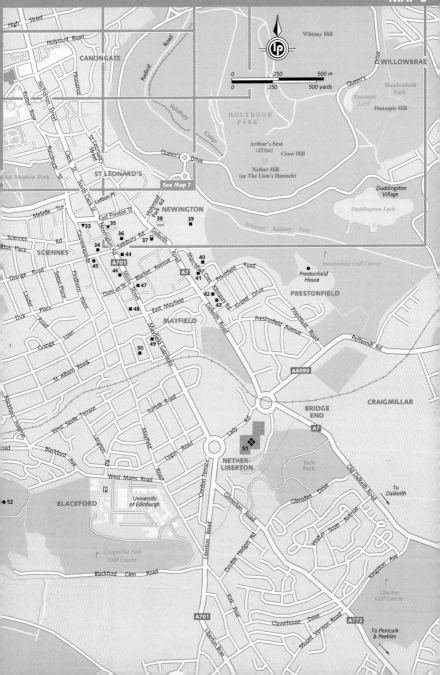

CANONGATE

Whinny Hill

WILLOWBRAE

Drive

Meadowfield
Park

Dunsapie
Loch

Dunsapie Hill

High Street

Holyrood Road

Radical Road

Salisbury

HOLYROOD
PARK

Queen's

0   250   500 m
0   250   500 yards

Nicholson Street

Pleasance

Potter Row

Clerk St

Buccleuch St

St Leonard's Street

South Clerk St

East Meadow Park

ST LEONARD'S

See Map 7

Queen's Drive

Crags

Arthur's Seat
(251m)   Crow Hill

Nether Hill
(or The Lion's Haunch)

Duddingston
Village

Duddingston Loch

Innocent Railway Path

Melville Tce

East Preston St

▼33

35

36

38 ■

39 ■

NEWINGTON

Sciennes Rd

Clarendon

SCIENNES

34

45

44 ■

46 ■

A701

Blacket Avenue

A7

40 ■
41 ■

Marchhall Cres

Kilmaury Rd

Priestfield

Road

Prestonfield
House

Prestonfield Golf Course

PRESTONFIELD

Orange Road

Seton Place

Findhorn Place

Duncan St

47 ■

East Mayfield

42 ■

43 ■

Kirkhill Drive

Dalkeith Road

Prestonfield Avenue

Priestfield Road

Peffermill Rd

Laird Place

Dick Place

48 ■

MAYFIELD

Grange Loan

St Albans Road

Mayfield Gardens

49 ■

50 ■

A6095

BRIDGE
END

A7

CRAIGMILLAR

Blackford Avenue

West Savile Terrace

Blackford Ave

Suffolk Road

Mayfield

Lygon Road

Lady Rd

51 ■

NETHER-
LIBERTON

Inch
Park

West Mains Road

University
of Edinburgh

BLACKFORD

52

Cordon Terrace

Gilmerton Road

Glenallan Drive

Old Dalkeith Road

Walter Scott Avenue

To
Dalkeith

Craigmillar Park
Golf Course

Blackford   Glen   Road

Liberton Road

Kirk Brae

Liberton Brae

Double Hedges Rd

Liberton
Golf Course

Kingston Ave

A701

Claverhouse Drive

Mount Vernon Road

A772

To Penicuik
& Peebles

MAP 4

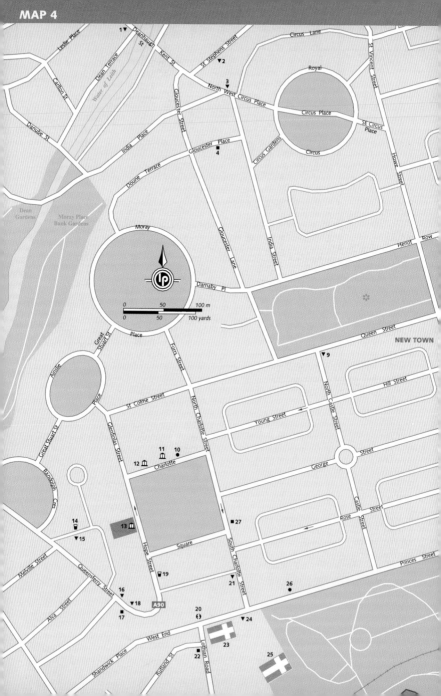

MAP 4

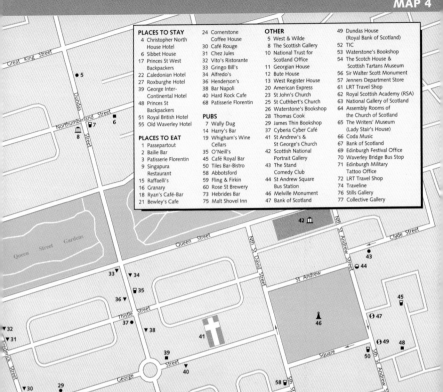

PLACES TO STAY
4 Christopher North House Hotel
6 Sibbet House
17 Princes St West Backpackers
22 Caledonian Hotel
27 Roxburghe Hotel
39 George Inter-Continental Hotel
48 Princes St Backpackers
51 Royal British Hotel
55 Old Waverley Hotel

PLACES TO EAT
1 Passepartout
2 Bailie Bar
3 Patisserie Florentin
9 Singapura Restaurant
15 Raffaelli's
16 Granary
18 Ryan's Café-Bar
21 Bewley's Cafe
24 Cornerstone Coffee House
30 Café Rouge
31 Chez Jules
32 Vito's Ristorante
33 Gringo Bill's
34 Alfredo's
36 Henderson's
38 Bar Napoli
40 Hard Rock Cafe
68 Patisserie Florentin

PUBS
7 Wally Dug
14 Harry's Bar
19 Whigham's Wine Cellars
35 O'Neill's
45 Café Royal Bar
50 Tiles Bar-Bistro
58 Abbotsford
59 Fling & Firkin
60 Rose St Brewery
73 Hebrides Bar
75 Malt Shovel Inn

OTHER
5 West & Wilde
8 The Scottish Gallery
10 National Trust for Scotland Office
11 Georgian House
12 Bute House
13 West Register House
20 American Express
23 St John's Church
25 St Cuthbert's Church
26 Waterstone's Bookshop
28 Thomas Cook
29 James Thin Bookshop
37 Cyberia Cyber Café
41 St Andrew's & St George's Church
42 Scottish National Portrait Gallery
43 The Stand Comedy Club
44 St Andrew Square Bus Station
46 Melville Monument
47 Bank of Scotland
49 Dundas House (Royal Bank of Scotland)
52 TIC
53 Waterstone's Bookshop
54 The Scotch House & Scottish Tartans Museum
56 Sir Walter Scott Monument
57 Jenners Department Store
61 LRT Travel Shop
62 Royal Scottish Academy (RSA)
63 National Gallery of Scotland
64 Assembly Rooms of the Church of Scotland
65 The Writers' Museum (Lady Stair's House)
66 Coda Music
67 Bank of Scotland
69 Edinburgh Festival Office
70 Waverley Bridge Bus Stop
71 Edinburgh Military Tattoo Office
72 LRT Travel Shop
74 Traveline
76 Stills Gallery
77 Collective Gallery

MAP 5

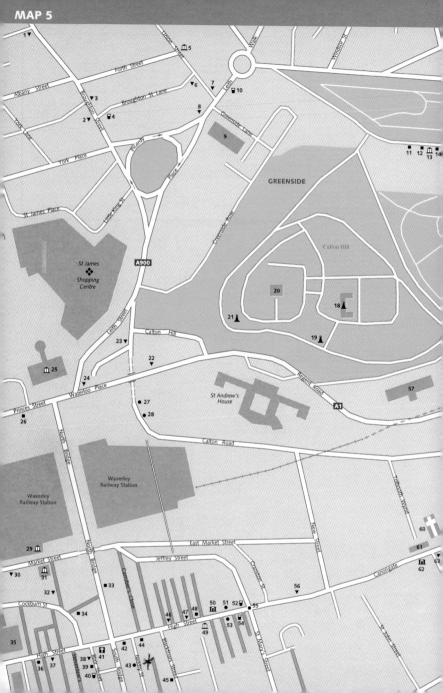

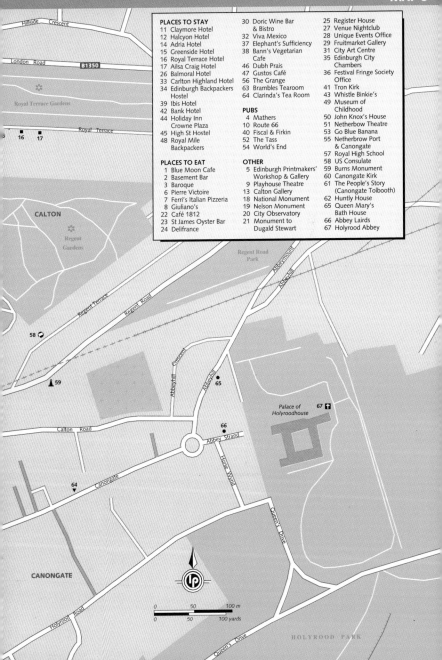

MAP 5

PLACES TO STAY
11 Claymore Hotel
12 Halcyon Hotel
14 Adria Hotel
15 Greenside Hotel
16 Royal Terrace Hotel
17 Ailsa Craig Hotel
26 Balmoral Hotel
33 Carlton Highland Hotel
34 Edinburgh Backpackers Hostel
39 Ibis Hotel
42 Bank Hotel
44 Holiday Inn Crowne Plaza
45 High St Hostel
48 Royal Mile Backpackers

PLACES TO EAT
1 Blue Moon Cafe
2 Basement Bar
3 Baroque
6 Pierre Victoire
7 Ferri's Italian Pizzeria
8 Giuliano's
22 Café 1812
23 St James Oyster Bar
24 Delifrance
30 Doric Wine Bar & Bistro
32 Viva Mexico
37 Elephant's Sufficiency
38 Bann's Vegetarian Cafe
46 Dubh Prais
47 Gustos Café
56 The Grange
63 Brambles Tearoom
64 Clarinda's Tea Room

PUBS
4 Mathers
10 Route 66
40 Fiscal & Firkin
52 The Tass
54 World's End

OTHER
5 Edinburgh Printmakers' Workshop & Gallery
9 Playhouse Theatre
13 Calton Gallery
18 National Monument
19 Nelson Monument
20 City Observatory
21 Monument to Dugald Stewart
25 Register House
27 Venue Nightclub
28 Unique Events Office
29 Fruitmarket Gallery
31 City Art Centre
35 Edinburgh City Chambers
36 Festival Fringe Society Office
41 Tron Kirk
43 Whistle Binkie's
49 Museum of Childhood
50 John Knox's House
51 Netherbow Theatre
53 Go Blue Banana
55 Netherbow Port & Canongate
57 Royal High School
58 US Consulate
59 Burns Monument
60 Canongate Kirk
61 The People's Story (Canongate Tolbooth)
62 Huntly House
65 Queen Mary's Bath House
66 Abbey Lairds
67 Holyrood Abbey

MAP 6

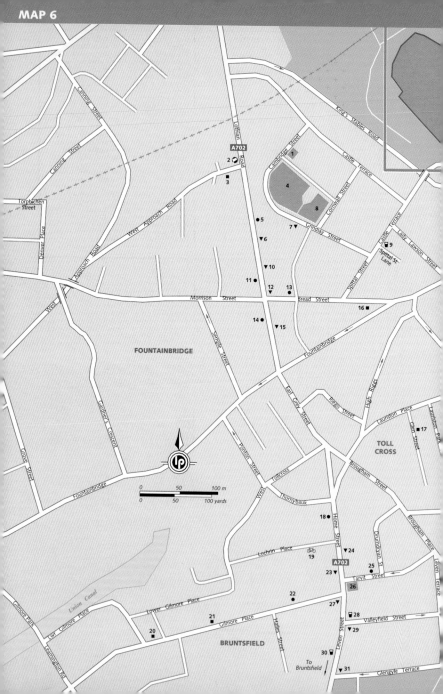

Torphichen
Street

A702

Lothian Road

Cambridge Street

King's Stables Road

Castle Terrace

Cornwall Street

1

2

3

4

8

5

7

6

Grindlay Street

9

Spittal St.
Lane

Lady Lawson Street

Castle Terrace

10

11

12

13

14

15

16

Morrison   Street

Bread   Street

Spittal Street

West Approach Road

Canning Street

Canning Street

Dewar Place

West   Approach   Road

West

FOUNTAINBRIDGE

Fountainbridge

Semple   Street

Earl   Grey   Street

Tobago   Street

High   Riggs

Gardner's   Crescent

Grove   Street

Fountainbridge

Fountainbridge

Tarvit   Street

Lauriston   Place

Chalmers   Street

Lauriston   Park

17

TOLL
CROSS

Tollcross

Thornybauk

Ponton   Street

Riego   Street

Brougham   Street

Brougham   Place

Leven   Terrace

18

Home   Street

19
dab

20

21

22

Union   Canal

Lower   Gilmore   Place

Gilmore   Place

Leamington Rd

Gilmore   Park

Lwr   Gilmore Place

Hailes   Street

BRUNTSFIELD

To
Bruntsfield

Lochrin   Place

24

A702

23

25

26

27

28

29

30

31

Dundonald   Street

Valleyfield   Street

Glengyle   Terrace

Leven   Street

0   50   100 m

0   50   100 yards

MAP 6

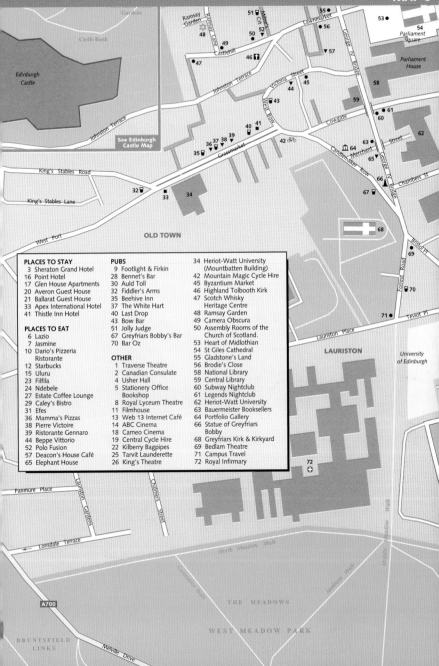

Edinburgh Castle

Castle Bank

Gardens

Ramsay Garden

Lawnmarket

Parliament Square

Parliament House

Johnston Terrace

Victoria Street

West Bow

Cowgate

See Edinburgh Castle Map

Grassmarket

Candlemaker Row

George IV Bridge

Chambers St.

King's Stables Road

King's Stables Lane

West Port

OLD TOWN

Forrest Road

Lauriston Place

LAURISTON

University of Edinburgh

Panmure Place

Lauriston Gardens

Chalmers Street

Lonsdale Terrace

North Meadow Walk

Middle Meadow Walk

Jawbone Walk

THE MEADOWS

WEST MEADOW PARK

A700

Melville Drive

BRUNTSFIELD LINKS

PLACES TO STAY
3 Sheraton Grand Hotel
16 Point Hotel
17 Glen House Apartments
20 Averon Guest House
21 Ballarat Guest House
33 Apex International Hotel
41 Thistle Inn Hotel

PLACES TO EAT
6 Lazio
7 Jasmine
10 Dario's Pizzeria Ristorante
12 Starbucks
15 Uluru
23 Filfila
24 Ndebele
27 Estate Coffee Lounge
29 Caley's Bistro
31 Efes
36 Mamma's Pizzas
38 Pierre Victoire
44 Beppe Vittorio
52 Polo Fusion
57 Deacon's House Café
65 Elephant House

PUBS
9 Footlight & Firkin
28 Bennet's Bar
30 Auld Toll
32 Fiddler's Arms
35 Beehive Inn
37 The White Hart
40 Last Drop
43 Bow Bar
51 Jolly Judge
67 Greyfriars Bobby's Bar
70 Bar Oz

OTHER
1 Traverse Theatre
2 Canadian Consulate
4 Usher Hall
5 Stationery Office Bookshop
8 Royal Lyceum Theatre
11 Filmhouse
13 Web 13 Internet Café
14 ABC Cinema
18 Cameo Cinema
19 Central Cycle Hire
22 Kilberry Bagpipes
25 Tarvit Launderette
26 King's Theatre
34 Heriot-Watt University (Mountbatten Building)
42 Mountain Magic Cycle Hire
45 Byzantium Market
46 Highland Tolbooth Kirk
47 Scotch Whisky Heritage Centre
48 Ramsay Garden
49 Camera Obscura
50 Assembly Rooms of the Church of Scotland.
53 Heart of Midlothian
54 St Giles Cathedral
55 Gladstone's Land
56 Brodie's Close
58 National Library
59 Central Library
60 Subway Nightclub
61 Legends Nightclub
62 Heriot-Watt University
63 Bauermeister Booksellers
64 Portfolio Gallery
66 Statue of Greyfriars Bobby
68 Greyfriars Kirk & Kirkyard
69 Bedlam Theatre
71 Campus Travel
72 Royal Infirmary

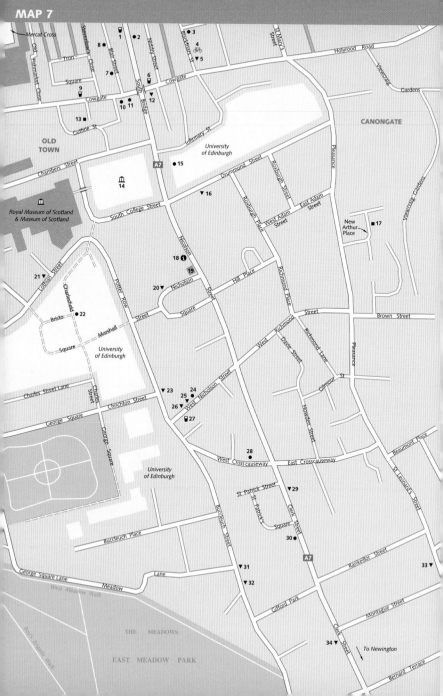

MAP 7

Mercat Cross

Steenlaw's Close

Tron

Square

Old Fishmarket Close

Blair Street

Blackfriars St

Niddry Street

South Bridge

Cowgate

St Mary's Street

Holyrood Road

Viewcraig

Gardens

OLD TOWN

Chambers Street

Guthrie St

Cowgate

Infirmary St

University of Edinburgh

CANONGATE

Pleasance

Viewcraig Gardens

Viewcraig Gardens

Royal Museum of Scotland & Museum of Scotland

South College Street

Drummond Street

Roxburgh Street

East Adam Street

West Adam Street

New Arthur Place

Lothian Street

Charlesfield

Potter Row

Nicolson Street

Nicolson Square

Hill Place

Richmond Place

Brown Street

Bristo

Marshall

Street

Square

University of Edinburgh

Richmond Street

West Richmond Street

Davie Street

Richmond Lane

Gilmour St

Pleasance

Charles Street Lane

Crichton Street

West Nicolson Street

Howden Street

Beaumont Place

George Square

George Square

University of Edinburgh

West Cross causeway

East Crosscauseway

St Leonard's Street

Buccleuch Place

Buccleuch Street

St Patrick Street

St Patrick's Square

Clerk Street

Beaumont Place

George Square Lane

Lane

Meadow

West Meadow Walk

Clifford Park

Rankeillor Street

Montague Street

THE MEADOWS

EAST MEADOW PARK

Clerk Street

To Newington

Bernard Terrace

Map markers: 1, 2, 3, 4, 5, 6, 7, 8, 9, 10, 11, 12, 13, 14, 15, 16, 17, 18, 19, 20, 21, 22, 23, 24, 25, 26, 27, 28, 29, 30, 31, 32, 33, 34

A7

MAP 7

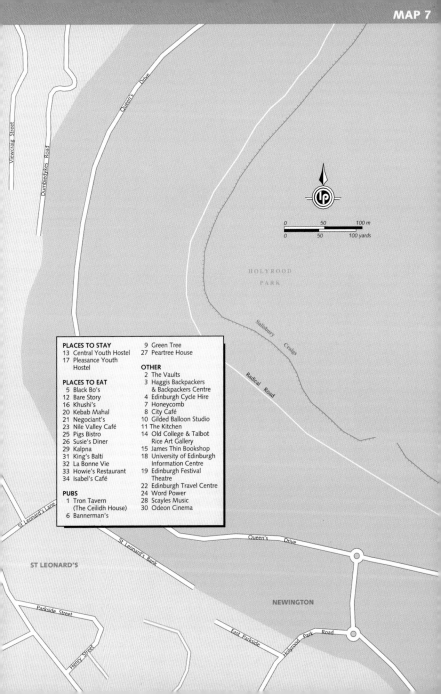

PLACES TO STAY
13 Central Youth Hostel
17 Pleasance Youth
   Hostel

PLACES TO EAT
5 Black Bo's
12 Bare Story
16 Khushi's
20 Kebab Mahal
21 Negociant's
23 Nile Valley Café
25 Pigs Bistro
26 Susie's Diner
29 Kalpna
31 King's Balti
32 La Bonne Vie
33 Howie's Restaurant
34 Isabel's Café

PUBS
1 Tron Tavern
  (The Ceilidh House)
6 Bannerman's

9 Green Tree
27 Peartree House

OTHER
2 The Vaults
3 Haggis Backpackers
  & Backpackers Centre
4 Edinburgh Cycle Hire
7 Honeycomb
8 City Café
10 Gilded Balloon Studio
11 The Kitchen
14 Old College & Talbot
   Rice Art Gallery
15 James Thin Bookshop
18 University of Edinburgh
   Information Centre
19 Edinburgh Festival
   Theatre
22 Edinburgh Travel Centre
24 Word Power
28 Scayles Music
30 Odeon Cinema

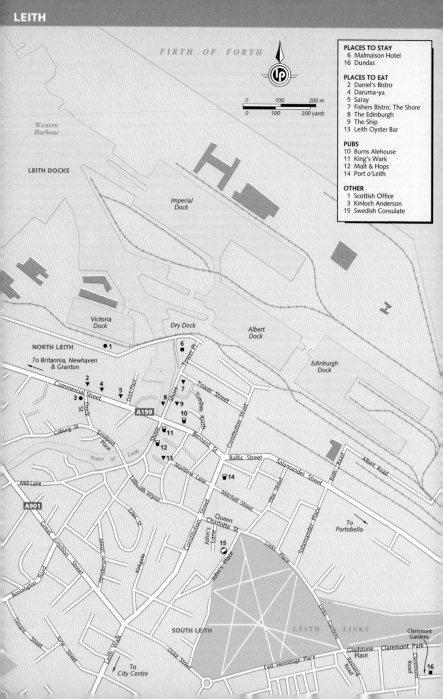

LEITH

FIRTH OF FORTH

PLACES TO STAY
6 Malmaison Hotel
16 Dundas

PLACES TO EAT
2 Daniel's Bistro
4 Daruma-ya
5 Saray
7 Fishers Bistro; The Shore
8 The Edinburgh
9 The Ship
13 Leith Oyster Bar

PUBS
10 Burns Alehouse
11 King's Wark
12 Malt & Hops
14 Port o'Leith

OTHER
1 Scottish Office
3 Kinloch Anderson
15 Swedish Consulate

Western
Harbour

LEITH DOCKS

Imperial
Dock

Victoria
Dock

Dry Dock

Albert
Dock

Edinburgh
Dock

NORTH LEITH

To Britannia, Newhaven
& Granton

Commercial Street

Tower Pl
Tower Street

Shore
Timber Bush
Bernard St
Constitution Street

A199

Coburg St
Sandport
Place

Water of Leith

Baltic Street
Salamander Street
Albert Road

Mill Lane

A901

Great Junction Street

Bonnington Road

Henderson Street

Tolbooth Wynd

Maritime Lane

Mitchell Street

The Shore

Salamander Place

Bath Road

To
Portobello

Cables
Wynd

Giles St

Kirkgate

Constitution Street

John's Lane

Queen
Charlotte St

John's Place

15

Links Place

Leith Links

LEITH LINKS

SOUTH LEITH

Leith Walk

Duke Street

Tennant Street

Iona Street

To
City Centre

East Hermitage Place

Gladstone
Place

Claremont Park

Reading Road

Claremont
Gardens

Claremont Road

16

The cruise ship *Edinburgh*, docked at The Shore, Leith, Edinburgh's main port

The Shore, Leith, is a distinctive corner of Edinburgh noted for its interesting pubs and eateries

MAP LEGEND

BOUNDARIES

- —··—··—·· International
- —··—··—·· State
- — — — — Disputed

HYDROGRAPHY

- Coastline
- River
- Creek
- Lake
- Intermittent Lake
- Canal
- Spring, Rapids
- Waterfalls
- Swamp

ROUTES & TRANSPORT

- Freeway
- Highway
- Major Road
- Minor Road
- Unsealed Road
- City Freeway
- City Highway
- City Road
- City Street, Lane
- Pedestrian Mall
- Tunnel
- Train Route & Station
- Metro & Station
- Tramway
- Cable Car or Chairlift
- Walking Track
- Walking Tour
- Ferry Route

AREA FEATURES

- Building
- Park, Gardens
- Cemetery
- Market
- Beach
- Urban Area

MAP SYMBOLS

○ CAPITAL	National Capital
◉ CAPITAL	State Capital
● CITY	City
● Town	Town
● Village	Village
○	Point of Interest
■	Place to Stay
▲	Camping Ground
⌂	Caravan Park
⌂	Hut or Chalet
▼	Place to Eat
♜	Pub or Bar

✈	Airport
⊕	ATM, Bank
✿	Beach
⬲	Bike Rental
⛫	Castle or Fort
✚ 🛈	Church
	Cliff or Escarpment
◔	Embassy
✛	Hospital
⚑	Monument
☪	Mosque
▲	Mountain or Hill
🏛	Museum
⚘	National Park

⟵	One Way Street
🅿	Parking
⛽	Petrol
★	Police Station
✉	Post Office
❖	Shopping Centre
🏛	Stately Home
	Swimming Pool
✡	Synagogue
☎	Telephone
⊖	Toilet
❶	Tourist Information
◒	Transport
🐾	Zoo

Note: not all symbols displayed above appear in this book

LONELY PLANET OFFICES

Australia
PO Box 617, Hawthorn, Victoria 3122
☎ (03) 9819 1877 fax (03) 9819 6459
email: talk2us@lonelyplanet.com.au

UK
10a Spring Place, London, NW5 3BH
☎ (0171) 428 4800 fax (0171) 428 4828
email: go@lonelyplanet.co.uk

USA
150 Linden St, Oakland, CA 94607
☎ (510) 893 8555 TOLL FREE: 800 275 8555
fax (510) 893 8572
email: info@lonelyplanet.com

France
1 rue du Dahomey, 75011 Paris
☎ 01 55 25 33 00 fax 01 55 25 33 01
email: bip@lonelyplanet.fr
3615 lonelyplanet *(1,29 F TTC/min)*

World Wide Web: www.lonelyplanet.com *or* AOL keyword: lp
Lonely Planet Images: lpi@lonelyplanet.com.au